PENGUIN CLASSICS

THE PRE-RAPHAELITES

DINAH ROE is an independent scholar and freelance writer whose interests include the nineteenth-century novel, Victorian poetry, and women's writing. Born and raised in the United States, she holds degrees from Vassar College (USA) and University College London. She has taught English Literature at UCL and the University of Hertfordshire. She has written *Christina Rossetti's Faithful Imagination* (2006), edited *Christina Rossetti: Selected Poems* for Penguin Classics (2008) and is currently working on a biography of the Rossetti family.

11-10

The Pre-Raphaelites

From Rossetti to Ruskin

Selected with an Introduction by
DINAH ROE

PENGUIN BOOKS

PENGUIN CLASSICS

Published by the Penguin Group
Penguin Books Ltd, 80 Strand, London WC2R ORL, England
Penguin Group (USA) Inc., 375 Hudson Street, New York, New York 10014, USA
Penguin Group (Canada), 90 Eglinton Avenue East, Suite 700, Toronto, Ontario,
Canada M4P 2Y3 (a division of Pearson Penguin Canada Inc.)
Penguin Ireland, 25 St Stephen's Green, Dublin 2, Ireland (a division of Penguin Books Ltd)
Penguin Group (Australia), 250 Camberwell Road, Camberwell, Victoria 3124, Australia
(a division of Pearson Australia Group Pty Ltd)
Penguin Books India Pvt Ltd, 11 Community Centre, Panchsheel Park, New Delhi – 110 017, India
Penguin Group (NZ), 67 Apollo Drive, Rosedale, North Shore 0632, New Zealand
(a division of Pearson New Zealand Ltd)
Penguin Books (South Africa) (Pty) Ltd, 24 Sturdee Avenue, Rosebank, Johannesburg 2196,
South Africa

Penguin Books Ltd, Registered Offices: 80 Strand, London WC2R ORL, England

www.penguin.com

This selection first published in Penguin Classics 2010
1

Selection and editorial material copyright © Dinah Roe, 2010

Set in 10.25/12.25 PostScript Adobe Sabon
Typeset by Ellipsis Books Limited, Glasgow
Printed in England by Clays Ltd, St Ives plc

ISBN: 978-0-141-19240-6

www.greenpenguin.co.uk

Mixed Sources
Product group from well-managed
forests and other controlled sources
www.fsc.org Cert no. SA-COC-1592
© 1996 Forest Stewardship Council

Penguin Books is committed to a sustainable future
for our business, our readers and our planet.
The book in your hands is made from paper
certified by the Forest Stewardship Council.

Contents

COVENTRY PATMORE

WILLIAM ALLINGHAM

JAMES COLLINSON

THOMAS WOOLNER

JOHN TUPPER

WALTER HOWELL DEVERELL

GEORGE MEREDITH

DANTE GABRIEL ROSSETTI

ELIZABETH SIDDAL

WILLIAM MICHAEL ROSSETTI

CHRISTINA GEORGINA ROSSETTI

ARTHUR HUGHES

WILLIAM MORRIS

ALGERNON CHARLES SWINBURNE

JOHN PAYNE

Acknowledgements

No work of this kind is ever produced alone, and thanks are owed to enough friends and colleagues to fill a separate collection. But I would like to acknowledge the following: my parents Ralph and Kathy Roe (as always) and Hamish and Dors Kidd for their humbling generosity and support; the magnificent, indispensable James Kidd; Oliver and Alyse Roe; David Shelley and his father Alan, a man whose love of books will always be an inspiration; the irrepressible Darren Cohen, Rhian Edwards and Fran Varian; Stephen Gerson, whose kindness and intelligence are reflected in his daughter Meredith.

I would also like to thank Diane D'Amico, Mary Arseneau, Joseph Bristow and Margaret Reynolds for their valuable advice and encouragement. Their generosity with both their time and experience has enriched this selection. Special thanks goes to Daniel Karlin, who has long helped to transform my ugly-duckling thoughts into elegant swans. In particular, I am grateful to him for casting his keen editorial eye over this selection's introduction, and for his fine reading of 'The Blessed Damozel'. Thanks also to Kate Parker and Alexis Kirschbaum, whose professionalism and support have helped make this project a pleasure.

Chronology

1830 Publication of Alfred Tennyson's *Poems, Chiefly Lyrical*.

1833 Anonymous publication of *Pauline: A Fragment of a Confession*. Dante Gabriel Rossetti correctly identifies Robert Browning as the author.

1837 Coronation of Queen Victoria.

1842 Publication of Tennyson's *Poems* and Browning's *Dramatic Lyrics*.

1843 Publication of John Ruskin's *Modern Painters I*. William Wordsworth becomes Poet Laureate.

1846 Publication of Ruskin's *Modern Painters II* and *Poems by Currer, Ellis and Acton Bell* (Charlotte, Emily and Anne Brontë).

1848 Publication of the *Communist Manifesto* in London. Revolution in France, Germany and Italy. Chartist mass demonstration on Kennington Common in London. Publication of Richard Monckton Milnes's *Life, Letters and Literary Remains of John Keats*. Formation of the Pre-Raphaelite Brotherhood (PRB).

1849 PRB members William Holman Hunt and John Everett Millais exhibit at the Royal Academy (RA). Rossetti exhibits at the Free Exhibition, Hyde Park Corner, London.

1850 Death of Wordsworth. Tennyson becomes Laureate. Publication of Elizabeth Barrett Browning's *Sonnets from the Portuguese*. Exhibitions of PRB paintings attract adverse criticism. Publication of Pre-Raphaelite magazine the *Germ*. James Collinson resigns from the PRB.

1851 Ruskin's letter to *The Times* and his pamphlet *Pre-Raphaelitism* published. The Great Exhibition takes place at Crystal Palace.

1852 Thomas Woolner sails for Australia.

1853 Millais elected Associate Member of the RA.

1854 Holman Hunt leaves for his tour of the Holy Land. Working Men's College established in London; Ruskin, Rossetti, Ford Madox Brown and Arthur Hughes teach here. Publication of Coventry Patmore's *The Angel in the House*, part 1.

1855 Publication of Browning's *Men and Women* and Tennyson's *Maud and Other Poems*. William Bell Scott begins painting the Northumbrian History Cycle murals at Wallington.

1856 Holman Hunt returns from the Middle East. The *Oxford and Cambridge Magazine* created by second-wave Pre-Raphaelites Edward Burne-Jones and William Morris at Oxford. Publication of Ruskin's *Modern Painters III* and *IV*.

1857 Rossetti, Burne-Jones, Morris, Hughes, Valentine Prinsep and others begin to paint the Oxford Union murals. Exhibition of Pre-Raphaelite paintings held at Fitzroy Square, London, including works by Elizabeth Siddal. Pre-Raphaelite exhibition held in New York. Publication of the Moxon edition of Tennyson's *Poems* and Charles Baudelaire's *Les Fleurs du mal*.

1858 Publication of Morris's *The Defence of Guenevere and Other Poems*. Formation of the Hogarth Club.

1859 Publication of the first version of Tennyson's *Idylls of the King* and Charles Darwin's *On the Origin of Species*.

1860 Publication of Ruskin's *Modern Painters V*.

1861 Morris, Rossetti, Burne-Jones and Ford Madox Brown, among others, form the decorating firm William Morris, Marshall, Faulkner & Co.

1862 Death of Elizabeth Siddal. Publication of Christina Rossetti's *Goblin Market and Other Poems* and George Meredith's *Modern Love and Poems of the English Roadside*.

1865 Ford Madox Brown's *Work* exhibited. Publication of Lewis Carroll's *Alice's Adventures in Wonderland*.

1866 Algernon Charles Swinburne's *Poems and Ballads*, dedicated to Burne-Jones, is published then withdrawn by Moxon. Republished by John Camden Hotten. William Michael Rossetti publishes a pamphlet defending Swinburne.

1867 Publication of Morris's *The Life and Death of Jason*.

1868 Publication of Browning's *The Ring and the Book*. William Gladstone becomes Prime Minister.

1869 Publication of the second version of Tennyson's *Idylls of the King*.

1870 Rossetti publishes his first collection, *Poems*.

1871 Robert Buchanan's article 'The Fleshly School of Poetry' appears in the October issue of *Contemporary Review*. Buchanan expands this article for a pamphlet in 1872. Rossetti's reply, 'The Stealthy School of Criticism', appears in the December issue of the *Athenaeum*.

1872 Publication of Swinburne's reply to Buchanan, *Under the Microscope*.

1873 Publication of Walter Pater's *The Renaissance: Studies in Art and Poetry*.

1874 Woolner elected as a member of the RA. Disraeli becomes Prime Minister.

1875 Morris becomes the sole owner of the reorganized 'William Morris & Co.'.

1880 Gladstone becomes Prime Minister.

1881 Publication of *Dalziels' Bible Gallery* with illustrations by Ford Madox Brown, Burne-Jones, Holman Hunt, Simeon Solomon and George Frederick Watts, among others.

1882 Death of Rossetti; Buchanan publicly retracts his criticism of Rossetti in a poem and preface to the second edition of his novel *God and the Man*.

1885 Burne-Jones becomes an Associate of the RA. Publication of the final 'Idyll' of Tennyson's *Idylls of the King*.

1891 Publication of Oscar Wilde's *The Picture of Dorian Gray*. Formation of the Rhymers' Club. Morris sets up the Kelmscott Press.

1892 George Meredith elected President of the Society of Authors. Death of Tennyson. Publication of Bell Scott's *Autobiographical Notes*.

1894 The *Yellow Book* literary magazine begins.

1896 Millais elected President of the RA.

1897 Tate Gallery (the National Gallery of British Art) opens.

1901 Death of Queen Victoria.

1905 Publication of Holman Hunt's autobiography, *Pre-Raphaelitism and the Pre-Raphaelite Brotherhood.*

1906 Holman Hunt retrospective exhibitions held in London and Manchester.

Introduction

In 1872, W. H. Mallock published a mock-literary cookbook for aspiring poets. One 'recipe' was entitled 'How to Write a Modern Pre-Raphaelite Poem'. Among the recommended ingredients were: 'obsolete and unintelligible' words, 'a perfectly vacant atmosphere', 'three damozels, dressed in straight nightgowns', 'a stone wall', 'trees and flowers', as well as stars, aureoles and lilies. 'When you have arranged all these objects rightly,' the recipe continued, 'take a cast of them in the softest part of your brain, and pour in your word-composition.'[1]

Mallock was not the first critic to accuse Pre-Raphaelite poetry of being soft in the head. From the outset, Pre-Raphaelitism was taken to task for its pretentiousness and unreality, aggravated by a self-opinion at odds with the Victorian virtues of modesty and reserve. Championed by the Aesthetes and Decadents of the *fin de siècle*, Pre-Raphaelite poetry has yet to shake off its reputation as a 'fleshly', self-indulgent trend enjoyed 'by young gentlemen with animal faculties morbidly developed by too much tobacco and too little exercise'.[2]

It is true that if we ask such poetry to emulate the engagement of the Victorian novel with contemporary social and political issues, we shall (with rare exceptions such as Dante Gabriel Rossetti's 'Jenny') be disappointed. Pre-Raphaelitism helped to popularize the notion of 'art for art's sake' (in painting and the decorative arts as well as poetry), often explicitly in opposition to the utilitarian ethos which, we should not forget, formed the dominant ideology of the mid-century.[3] This helps to explain the concentration of Pre-Raphaelite poems on sexual yearning and artistic introspection, and the movement's consciously idealized medievalism. Devoid of the political edge of Benjamin Disraeli's Young England, Pre-Raphaelite writing explored a world where art and beauty were more important than the growth of the railway, market fluctuations or the 'Two Nations'.[4] At the time, Pre-Raphaelitism (and especially its poetry) was dismissed as naïve, over-sexualized, immoral and, most damningly, 'unmanly'; since then, the movement's atmosphere of middle-class Bohemianism has made it an easy target for satire. Yet this 'counter-culture' also had an aspect of recognizably 'Victorian' earnestness and high-mindedness, and, as we shall see, its artistic programme originally promoted a 'modern' aesthetic which was found shocking not because it was dreamy and nostalgic, but quite the reverse: because it was hyper-realistic and given to recording supposedly sacred events in repulsive detail. Like many such movements, in other words, it is a compound phenomenon, and its principal figures are not easily categorized, whether according to the preconceptions of their own day or of ours.

While new schools of poetry regularly find themselves the subject of critical scorn in their own time, their work is often recognized and rehabilitated in later years. The Pre-Raphaelites, however, suffered blows from which they have yet to recover. Part of the problem is that such attacks were seldom unprovoked. Even in its beginnings as a fine-art movement, Pre-Raphaelitism courted controversy, goading the critical establishment with paintings representing, for example, the Virgin Mary as a rangy adolescent in a nightgown.[5] Oscar Wilde noted that the painters 'had on their side three things that the English public never forgives: youth, power and enthusiasm'.[6] Pre-Raphaelite poets proved equally unforgivable.

Defining just who these poets were is a tricky business. From the outset, the group was characterized by protean shifts in membership, parameters and objectives. Some Pre-Raphaelite poets were self-appointed while others had Pre-Raphaelitism thrust upon them, often by hostile contemporary critics. Between the movement's beginnings in the late 1840s and its end (around the turn of the century), its ranks would include Dante Gabriel Rossetti, William Morris, Algernon Charles Swinburne, George Meredith, Christina Rossetti, William Bell Scott, William

Allingham, Arthur O'Shaughnessy and John Payne, among others. As befits this loose and baggy collective, many of these would reject the term later in life.

Although its end date is harder to define, Pre-Raphaelitism's origins are well documented. Frustrated with the traditional approach to painting taught at London's Royal Academy of Arts, seven young artists formed a group called the Pre-Raphaelite Brotherhood (PRB) in 1848.[7] The painters were: Dante Gabriel Rossetti, William Holman Hunt, John Everett Millais, James Collinson and Frederic Stephens. The non-painters were sculptor Thomas Woolner and PRB secretary William Michael Rossetti, Dante Gabriel's brother.

Although the Brotherhood was formed in 1848, it was not particularly exercised by the revolutions breaking out in Europe or the Chartist uprisings at home. Its rebellion was artistic rather than political; the 1848 release of Richard Monckton Milnes's *Life, Letters and Literary Remains of John Keats* was far more significant to the PRB than the London publication of the *Communist Manifesto* in the same year. This apolitical stance would remain characteristic of Pre-Raphaelite work, though some of its associates would develop an interest in politics. William Morris, for example, became an outspoken socialist while Swinburne supported the Italian liberation movement.

The PRB's original aims were to rebel against Royal Academy conventions governing composition, technique and subject matter. With youthful arrogance, these painters, the eldest of whom was only twenty-four, rejected Academy-approved work as the 'sloshy' legacy of 'Sir Sloshua' himself, better known as the first RA President, Sir Joshua Reynolds (1723–92). They advocated a rejection of classicism and a self-conscious return to the traditions of medieval painting that came 'before Raphael' and the Renaissance, hence 'Pre-Raphaelite'.[8] Though they did not have a definite methodology, the PRB painters were determined to follow a programme of 'truth to nature', as earnestly outlined by William Michael Rossetti:

> 1, to have genuine ideas to express; 2, to study Nature attentively, so as to know how to express them; 3, to sympathize with what

is direct and serious and heartfelt in previous art, to the exclu-
sion of what is conventional and self-parading and learned by
rote; and 4, most indispensable of all, to produce thoroughly
good pictures and statues.[9]

Comparable, at least in spirit, to the Young British Artists of
the 1990s, members of the PRB were in open rebellion against
what they saw as the tired, derivative traditions of British art.
They actively sought to shock, and found a strength in numbers
that they would not have had as individuals. Instead of painting
idealized figures, the PRB used live models whose faces were
recognizably 'modern' rather than classical. They pioneered a
striking technique of painting, using vivid colours on a wet white
ground, with flattened figures outlined in almost photographic
detail. Many of their early works show that Pre-Raphaelitism
was intimately connected with literature from the very beginning.
Alongside biblical subjects, PRB painters depicted scenes and
characters from Shakespeare, Keats and Tennyson.

Though Rossetti, Holman Hunt and Millais had signed their
pictures with the initials 'PRB' as early as 1849, it was not until
they were recognized as a movement in 1850 that their pictures
attracted the ire of contemporary critics. They were reprimanded
for their use of detailed imagery and symbolism, which was
perceived as being dangerously close to 'Romanism'. At the same
time, their unidealized subjects, such as the skinny red-headed
Christ child in Millais's *Christ in the House of His Parents*
(1849–50), were considered blasphemous. Encouraged by PRB
associate Coventry Patmore, John Ruskin, the influential art
critic and author of *Modern Painters* (1843–60), defended the
Brotherhood in the *Times* in 1851. Though the short-lived PRB
disbanded that year, its impact on art and literature continued
throughout the century.

Literary Pre-Raphaelitism ran concurrently with the artistic
movement, and, like the visual artists, the early poets took an
interest in both the medieval and the very modern. In 1848,
Rossetti and Holman Hunt drew up a list of 'Immortals' whose
work demonstrated 'that there was no immortality for humanity
except in reputation gained by man's own genius or heroism'.[10]

While Jesus Christ headed the list, the majority of these heroes were painters or poets. The poets predictably included Homer, Dante Alighieri, Boccaccio and Shakespeare. But established, canonical names were balanced by those of more contemporary writers. The list included the recent Romantic poets Byron, Keats and Shelley, as well as living writers like William Wordsworth, Elizabeth Barrett Browning, Robert Browning, Alfred Tennyson, William Makepeace Thackeray, Edgar Allan Poe, Henry Wadsworth Longfellow, Ralph Waldo Emerson and Coventry Patmore. Particularly admired figures were given a star-rating, with the result that Robert Browning, whose work was by no means universally praised at the time, was placed on equal footing with Dante and Homer. Minor poet and Pre-Raphaelite associate Coventry Patmore received the same number of stars as Boccaccio.

This diversity was reflected in the poetry which grew out of the Pre-Raphaelite Brotherhood. From 1850, the group published a literary magazine, *The Germ: Thoughts Towards Nature in Poetry, Literature, and Art*. This contained poems, essays and pictures, some of which were directly about fine art, but most of which reflected a more general desire to challenge the status quo. In literary as well as pictorial terms, this meant making art utterly modern by a paradoxical return to the 'serious and heartfelt' philosophy and practices of the medieval age, and the transcendent, symbolic beauty of nature.

The poems are generally set in rural landscapes whose natural details, true to PRB principles, are minutely expressed, as in the sixth stanza of Thomas Woolner's 'Of My Lady in Death':

> Speargrass stoops with watery beads:
> > The weight from its fine tips
> > Occasionally drips:
> The bee drops in the mallow-bloom, and feeds.

Curiously, while most of the poetry focuses on rural scenes, Pre-Raphaelitism was an urban movement. The natural world to which it swore fealty was not experienced on a daily basis, but was a landscape remembered, imagined or conjured out of time spent in London's parks and green spaces or the rural retreats of friends, reached by the ever-expanding network of the new railway. In the hands of the early Pre-Raphaelite poets, nature functioned allegorically. Following the precedent set by the Romantic poets, the Pre-Raphaelite natural world often reflected a speaker's state of mind, as in Woolner's 'Emblems' and William Bell Scott's 'Morning Sleep', or was freighted with suggestive symbols, as in Walter Deverell's 'The Sight Beyond' and Christina Rossetti's 'Sweet Death'. But the debt to Romanticism needs qualifying. Very few Pre-Raphaelite poems sound remotely like Wordsworth, whose influence was overlaid by that of his successor as Poet Laureate, Alfred Tennyson. In terms of poetic language, the Pre-Raphaelites looked to the 'second generation' of Romantic poets, especially to Keats, rather than Wordsworth and Samuel Taylor Coleridge.

The medievalism which would come to dominate mid-century Pre-Raphaelite writing was also in evidence in the *Germ*, in titles such as 'My Beautiful Lady', 'Of My Lady in Death', 'The Blessed Damozel'; and in poems whose chivalrous heroes pined for unattainable ladies. Even Christina Rossetti, sister to Dante Gabriel and William Michael and the only woman to publish with the Brotherhood, was not immune to this neo-medievalist influence, writing under a pseudonym borrowed from an old ballad, 'Ellen Alleyn'. Other significant non-PRB contributors were Ford Madox Brown, Coventry Patmore and John Tupper.

A cultivated melancholy was another notable feature of the *Germ* poems, and would become a leading characteristic of Pre-Raphaelite writing. It is typified by Christina Rossetti's 'Dream Land', 'A Pause of Thought' and 'An End', poems whose mournful tone would influence the work of Elizabeth Siddal, Philip Bourke Marston and John Payne. Contemporary critics often pointed to this elegiac strain as a sign of Pre-Raphaelitism's unhealthy and 'morbid' tendencies, particularly in the love poetry.

As much a social network as a poetic or artistic school, Pre-Raphaelitism always permitted works of less obvious merit to ride on the coat-tails of its better productions. Along with innovative contributions by Christina and Dante Gabriel Rossetti, the *Germ* contains its share of clanking lines: 'The uncouth moth upon the window-panes / Hath ceased to flap . . .'; 'When Viola, a servant of the Duke, / Of him she loved the page, went, sent by him'; 'Like those who in dense theatre and hall, / When fire breaks out or weight-strained rafters fall, / Towards some egress struggle doubtfully'.[11]

Pre-Raphaelite poetry in the *Germ* was, appropriately enough, very much a work-in-progress, but some of its enduring qualities were already manifest. Anticipating the direction Pre-Raphaelite poetry would take after the dissolution of the PRB, Dante Gabriel Rossetti's 'The Blessed Damozel' successfully binds together elements which in other poems are disparate and clashing. It has a consistency of tone and a painterly attention to detail which make its stylized gestures convincing in their own terms:

> The blessed Damozel leaned out
>   From the gold bar of Heaven:
> Her blue grave eyes were deeper much
>   Than a deep water, even.
> She had three lilies in her hand,
>   And the stars in her hair were seven.
>
> Her robe, ungirt from clasp to hem,
>   No wrought flowers did adorn,
> But a white rose of Mary's gift,
>   On the neck meetly worn;
> And her hair, lying down her back,
>   Was yellow like ripe corn.[12]
>
>   (ll. 1–12)

The core of Rossetti's technique is here: the Damozel's hair, for example, is both a mystical attribute and an emblem of natural fertility; verbal patterning (the way the word 'even' sits oddly between 'Heaven' and 'seven', the slide from 'robe' to 'wrought' to 'rose', the half-rhyme of 'neck' and 'back') is powerful but controlled and purposive. Rossetti was not always as good as this, but this is what he could do.

The influence of the *Germ* on other young artists far exceeded its poor sales, which brought the magazine to an end after only four issues. One important effect of the magazine, which included pictures by Holman Hunt, Collinson, Deverell and Ford Madox Brown, was the creation of permanent links between Pre-Raphaelite illustration and poetry. As Lorraine Kooistra points out, the subsequent Pre-Raphaelite illustrations provided for William Allingham's *The Music Master* (1855) and the edition of Tennyson's *Poems* published by Edward Moxon (1857) brought a collaborative spirit and a new respectability to the commercial art of book illustration in the nineteenth century.[13]

There has been a tendency among later critics to keep Pre-Raphaelite painting in a separate compartment from poetry; its originators perceived no such necessity. Inspired by the work of poet-painter William Blake, the group were especially interested in how text and image worked together to create meaning.[14] Members of the Brotherhood were in the habit of writing poems to accompany their paintings, and producing paintings to illustrate each other's poems. Dante Gabriel Rossetti would even inscribe verses directly on to his picture frame. This juxtaposition of text and image, found in illuminated manuscripts and stained glass, forms part of the 'medievalism' that the Pre-Raphaelites helped to popularize, but its significance goes well beyond this phenomenon: it influenced not just a 'Gothic' but a 'graphic' revival in English literary culture.

In 1856, another phase of Pre-Raphaelitism began, once again as a collaboration between painters and poets. Oxford undergraduates and aspiring painters Edward Burne-Jones and William Morris produced a periodical called the *Oxford and Cambridge Magazine*, whose medievalist writing was so deeply influenced by the *Germ* that Dante Gabriel Rossetti referred to it as 'The Oxford and Cambridge Germ'.[15] In 1857, this trio, along with Valentine Prinsep, Arthur Hughes and others, painted Arthurian murals on the walls of the Oxford Union Debating Room.[16] During this sojourn, another Oxford undergraduate, Algernon Charles Swinburne, introduced himself. This new group formed Pre-Raphaelitism's second wave, which crested with the publication of Morris's *The Defence of Guenevere* in 1858.[17]

Dedicated to Rossetti, this work was identified by contemporary critics as the first Pre-Raphaelite book of poetry. Swinburne would later note in the *Fortnightly Review* that the volume 'seems to have been now lauded and now decried as the result and expression of a school rather than a man'.[18] A positive review in the *Tablet* pointed out that the 'dedication . . . suggests already the Pre-Rafaelite sympathies of the author, and the book itself fully establishes them'.[19] These 'sympathies' were viewed with a suspicion that set the tone for future criticism of Pre-Raphaelite poetry. The *Athenaeum* rejected Morris's 'book of Pre-Raphaelite minstrelsy as a curiosity which shows how far affectation may mislead an earnest man towards the fog-land of Art'.[20] With some exceptions, Morris's first volume was either ignored or badly received, and was neither a critical nor a commercial success. One admirer, however, came directly from the 'List of Immortals'. Robert Browning, whose dramatic monologues heavily influenced *The Defence of Guenevere*, wrote to William Michael Rossetti that Morris's were 'the only new poems to my mind since there's no telling when'.[21] It took Browning, a poet equally underappreciated in his own time, to perceive the modern innovations beneath the 'fog-land' of Morris's medieval locations and protagonists.

Formally inventive, the title poem combines *terza rima* and elements of dramatic monologue. Beginning *in medias res*, it embodies the medievalism, eroticism, immediacy and pictorial detail that had come to be associated with the Pre-Raphaelites:

> But, knowing now that they would have her speak,
> She threw her wet hair backward from her brow,
> Her hand close to her mouth touching her cheek . . .
>
> (ll. 1–3)

On trial for her life, the adulterous Queen Guenevere prepares to defend herself, using her beauty to distract her voyeuristic accusers. She invites them to 'see my breast rise, / Like waves of purple sea' and to observe 'through my long throat how the words go up / In ripples to my mouth . . .' (ll. 226–7, 230–31). This kind of knowing female sexuality, which never ceased to attract attention, would become a major theme of later Pre-Raphaelite work.

Although its poetry was becoming increasingly significant, Pre-Raphaelitism's fine-art connections were by no means on the wane. No longer just young pretenders, Rossetti and Holman Hunt had become commercially successful painters and Millais was a member of the RA. In 1861, Morris, Rossetti, Burne-Jones, Ford Madox Brown and others formed a decorative arts firm which in 1875 became the famous and influential Morris & Co. Its formation inaugurated the Arts and Crafts Movement, which, in opposition to the rise of mechanically mass-produced items, advocated the design of hand-crafted, individualized pieces for the home as well as for public buildings. In this way, a Pre-Raphaelite resistance to the increasingly mechanized Victorian age influenced the private domestic environment as well as public spaces.

The first successful Pre-Raphaelite publication came neither from the original Brotherhood nor the second wave of Oxford painters and poets. Christina Rossetti's *Goblin Market* (1862), with illustrations by Dante Gabriel, was so well received that Swinburne breathlessly dubbed her 'the Jael who led their [Pre-Raphaelite] host to victory'.[22] Christina's subsequent devotional work would gradually abandon the medievalist, fantasy spirit that animates poems like 'Goblin Market' and 'The Prince's Progress'. But her early poems were received as distinctly Pre-Raphaelite. Such was the impact of *Goblin Market* that in 1894 she was still being referred to as 'Queen of the Pre-Raphaelites'.[23]

Though she may have been its temporary queen, Christina had reservations about the movement that caused her eventually to abdicate her throne. She was a devout Christian, and probably objected to her brother's habit of co-opting sacramental language and imagery for his secular love poetry. But her religious sensibilities were not the only cause of her scepticism. As both a poet and a muse (she modelled for various paintings) she offered a distinctive, female perspective on Pre-Raphaelite obsessions such as the intersection of life and art, of real and ideal love, and of creator and created.

Christina's 1856 sonnet 'In an Artist's Studio' describes the unsettling experience of viewing a male artist's multiple portraits of one model. Each canvas evokes 'The same one meaning, neither more nor less' as the artist 'feeds upon her face by day and night', and paints the woman 'Not as she is, but as she fills his dream' (ll. 8, 9, 14). The concluding lines of Dante Gabriel's 1869 sonnet 'The Portrait' (included in *The House of Life* sequence) seem like a defiant rebuttal to Christina's poem: 'Her face is made her shrine. Let all men note / That in all years (O Love, thy gift is this!) / They that would look on her must come to me' (ll. 12–14). The 'quarrel' between brother and sister is not so much about the objectification of women as about the male artist's self-worship. Or, to put it another way, at issue is the price paid by the imagination for the triumph Dante Gabriel celebrates, and which (in Christina's trenchant words) limits him to 'The same one meaning'.

Pre-Raphaelite poetry was poised to achieve mainstream acceptance, surviving even the scandalized critical reception of George Meredith's 1862 sonnet sequence *Modern Love*. It is significant that this dissection of adultery and marital breakdown, set in the bedrooms and at the dinner-tables of recognizably contemporary middle-class homes, and about as far from pseudo-medieval romance as it was possible to get, was still identified as a 'Pre-Raphaelite' poem. The reference on this occasion was not to dreamy eroticism but to something the *Spectator* dismissed as a 'confusion between a "fast" taste and what Mr Meredith mistakes for courageous realism – poetic pre-Raphaelitism'.[24]

In that same year, and writing in the same journal, Swinburne published a ground-breaking review of Charles Baudelaire's verse. Its ideas about the purpose of poetry would be embraced by the Pre-Raphaelites and later by the Aesthetes. Swinburne asserted that a 'poet's business is presumably to write good verses, and by no means to redeem the age and remould society'. By this he did not mean that poets should be oblivious to the world around them, but rather that poetry should not be bound by a sort of Protestant work ethic which insisted that 'a poem is the better for containing a moral lesson or assisting in a tangible and material good work'.[25]

Swinburne's next significant publication, *Poems and Ballads* (1866), tested this theory to the limits of critical tolerance. Poems whose subject matter included sado-masochism, blasphemy, homosexuality and necrophilia certainly could not be accused of 'containing a moral lesson', or at least not one that recommended itself to a reading public that had barely begun to accept Robert Browning. As David Riede notes, Swinburne's attention-seeking poetry helped to position Pre-Raphaelitism (with which he was associated) in opposition to mainstream Victorian culture.[26] In Swinburne's hands, Pre-Raphaelite close attention to detail becomes positively forensic, as is evident in 'Laus Veneris':

> Asleep or waking is it? for her neck,
> Kissed over close, wears yet a purple speck
>   Wherein the pained blood falters and goes out;
> Soft, and stung softly – fairer for a fleck.
>
> But though my lips shut sucking on the place,
> There is no vein at work upon her face;
>   Her eyelids are so peaceable, no doubt
> Deep sleep has warmed her blood through all its ways.
>
> (ll. 1–8)

Withdrawn by its original publisher, *Poems and Ballads* was defended in pamphlets by Swinburne himself and by William Michael Rossetti, who bemoaned 'times like ours, when the advent of even so poor and pretentious a poetaster as a Robert Buchanan stirs storms in teapots'.[27] From this aside, a major literary controversy was brewed.

Buchanan, a minor poet and critic, struck back with 'The Fleshly School of Poetry', his infamous 1871 review of Dante Gabriel Rossetti's first volume of original poems. The book had been critically well received, though it should be noted that its reviewers were mostly Rossetti's friends. Influenced by the medieval Italian poetry of Dante and Petrarch, *Poems* (1870) included the first half of Rossetti's sonnet sequence *The House of Life* (published in complete form in 1881) and sonnets written to accompany his paintings. Alongside medievalist fare such as revised versions of 'The Blessed Damozel' and 'The Staff and the Scrip' were poems dealing with contemporary matters, such as

'Jenny', a dramatic monologue spoken by a young man to the prostitute with whom he spends the night, and 'The Burden of Nineveh', a Shelleyan meditation on man, his monuments and the passage of time.

Buchanan's strongly worded review attacked both Rossetti and his Pre-Raphaelite associates, whom he dubbed 'the fleshly school'. Comparing Rossetti's paintings and poetry, Buchanan found they shared 'the same thinness and transparence of design, the same combination of the simple and the grotesque, the same morbid deviation from healthy forms of life'. His poems were even worse than those of the 'glibly imitative' Morris and the 'transcendently superficial' Swinburne. The fleshly school were further condemned for 'their droll medieval garments' and 'their funny archaic speech'. Their work was a contagion, spreading like 'measles' through younger poetic 'imitators' such as Arthur O'Shaughnessy, John Payne and Philip Bourke Marston.[28]

Pre-Raphaelite poetry was denounced for its intellectual weakness, sexual obsession and downright weirdness. The poets, in pursuit of their determination to 'extol fleshliness', were trying to claim that 'poetic expression is greater than poetic thought' and that 'the body is greater than the soul, and sound superior to sense'. The fleshly school promoted the idea 'that the poet, properly to develop his poetic faculty, must be an intellectual hermaphrodite, to whom the very facts of day and night are lost in a whirl of aesthetic terminology'.[29]

Although Rossetti wrote a stinging reply, 'The Stealthy School of Criticism', in the *Athenaeum*, the damage was done. Pre-Raphaelite poetry would be inextricably linked with the pornographic, the unhealthy, the morbid and the feminized. As late as 1900, William Michael was still emphasizing his brother's 'masculine traits', insisting rather sternly: 'He did not "yearn".' The more readers learned about Dante Gabriel the man, 'the less room will be left for the notion of a pallid and anaemic "aesthete"'.[30]

In some ways, Pre-Raphaelite poetry is an invention of Buchanan's essay, which unwittingly helped immortalize it by grouping the poets together and suggesting common aims, methods and objectives. Ironically, the same 'deliberately abnormal'

characteristics derided by Buchanan would attract Aesthetes and
Decadents like Oscar Wilde, Aubrey Beardsley, Arthur Symons
and Ernest Dowson, not to mention W. B. Yeats.[31] It may seem
strange that a movement founded on principles of 'truth to nature'
should be taken up with enthusiasm by the Aesthetes, who
championed the artificial and the unnatural. But it was Pre-
Raphaelitism in its later stages, with its worship of beauty, fusion
of the visual and the literary, and rebellion against cultural norms
which held the greatest appeal. Pre-Raphaelitism had provided a
bridge between Romantic poetry and the poetry of the *fin de siècle*.
The spirit of the *Germ* informed magazines such as the *Yellow
Book* (1894–7) and the *Savoy* (1896), publications which presented
a mix of poems, prose and illustration by such figures as Yeats,
Beardsley, Symons, Walter Sickert and Joseph Conrad. The
Rhymers' Club, a literary dining club begun in 1891 by Yeats and
Ernest Rhys, produced anthologies of poetry in 1892 and 1894.
The club's informal, shifting membership, social nature and loose
but passionate literary aims recalled the early days of the PRB.

In the twentieth century, the Pre-Raphaelite poets fell into
disregard. Dismissed by the Modernists, they have yet to be re-
admitted to the realms of serious English poetry. Pre-Raphaelitism
remains widely perceived as a movement which never really grew
up. Even Dante Gabriel Rossetti tried to disown it in later life:
'As for all the prattle about Pre-Raphaelitism, I confess to you I
am weary of it, and long have been. Why should we go on talking
about the visionary vanities of half-a-dozen boys? We've all
grown out of them, I hope, by now.'[32] Swinburne asserted that
'Pre-Raphaelite' was 'never applicable to any but the work of my
earliest youth written at college' and had 'long ceased to be
applicable . . . to the poetic work of my two elders [Rossetti and
Morris]'.[33] Both Yeats and T. S. Eliot regarded Pre-Raphaelitism
as a sort of childish thing which a writer must put away upon
achieving literary maturity.

If there is still no critical consensus on these issues, this is in
part because there is no agreement as to the exact parameters of
the term 'Pre-Raphaelitism' itself. The Pre-Raphaelites themselves
set the tone for this debate, though some of them at least had
ulterior motives for rewriting history. William Michael Rossetti

(by this time the guardian of the siblings' literary heritage) argued in 1895 that 'the name still subsists in a very active condition – which is also a very lax and undefined one'.[34] This echoes Swinburne's opinion twenty years earlier of the 'rather foolish and now long since obsolete word Pre-Raphaelite', which 'for the sake of common accuracy ... should now be disused'.[35] Scholars like Ifor Evans, William E. Fredeman, James Sambrook, Jerome McGann, David Riede and Isobel Armstrong have commented on this imprecision, but none has succeeded in formulating a definition with which everyone would agree. The movement's life-span may plausibly be argued to cover one decade or six, and the body of work associated with it will expand or shrink accordingly. Those who draw a distinction between the movement's literary and visual aspects, for example, and who at least in art-historical terms are keen to divide it into distinct chronological phases, find themselves at odds with those who see it as a broad, shifting cultural phenomenon whose development and effects should be studied holistically. With specific regard to Pre-Raphaelite poetry, the diversity of figures and the difficulty of identifying membership of a specific group (whether defined by social ties or intellectual affinity) make the drawing of boundaries seem pointless.

It is not my aim to propose a neat resolution of this difficulty. Rather, I wish to suggest that the difficulty itself offers a kind of opportunity. The commonalities of theme which are discernible in my selection (the difference between real and ideal love, the relationship of dreams to reality, the role of the artist in a changing world, the disparity between intellect and emotion, the conflict between body and soul, and the function of history in the present) are not meant to suggest that Pre-Raphaelite poetry is a unified or homogenous entity. Shared themes mask a radical diversity of style and tone, a stubborn clinging to individual vision.

Although working with roughly similar themes and ideas, the Pre-Raphaelite poets are not simply dogmatic 'imitators' of each other, as Buchanan's essay would have it. Despite their shared medievalist trappings, it would be difficult, for instance, to confuse Rossetti's languid Damozel with Morris's defiant Guenevere. The

Pre-Raphaelites were, paradoxically perhaps, a group movement that enshrined individuality. They self-consciously (some would say naïvely) strove to place individual artistic merit above other considerations of taste and belief, an aspiration sympathetic to the doctrine of 'art for art's sake'.

Like many Victorian projects, Pre-Raphaelitism is characterized as much by contradiction as agreement, deriving both strengths and weaknesses from its diverse, informal and kaleidoscopic membership. This movement's continuing involvement with other arts, such as painting, illustration and decoration, adds further layers of complexity. Its approach resists our twenty-first-century practice of separating the arts into distinct disciplines. Pre-Raphaelite images and poems illuminate each other, which may suggest a more prosaic obstacle in the rediscovery of the poetry: the prohibitive cost of illustrated, colour anthologies. I have included a list of key paintings and illustrations, all widely available in book form and searchable on the internet, as a starting point for readers interested in exploring Pre-Raphaelite visual culture.

Selections have been made from both early and later works, and from both major and minor figures. Pre-Raphaelitism's most famous poets are Dante Gabriel Rossetti, William Morris and Algernon Charles Swinburne, but I have also included work by Coventry Patmore and George Meredith as well as lesser-known figures like William Allingham, William Bell Scott and Arthur O'Shaughnessy. Although most of these did not remain lifelong Pre-Raphaelite acolytes or friends, their poetry makes it plain that they all came under its influence at one time or another. A diversity of subject matter and style is represented, from the lush ballads of Swinburne to the stark medievalist narratives of Morris; from Rossetti's erotic dreamscapes to his sister Christina's cautionary allegories. Also included are poems which the Pre-Raphaelites wrote to and about themselves, both during their early heyday in the 1860s and in their twilight years.

Pre-Raphaelitism, based as it was on social networking and a dining-club atmosphere, was an almost exclusively male movement, which has made its near-obsession with the portrayal of women a heated topic in Victorian studies. In an era which saw an unprecedented number of women entering the literary marketplace, Pre-Raphaelitism maintained strict demarcations between women's roles (as muses) and men's (as creators). In this volume, poems about women have been chosen to demonstrate a range of attitudes and approaches: Coventry Patmore's veneration of monogamous love in 'The Gracious Chivalry'; Rossetti's studies of women as the embodiment of the poet's soul in *The House of Life* sonnets; Swinburne's call for a kind of sado-masochistic gender equality in 'A Match'; Christina Rossetti and Elizabeth Siddal's critiques of female objectification in *Monna Innominata* and 'The Lust of the Eyes'.

My selection acknowledges both the justice, and the limitations, of W. H. Mallock's recipe for making a 'modern Pre-Raphaelite poem'. All the stock ingredients have been provided. There are plenty of damozels, flowers, archaic words, stars and lilies. But I have also taken the word *modern* in a sense Mallock did not intend. In idiom, in voice, in poetic form, the Pre-Raphaelites were innovators as well as dreamers. Their work represented an irruption of energy, unrespectable and still resonant, if we choose to listen. What Arthur O'Shaughnessy so memorably expressed, in his 1874 'Ode' on poetic ambition, stands as a tribute to the best, if not the whole, of Pre-Raphaelite poetry:

> We are the music makers,
>   And we are the dreamers of dreams,
> Wandering by lone sea-breakers,
>   And sitting by desolate streams; –
> World-losers and world-forsakers,
>   On whom the pale moon gleams:
> Yet we are the movers and shakers
>   Of the world for ever, it seems.
>
>   (ll. 1–8)

NOTES

1. W. H. Mallock, *Every Man His Own Poet: Or, the Inspired Singer's Recipe Book* (Shrimpton & Son, 1872), pp. 13–14.

2. Robert Buchanan (as 'Thomas Maitland'), 'The Fleshly School of Poetry: Mr D. G. Rossetti', *Contemporary Review* 18 (October 1871), p. 349 (referred to in subsequent notes as *FS*).

3. Dedicated to William Michael Rossetti, Swinburne's essay on Blake makes this doctrine explicit: 'Art for art's sake first of all, and afterwards we may suppose all the rest shall be added to her ...' (*William Blake: A Critical Essay*, John Camden Hotten, 1868, p. 91).

4. 'Young England' was a movement advocating a return to an idealized feudal relationship between the aristocracy and the working classes; 'Two Nations' refers to the rich and the poor; it is also the subtitle of Disraeli's *Sybil* of 1845, a polemic novel about the predicament of England's working classes.

5. See Dante Gabriel Rossetti's *The Annunciation* (or *Ecce Ancilla Domini!*) (1849–50).

6. 'The English Renaissance of Art', *Essays and Lectures by Oscar Wilde* (Methuen, 1908), p. 120. Originally delivered in New York, 1882.

7. With the exception of W. M. Rossetti, all of the Brotherhood had also been members of the Cyclographic Society, a sketching and drawing club which was the forerunner of the PRB.

8. According to William Holman Hunt, this name 'had first been used as a term of contempt by our enemies' (quoted in W. M. Rossetti, *Dante Gabriel Rossetti: His Family Letters with a Memoir*, 2 vols., Ellis and Elvey, 1895, vol. 1, p. 127; referred to in subsequent notes as *FLM*).

9. *FLM* 1, 135.

10. Holman Hunt, *Pre-Raphaelitism and the Pre-Raphaelite Brotherhood*, 2 vols. (Macmillan, 1905–6), vol. 1, pp. 110–11.

11. ll. 24–5, 'Morning Sleep', William Bell Scott; ll. 1–2, 'Viola and Olivia', John Tupper; ll. 6–8, 'The Sight Beyond', Walter Deverell.

12. The extract quoted here is from the *Germ* 2 (February 1850). The poem was revised for its appearance in Rossetti's *Poems* (1870), the version given later in this collection.

13. Lorraine Janzen Kooistra, 'Poetry and Illustration' in *A Companion to Victorian Poetry*, ed. Richard Cronin, Alison Chapman and Antony H. Harrison (Blackwell, 2002), pp. 246–61.

14. The Pre-Raphaelites were largely responsible for reviving Blake's

reputation in the Victorian era. Rossetti owned one of the most important of Blake's manuscripts, his 'Notebook', which he bought for ten shillings in 1847 (now in the British Library, Add. MS 49460); along with William Michael Rossetti, he subsequently helped Anne Gilchrist to finish her late husband Alexander's life of Blake (1863), the first major biography of him.

15. W. M. Rossetti (ed.), *Ruskin: Rossetti: Preraphaelitism: Papers 1854–1862* (George Allen, 1899), p. 135 (referred to in subsequent notes as *RRP*).

16. Now known as the 'Old Library'; the project was a failure as the paintings quickly faded because of poor preparation and technical inexperience.

17. Both Burne-Jones and Morris joined the Hogarth Club (1858–61), which organized meetings and exhibitions, allowing artists to network with each other and with patrons. Most of the PRB were members.

18. 'Morris's *Life and Death of Jason*', *Fortnightly Review* 8 (July 1867), p. 20.

19. Unsigned review, *Tablet* 19 (April 1858), p. 266.

20. H. F. Chorley, '*The Defence of Guenevere and Other Poems*, by William Morris', *Athenaeum* 1588 (3 April 1858), p. 428.

21. *RRP*, 219.

22. Edmund Gosse, *The Life of Algernon Charles Swinburne* (Macmillan, 1917), p. 137.

23. Article by Sarah A. Tooley in the *Young Woman* (November 1894), quoted in *FLM* 1, 138.

24. R. H. Hutton, *Spectator* 35 (24 May 1862), p. 580.

25. 'Charles Baudelaire: *Les Fleurs du Mal*', *Spectator* 35 (6 September 1862), p. 998.

26. See David Riede, 'The Pre-Raphaelite School' in *A Companion to Victorian Poetry*, pp. 317–18.

27. W. M. Rossetti, *Swinburne's Poems and Ballads: A Criticism* (John Camden Hotten, 1866), p. 7. Buchanan had anonymously contributed a poor review of Swinburne's work in the *Athenaeum*.

28. *FS*, 337, 350 and 347.

29. *FS*, 335.

30. W. M. Rossetti, introduction to *Praeraphaelite Diaries and Letters* (Hurst and Blackett, 1900), p. 4. Buchanan's insinuations of a

homosexual milieu were wide of the mark; Pre-Raphaelitism itself was not particularly tolerant of overt homosexuality. For example, Simeon Solomon, a gay, commercially successful Pre-Raphaelite painter, was abandoned by the group following his conviction for 'indecency' after being arrested, along with another man, at a public urinal in London.

31. In an essay on George Meredith, Symons praises him as a Decadent poet, defining Decadence as 'learned corruption of language by which style ceases to be organic, and becomes, in the pursuit of some new expressiveness or beauty, deliberately abnormal'. *Studies in Prose and Verse* (J. M. Dent, 1904), p. 149.

32. Reportedly D. G. Rossetti to Hall Caine, *Recollections of Dante Gabriel Rossetti* (Elliot Stock, 1882), p. 219.

33. Letter to John Nichol, 2 April 1876, quoted in Georges Lafourcade, *La Jeunesse de Swinburne*, vol. 2 (Oxford University Press, 1928), p. 38.

34. *FLM* 1, 137.

35. Letter to John Nichol, 2 April 1876.

Further Reading

COLLECTIONS OF PRE-RAPHAELITE WRITING

The first anthology of Pre-Raphaelite poetry, *The Painter-Poets*, ed. Kineton Parkes (Walter Scott, 1890), was compiled while some of the poets were still living, and is valuable for its inclusion of previously unpublished poems by Arthur Hughes and Ford Madox Brown, as well as reprints of poetry unseen since the *Germ* (January–April 1850). Derek Stanford includes prose and critical works in *Pre-Raphaelite Writing* (Dent, 1973), while Cecil Y. Laing concentrates on the poetry for the first and second editions of *The Pre-Raphaelites and Their Circle* (University of Chicago Press, 1968 and 1975). Good recent anthologies include *An Anthology of Pre-Raphaelite Writing*, ed. Carolyn Hares-Stryker (Sheffield Academic Press, 1997), and *The Pre-Raphaelites: Writings and Sources*, ed. Inga Bryden, 4 vols. (Routledge, 1998).

SHORT STORIES BY THE PRE-RAPHAELITES

Originally appearing in the *Germ* 1 (January 1850), Dante Gabriel Rossetti's 'Hand and Soul' is regarded as a Pre-Raphaelite manifesto in fiction and can be found in vol. 3 of Inga Bryden's *The Pre-Raphaelites*. Published originally in the *Oxford and Cambridge Magazine* (1856), William Morris's 'The Story of the

Unknown Church' is in vol. 1 of Bryden's collection, but Edward Burne-Jones's 'The Cousins' and 'A Story of the North' have not been republished, as far as I know, since their appearance in the *Oxford and Cambridge Magazine*. Christina Rossetti's 'The Lost Titian' first appeared in *Commonplace, and Other Short Stories* (F. S. Ellis, 1870), and can be found in Jan Marsh's *Christina Rossetti: Poems and Prose* (Dent, 1994). Vol. 1 of Bryden's anthology also contains Oliver Madox Brown's tale of art student antics, 'Dismal Jemmy'.

CONTEMPORARY ARTICLES, ESSAYS AND LECTURES ON THE PRE-RAPHAELITES

Reading contemporary reviews of the Pre-Raphaelites alongside passionate defences of their work is a useful way to become acquainted with Pre-Raphaelitism's controversies. For the best art criticism, see Charles Dickens's review of PRB painting, 'Old Lamps for New Ones', *Household Words* 12 (15 June 1850); John Ruskin's defence of the Brotherhood in his letter to *The Times* on 13 May 1851 and *Pre-Raphaelitism* (pamphlet, Smith, Elder & Co., 1851); William Michael Rossetti, 'Praeraphaelitism', *Spectator* 24.1214 (4 October 1851), pp. 955–7. See also John Ruskin's lectures: 'Lecture 4: Pre-Raphaelitism', *Lectures on Architecture and Painting* (John Wiley, 1854), and 'Realistic Schools of Painting: Dante Gabriel Rossetti and William Holman Hunt', *The Art of England: Lectures Given in Oxford* (George Allen, 1883). Oscar Wilde praises the PRB in his 1882 lecture 'The English Renaissance of Art', *Essays and Lectures* (Methuen, 1908). The developing Pre-Raphaelite philosophy can be glimpsed in two *Germ* essays: J. L. Tupper's 'The Subject in Art', parts 1 and 3 (January and March 1850), and F. G. Stephens's 'Modern Giants', part 4 (April 1850). For literary controversies, see W. M. Rossetti's defence of Algernon Charles Swinburne, *Swinburne's Poems and Ballads: A Criticism* (pamphlet, John Camden Hotten, 1866). See also Robert Buchanan (as 'Thomas Maitland'), 'The Fleshly School of Poetry: Mr. D. G. Rossetti', *Contemporary Review* 18 (October 1871), pp. 334–50, and the responses to it: Rossetti's 'The Stealthy School of Criticism' in the *Athenaeum* (December 1871) and Swinburne's *Under the Microscope* (pamphlet, D. White, 1872). See also Walter Pater's influential essay on Rossetti's poetry 'Dante Gabriel Rossetti', *Appreciations* (Macmillan, 1890).

CRITICAL AND SCHOLARLY BOOKS ON THE PRE-RAPHAELITES

Although books such as H. Buxton Forman's *Our Living Poets: An Essay in Criticism* (Tinsley, 1871) and G. S. Layard's *Tennyson and His Pre-Raphaelite Illustrators: A Book about a Book* (Stock, 1894) reflect a contemporary interest in Pre-Raphaelite poetry, critical works in the following decades were few and far between. Notable exceptions are Earle T. Welby's *The Victorian Romantics, 1850–1870: The Early Work of Dante Gabriel Rossetti, William Morris, Burne-Jones, Swinburne, Simeon Solomon and Their Associates* (Howe, 1929) and Ifor Evans's *English Poetry in the Later Nineteenth Century* (Methuen, 1933). The 1948 centenary of the PRB inspired significant re-evaluations of Pre-Raphaelite poetry such as Graham Hough's *The Last Romantics* (Duckworth, 1949), John Heath-Stubbs's *The Darkling Plain* (Eyre & Spottiswoode, 1950), D. S. Welland's *The Pre-Raphaelites in Literature and Art* (George Harrap, 1953) and David H. Dickason's *The Daring Young Men: The Story of the American Pre-Raphaelites* (Indiana University Press, 1953). Pre-Raphaelite scholar, collector and enthusiast William E. Fredeman's indispensable *Pre-Raphaelitism: A Bibliocritical Study* (Harvard University Press, 1965) spurred another revival of interest, which saw the publication of John Dixon Hunt's *The Pre-Raphaelite Imagination 1848–1900* (Routledge & Kegan Paul, 1968), Lionel Stephenson's *The Pre-Raphaelite Poets* (University of North Carolina Press, 1972) and *Pre-Raphaelitism: A Collection of Critical Essays*, ed. James Sambrook (University of Chicago Press, 1974). Recent full-length studies of Pre-Raphaelite poetry are scarce, but excellent work on Pre-Raphaelite poets can be found in *The*

Victorian Poet: Poetics and Persona, ed. Joseph Bristow (Croom Helm, 1987), *The Cambridge Companion to Victorian Poetry*, ed. Joseph Bristow (Cambridge University Press, 2000), *A Companion to Victorian Poetry*, ed. Richard Cronin, Alison Chapman and Antony H. Harrison (Blackwell, 2002), *Haunted Texts: Studies in Pre-Raphaelitism*, ed. David Latham (University of Toronto Press, 2003), and Elizabeth Helsinger's *Poetry and the Pre-Raphaelite Arts: Dante Gabriel Rossetti and William Morris* (Yale University Press, 2008). *The Journal of Pre-Raphaelite Studies*, ed. David Latham (York University, Canada, 1977–), is also a good source of current work on Pre-Raphaelite art and literature.

GROUP BIOGRAPHIES AND MEMOIRS OF THE PRE-RAPHAELITES

More biographies have been written on individual Pre-Raphaelite writers and artists than can be included here, but there are several group biographies which provide a useful overview. William Bell Scott's *Autobiographical Notes* (Osgood, McIlvaine, 1892) challenges Rossetti's dominance of the group, as does William Holman Hunt's *Pre-Raphaelitism and the Pre-Raphaelite Brotherhood*, 2 vols. (Macmillan, 1905–6). William E. Fredeman's edition of W. M. Rossetti's *The P.R.B. Journal* (Clarendon Press, 1975) is a useful collection of contemporary papers relating to the Brotherhood, as is W. M. Rossetti's *Ruskin: Rossetti: Pre-Raphaelitism* (George Allen, 1899). W. M. Rossetti also published a memoir in two volumes, *Some Reminiscences* (London, 1906). Twentieth-century publications include Teresa Newman and Ray Watkinson's *Ford Madox Brown and the Pre-Raphaelite Circle* (Chatto & Windus, 1991) and Jan Marsh's compelling biography of the artists' female models, *Pre-Raphaelite Sisterhood* (Quartet, 1985), as well as her authoritative guide *The Pre-Raphaelite Circle* (National Portrait Gallery, 2005). The most recent group biography is Franny Moyle's entertaining and informative *Desperate Romantics* (John Murray, 2009).

A Note on the Texts

This selection is structured by author, the sequence by date of birth. First publication date guides the sequence within each individual poet's work. Exceptions are noted on an individual basis in the Notes.

The texts of these poems are taken from the original volumes or from collected editions published within the period. In order to give a sense of literary Pre-Raphaelitism as it was unfolding, I have chosen to preserve these poems as they were first presented to the reading public. Exceptions are where poems first appeared in contemporary magazines such as the *Germ* and the *Oxford and Cambridge Magazine*. Texts of these poems have been selected from the first volume of poetry in which they appeared, or from the magazine in which they first appeared if they weren't subsequently published in book form. Any exceptions to this are dealt with on an individual basis in the Notes. A number of poems taken from a particular publication are arranged in the order in which they appear within that publication. Poem texts taken from the *Germ* are from a reprint published by Thomas Mosher (1898).

A few basic elements of house style, mostly typographic, have been applied to the poem texts and any 'American' spellings ('gray', 'splendor', etc.) have been anglicized. Apart from this, original spelling and punctuation have been retained, including any inconsistencies, archaisms and other oddities – often deliberate on the part of the poets in order to reproduce a sense of the medieval. Any footnotes are part of the original texts.

In order to include as many authors and poems as possible, I have chosen to extract some of the longer works, for example Algernon Charles Swinburne's *Tristram of Lyonesse* and George

Meredith's *Modern Love*. Inevitably, something of the complete poems' richness is lost in this process, but I hope at least to draw attention to the existence and the appeal of the longer works. I particularly regret not being able to include Dante Gabriel Rossetti's *The House of Life* and Christina Rossetti's *Monna Innominata* in their entirety, but too much of their other work would have been left out in order to accommodate these lengthy sonnet sequences.

WILLIAM BELL SCOTT

From *Rosabell*

12

Down the wet pavement gleam the lamps,
While the cold wind whistles past;
A distant heel rings hurrying home,
It lessens into stillness now,
And she is left alone again.
The rain-drops from shop-eaves are blown
Against her face, she turns,
The wind lifts up the gaudy scarf,
Faded now, with ragged fringe,
And flings it blinding o'er her head.
Her lips are sharp, as if a scorn
Of all humanity had shrunk
And bitten them; her eyes
They are not sunk, for generous cares
Are no part of her misery:
They never weep, for she can think
Of long ago without a sigh,
But they are blind and insolent;
Then why measure tears in a cracked wine-cup,
Or blame the madman should he laugh
While his mother's funeral passes?
Can the outcast retrace her steps?
Would any mourn with her although
She watered the earth with tears?
She cannot wash Christ's feet with them,
For He has gone to heaven:
Perhaps she is without the pale,
And would not if she could.
Give her but heat, and food, and drink,
She needs no more; the sun but shines
That the shadow where she sits may be
The darker, so she feels the light
In which the insects all rejoice
Can unenlivening fall on such

As have a soul. But hark, she sings,   35
Sings a song we write not here.

Morning Sleep

Another day hath dawned
Since, hastily and tired, I threw myself
Into the dark lap of advancing sleep.
Meanwhile through the oblivion of the night
The ponderous world its old course hath fulfilled;   5
And now the gradual sun begins to throw
Its slanting glory on the heads of trees,
And every bird stirs in its nest revealed,
And shakes its dewy wings.

A blessed gift
Unto the weary hath been mine to-night,   10
Slumber unbroken: now it floats away:
But whether 'twere not best to woo it still,
The head thus properly disposed, the eyes
In a continual dawning, mingling earth
And heaven with vagrant fantasies, one hour,   15
Yet for another hour? I will not break
The shining woof; I will not rudely leap
Out of this golden atmosphere, through which
I see the forms of immortalities.
Verily, soon enough the labouring day   20
With its necessitous unmusical calls
Will force the indolent conscience into life.

The uncouth moth upon the window-panes
Hath ceased to flap, or traverse with blind whirr
The room's dusk corners; and the leaves without   25
Vibrate upon their thin stems with the breeze
Flying towards the light. To an Eastern vale
That light may now be waning, and across
The tall reeds by the Ganges lotus-paved,

30 Lengthening the shadows of the banyan-tree.
    The rice-fields are all silent in the glow,
    All silent the deep heaven without a cloud,
    Burning like molten gold. A red canoe
    Crosses with fan-like paddles and the sound
35 Of feminine song, freighted with great-eyed maids
    Whose unzoned bosoms swell on the rich air;
    A lamp is in each hand; some mystic rite
    Go they to try. Such rites the birds may see,
    Ibis or emu, from their cocoa nooks, –
40 What time the granite sentinels that watch
    The mouths of cavern-temples hail the first
    Faint star, and feel the gradual darkness blend
    Their august lineaments; – what time Haroun
    Perambulated Bagdat, and none knew
45 He was the Caliph who knocked soberly
    By Giafar's hand at their gates shut betimes; –
    What time prince Assad sat on the high hill
    'Neath the pomegranate-tree, long wearying
    For his lost brother's step; – what time, as now,
50 Along our English sky, flame-furrows cleave
    And break the quiet of the cold blue clouds,
    And the first rays look in upon our roofs.

    Let the day come or go; there is no let
    Or hindrance to the indolent wilfulness
55 Of fantasy and dream-land. Place and time
    And bodily weight are for the wakeful only,
    Now they exist not: life is like that cloud,
    Floating, poised happily in mid-air, bathed
    In a sustaining halo, soft yet clear,
60 Voyaging on, though to no bourne; all heaven
    Its own wide home alike, earth far below
    Fading still further, further. Yet we see,
    In fancy, its green fields, its towers and towns
    Smoking with life, its roads with traffic thronged
65 And tedious travellers within iron cars,
    Its rivers with their ships and labourers,

To whose raised eyes, as, stretched upon the sward,
They may enjoy some interval of rest,
That little cloud appears no living thing,
Although it moves, and changes as it moves.   70
There is an old and memorable tale
Of some sound sleeper being borne away
By banded fairies in the mottled hour
Before the cock-crow, through unknown weird woods
And mighty forests, where the boughs and roots   75
Opened before him, closed behind; thenceforth
A wise man lived he all unchanged by years.
Perchance again these fairies may return,
And evermore shall I remain as now,
A dreamer half awake, a wandering cloud!   80

The spell

Of Merlin old that ministered to fate,
The tales of visiting ghosts, or fairy elves,
Or witchcraft, are no fables. But his task
Is ended with the night; the thin white moon
Evades the eye, the sun breaks through the trees,   85
And the charmed wizard comes forth a mere man
From out his circle. Thus it is, whate'er
We know and understand hath lost the power
Over us; we are then the masters. Still
All Fancy's world is real; no diverse mark   90
Is on the stores of memory, whether gleaned
From childhood's early wonder at the charm
That bound the lady in the echoless cave
Where lay the sheath'd sword and the bugle horn, –
Or from the fullgrown intellect that works   95
From age to age, exploring darkest truths,
With sympathy and knowledge in one yoke
Ploughing the harvest land.

The lark is up,

Piercing the dazzling sky beyond the search
Of the acutest love: enough for me   100

To hear its song: but now it dies away,
Leaving the chirping sparrow to attract
The listless ear, – a minstrel, sooth to say,
Nearly as good. And now a hum like that
105   Of swarming bees on meadow-flowers comes up.
Each hath its just and yet luxurious joy,
As if to live were to be blessed. The mild
Maternal influence of nature thus
Ennobles both the sentient and the dead; –
110   The human heart is as an altar wreathed,
On which old wine pours, streaming o'er the leaves
And down the symbol-carved sides. Behold!
Unbidden, yet most welcome, who be these?
The high-priests of this altar, poet-kings; –
115   Chaucer, still young with silvery beard that seems
Worthy the adoration of a child;
And Spenser, perfect master, to whom all
Sweet graces ministered. The shut eye sees
Brave pictures! The immortals pass along
120   Into the heaven, and others follow still,
Each on his own ray-path, till all the field
Is threaded with the foot-prints of the great.
And now the passengers are lost; long lines
Only are left, all intertwisted, dark
125   Upon a flood of light . . . I am awake!
I hear domestic voices on the stair!

Already hath the mower finished half
His summer day's ripe task; already hath
His scythe been whetted often; and the heaps
130   Behind him lie like ridges from the tide.
In sooth, it is high time to wave away
The cup of Comus, though with nectar filled,
And sweet as odours to the mariner
From lands unseen, across the wide blank sea.

Sonnet
Early Aspirations

How many a throb of the young poet-heart,
   Aspiring to the ideal bliss of Fame,
   Deems that Time soon may sanctify his claim
Among the sons of song to dwell apart. –
   Time passes – passes! the aspiring flame   5
Of Hope shrinks down; the white flower Poesy
Breaks on its stalk, and from its earth-turned eye
   Drop sleepy tears instead of that sweet dew
   Rich with inspiring odours, insect wings
Drew from its leaves with every changing sky,   10
   While its young innocent petals unsunn'd grew.
   No more in pride to other ears he sings,
But with a dying charm himself unto: –
   For a sad season: then, to active life he springs.

To the Artists Called P.R.B.

I thank you, brethren in Sincerity, –
   One who, within the temperate climes of Art,
   From the charmed circle humbly stands apart,
Scornfully also, with a listless eye
Watching old marionettes' vitality;   5
   For you have shown, with youth's brave confidence,
   The honesty of true speech and the sense
Uniting life with 'nature,' earth with sky.

In faithful hearts Art strikes its roots far down,
   And bears both flower and fruit with seeded core;   10
   When Truth dies out, the fruit appears no more.
But the flower hides a worm within its crown.
   God-speed you onward! once again our way
   Shall be made odorous with fresh flowers of May.

'I Go to be Cured at Avilion'
(To a Picture Painted 1847)

Silently, swiftly the funeral barge
Homeward bears the brave and good,
His wide pall sweeping the murmuring marge,
 Flowing to the end of the world.
Kings' daughters watching round his head,
His brazen breastplate wet with blood
And tears by these kings' daughters shed,
 Watching to the end of the world.

A cresset of spices and sandal-wood
Fills the wake with an odour rare;
Two swans lead dimly athwart the flood,
 Lead on to the end of the world.
From the distant wold what brings the blast?
The trump's recall, the watch-fire's glare, –
Oh! let these fade into the past,
 As he fares to the end of the world.

From the misty woods a holier sound –
For the monks are singing their evensong –
Swoons faintly o'er the harvest-ground,
 As they pass to the end of the world.
From the minster where the steep roofs are,
The passing bell, that voice supreme,
Sends a farewell faintly far,
 As they fade to the end of the world.

It is gone, it is closed, the last red gleam,
Darkness shuts the fiery day;
Over the windless, boatless stream
The odours and embers have died away:
 They are gone to the end of the world.

Art for Art's Sake

'Art for art's sake,' – very well,
Your picture you don't care to sell?
Yes, yes, I do, and thus I try
To paint so bright they want to buy –
'Art for art's sake,' – then I fear   5
You want no sympathetic tear
From the stalls and boxes here?
Yes, yes, I do, I write it so,
A hundred nights the crowds shall go –
'Art for art's sake,' – Heavens! Once more,   10
You'd say again things said before?
And pray, why not? I wish I could
Stand as Shakespeare, Fletcher, stood –
Nay, dear, aspirant rather write
As Shakespeare were he here to-night,   15
That would be far more worth prizing: –
But who can rise to that high pass –
        Who can *rise*? alas, alas,
Shakespeare little thought of rising!

JOHN RUSKIN

The Last Smile

She sat beside me yesternight,
    With lip and eye so sweetly smiling,
So full of soul, of life, of light,
    So beautifully care-beguiling,
That she had almost made me gay,
Had almost charmed the thought away
(Which, like the poisoned desert wind,
Came sick and heavy o'er my mind),
That memory soon mine all would be,
And she would smile no more for me.

Christ Church,
Oxford Night

Faint from the bell the ghastly echoes fall,
    That grates within the grey cathedral tower –
Let me not enter through the portal tall,
    Lest the strange spirit of the moonless hour
Should give a life to those pale people, who
Lie in their fretted niches, two and two –
Each with his head on pillowy stone reposed,
And his hands lifted, and his eyelids closed.

A cold and starless vapour, through the night,
    Moves as the paleness of corruption passes
Over a corpse's features, like a light
    That half illumines what it most effaces;
The calm round water gazes on the sky,
Like the reflection of the lifeless eye
Of one who sleeps and dreams of being slain,
Struggling in frozen frenzy, and in vain.

From many a mouldering oriel, as to flout
    Its pale, grave brow of ivy-tressèd stone,

Comes the incongruous laugh, and revel shout –
   Above, some solitary casement, thrown   20
Wide open to the wavering night wind,
Admits its chill – so deathful, yet so kind
Unto the fevered brow and fiery eye
Of one, whose night-hour passeth sleeplessly.

Ye melancholy chambers! I could shun   25
   The darkness of your silence, with such fear,
As places where slow murder had been done.
   How many noble spirits have died here –
Withering away in yearnings to aspire,
Gnawed by mocked hope – devoured by their own   30
   fire!
Methinks the grave must feel a colder bed
To spirits such as these, than unto common dead.

The Mirror

I

It saw, it knew thy loveliness,
   Thy burning lip, and glancing eye,
Each lightning look, each silken tress
   Thy marble forehead braided by,
Like an embodied music, twined   5
About a brightly breathing mind.

II

Alas! its face is dark and dim;
   No more its lightless depth below
That glancing eye shall seem to swim,
   That brow to breathe or glow;
Its treacherous depth – its heartless hue –   5
Forgets the form that once it knew.

III

With many a changing shape and face
   Its surface may be marked and crossed –
Portrayed with as distinct a grace
   As thine, whose loveliness is lost;
But there's one mirror, good and true,
That doth not lose what once it knew.

IV

My thoughts are with that beauty blest,
   A breathing, burning, living vision,
That, like a dove with wings at rest,
   Still haunts the heart it makes Elysian;
And days and times pass like a sleep
Softly sad, and still, and deep;
And, oh! what grief would wakening be
From slumber bright with dreams of thee!

The Old Water-Wheel

It lies beside the river; where its marge
Is black with many an old and oarless barge;
And yeasty filth, and leafage wild and rank
Stagnate and batten by the crumbling bank.

Once, slow revolving by the industrious mill,
It murmured, only on the Sabbath still;
And evening winds its pulse-like beating bore
Down the soft vale, and by the winding shore.

Sparkling around its orbèd motion flew,
With quick, fresh fall, the drops of dashing dew;
Through noon-tide heat that gentle rain was flung,
And verdant round the summer herbage sprung.

Now dancing light and sounding motion cease,
In these dark hours of cold continual peace;
Through its black bars the unbroken moonlight
    flows,   15
And dry winds howl about its long repose;

And mouldering lichens creep, and mosses grey
Cling round its arms in gradual decay,
Amidst the hum of men – which doth not suit
That shadowy circle, motionless, and mute.   20

So, by the sleep of many a human heart,
The crowd of men may bear their busy part,
Where withered, or forgotten, or subdued,
Its noisy passions have left solitude:

Ah! little can they trace the hidden truth!   25
What waves have moved it in the vale of youth!
And little can its broken chords avow
How once they sounded. All is silent now.

The Hills of Carrara

I

Amidst a vale of springing leaves,
    Where spreads the vine its wandering root,
And cumbrous fall the autumnal sheaves,
    And olives shed their sable fruit,
    And gentle winds and waters never mute   5
Make of young boughs and pebbles pure
    One universal lute,
And bright birds, through the myrtle copse obscure,
Pierce, with quick notes, and plumage dipped in
    dew,
The silence and the shade of each lulled avenue, –   10

II

Far in the depths of voiceless skies,
    Where calm and cold the stars are strewed,
The peaks of pale Carrara rise.
    Nor sound of storm, nor whirlwind rude,
5 Can break their chill of marble solitude;
    The crimson lightnings round their crest
May hold their fiery feud –
    They hear not, nor reply; their chasmèd rest
No flowret decks, nor herbage green, nor breath
10 Of moving thing can change their atmosphere of death.

III

But far beneath, in folded sleep,
    Faint forms of heavenly life are laid,
With pale brows and soft eyes, that keep
    Sweet peace of unawakened shade;
5   Whose wreathèd limbs, in robes of rock arrayed,
Fall like white waves on human thought,
    In fitful dreams displayed;
Deep through their secret homes of slumber sought,
They rise immortal, children of the day,
10 Gleaming with godlike forms on earth, and her decay.

IV

Yes, where the bud hath brightest germ,
    And broad the golden blossoms glow,
There glides the snake, and works the worm,
    And black the earth is laid below.
5 Ah! think not thou the souls of men to know,
    By outward smiles in wildness worn:
The words that jest at woe
    Spring not less lightly, though the heart be torn –
The mocking heart, that scarcely dares confess,
10 Even to itself the strength of its own bitterness.

V

Nor deem that they, whose words are cold,
   Whose brows are dark, have hearts of steel;
The couchant strength, untraced, untold,
   Of thoughts they keep, and throbs they feel,
   May need an answering music to unseal;   5
Who knows what waves may stir the silent sea,
   Beneath the low appeal,
From distant shores, of winds unfelt by thee?
What sounds may wake within the winding shell,
Responsive to the charm of those who touch it well!   10

FORD MADOX BROWN

Angela Damnifera

Could I have known, that day I saw you first,
  How much my fate lay coiled within your eyes!
  How Nemesis spoke in your soft replies!
Could I have known – and so have shunned the worst?
Could I have known how for my bitter thirst
  Your coming brought but saltest tears and sighs,
  How going life seemed fled with you likewise.
Could I have known – oh angel love-accurs'd!

And now how name you, slayer of my peace?
  Life-giving basilisk? source of gladdest woe?
  Emblem of Fortune wrecked upon one throw?
O'er blessed and damned flame-hallowed Beatrice?
And cause of martyrdom without surcease?
  Alas! Alas! by me entreated so!

For the Picture 'The Last of England'

'The last of England! O'er the sea, my dear,
  Our homes to seek amid Australian fields,
  Us, not our million-acred island yields
The space to dwell in. Thrust out! Forced to hear
Low ribaldry from sots, and share rough cheer
  With rudely-nurtured men. The hope youth builds
  Of fair renown, bartered for that which shields
Only the back, and half-formed lands that rear

The dust-storm blistering up the grasses wild.
  There learning skills not, nor the poet's dream,
  Nor aught so loved as children shall we see.'
She grips his listless hand and clasps her child,
  Through rainbow tears she sees a sunnier gleam,
  She cannot see a void, where he will be.

For the Picture Called 'Work'

Work! which beads the brow, and tans the flesh
  Of lusty manhood, casting out its devils!
  By whose weird art transmuting poor men's evils,
Their bed seems down, their one dish ever fresh.
Ah me! For lack of it what ills in leash   5
  Hold us. 'Tis want the pale mechanic levels
  To workhouse depths, while Master Spendthrift revels.
For want of work, the fiends him soon inmesh!

Ah! beauteous tripping dame with bell-like skirts,
  Intent on thy small scarlet-coated hound,   10
  Are ragged wayside babes not lovesome too?
Untrained, their state reflects on thy deserts,
  Or they grow noisome beggars to abound,
  Or dreaded midnight robbers breaking through.

COVENTRY PATMORE

The Seasons

The crocus, in the shrewd March morn,
    Thrusts up his saffron spear;
And April dots the sombre thorn
    With gems, and loveliest cheer.

5   Then sleep the seasons, full of might;
    While slowly swells the pod,
And rounds the peach, and in the night
    The mushroom bursts the sod.

The winter comes: the frozen rut
10   Is bound with silver bars;
The white drift heaps against the hut;
    And night is pierced with stars.

Stars and Moon

Beneath the stars and summer moon
    A pair of wedded lovers walk,
Upon the stars and summer moon
    They turn their happy eyes, and talk.

EDITH

5   'Those stars, that moon, for me they shine
    With lovely, but no startling light;
My joy is much, but not as thine,
    A joy that fills the pulse, like fright.'

ALFRED

'My love, a darken'd conscience clothes
  The world in sackcloth; and, I fear,   10
The stain of life this new heart loathes,
  Still clouds my sight; but thine is clear.

'True vision is no startling boon
  To one in whom it always lies;
But if true sight of stars and moon   15
  Were strange to thee, it would surprise.

'Disease it is and dearth in me
  Which thou believest genius, wealth;
And that imagined want in thee
  Is riches and abundant health.   20

'O, little merit I my bride!
  And therefore will I love her more;
Renewing, by her gentle side,
  Lost worth: let this thy smile restore!'

EDITH

'Ah, love! we both, with longing deep,   25
  Love words and actions kind, which are
More good for life than bread or sleep,
  More beautiful than Moon or Star.'

FROM *THE ANGEL IN THE HOUSE: THE BETROTHAL*

The Gracious Chivalry

May these my songs inaugurate
   The day of a new chivalry
Which shall not feel the mortal fate
   Of fashion, chance, or phantasy.
The ditties of the knightly time,
   The deep-conceiving dreams of youth,
With sweet corroboration chime,
   And I believe that love's the truth.
I do and ever shall profess
   That I more tenderly revere
A woman in her gentleness
   Than all things else I love or fear;
And these glad songs are good to prove
   To loyal hearts convincingly,
That he who's orthodox in love
   Can hold no kind of heresy.
Long lease of his low mind befall
   The man who, in his wilful gust,
Makes waste for one, to others all
   Discourteous, frigid, and unjust!
Untrue to love and ladies he
   Who, scarf on arm and spear in rest,
Assail'd the world with proof that she,
   Being his, was also nature's best.
That chivalry do I proclaim
   Alone substantial, wise, and good,
Which scorns to help one woman's fame
   With treason against all womanhood.
Each maid, (albeit to me my own
   Appears and is past others rare,)
When aptness makes her beauty known,

May seem as singularly fair;
  And each is justly most desired;
    And no true Knight will care to prove
  That there is more of what's admired   35
    In his than in another's love.

Love Liberal

'Whenever I come where women are,
  How sad soe'er I was before,
Though like a ship frost-bound and far
  Withheld in ice from the ocean's roar,
Third-winter'd in that dreadful dock,   5
  With stiffen'd cordage, sails decay'd,
And crew that care for calm and shock
  Alike, too dull to be dismay'd;
Though spirited like that speedless bark,
  My cold affections like the crew,   10
My present drear, my future dark,
  The past too happy to be true;
Yet if I come where women are,
  How sad soever I was before,
Then is my sadness banish'd far,   15
  And I am like that ship no more;
Or like that ship if the ice-field splits,
  Burst by the sudden polar Spring,
And all thank God with their warmed wits,
  And kiss each other and dance and sing,   20
And hoist fresh sails that make the breeze
  Blow them along the liquid sea,
From the homeless North where life did freeze,
  Into the haven where they would be.'
So thought the melancholy boy,   25
  Whose love-sick mind, misreading fate,
Scarce hoped that any Queen of Joy
  Could ever stoop to be his mate.
Thus thinks the man, who deems, (tho' life

30   Has long been crown'd with youth's desire,)
        That he who has his Love to wife
            Has all that heart may well require: –
        Though bonded unto one, my best,
            My faith to whom is pleasure and ease,
35   Shall I despise or shun the rest
            Of nature's queens and priestesses?
        Rather by loving one I learn
            To love her like, who still recall
        My nuptial pale, and teach in turn
40   That faith to one is debt to all:
        For I'm not of so dull a wit
            As not to know that what I admire
        And the sweet joy of loving it
            Would both be slain by false desire;
45   Therefore, though singly her's till death,
            (And after, I hope,) with all I'm free,
        Inhaling love's delighted breath
            In the bright air of chastity.

WILLIAM ALLINGHAM

The Fairies
A Nursery Song

Up the airy mountain
  Down the rushy glen,
We daren't go a hunting
  For fear of little men;
Wee folk, good folk,
  Trooping all together;
Green jacket, red cap,
  And white owl's feather!

Down along the rocky shore
  Some make their home,
They live on crispy pancakes
  Of yellow tide-foam;
Some in the reeds
  Of the black mountain-lake,
With frogs for their watch-dogs,
  All night awake.

High on the hill-top
  The old King sits;
He is now so old and grey
  He's nigh lost his wits.
With a bridge of white mist
  Columbkill he crosses,
On his stately journeys
  From Slieveleague to Rosses;
Or going up with music
  On cold starry nights,
To sup with the Queen
  Of the gay Northern Lights.

They stole little Bridget
   For seven years long;   30
When she came down again
   Her friends were all gone.
They took her lightly back,
   Between the night and morrow,
They thought that she was fast asleep,   35
   But she was dead with sorrow.
They have kept her ever since
   Deep within the lakes,
On a bed of flag-leaves,
   Watching till she wakes.   40

By the craggy hill-side,
   Through the mosses bare,
They have planted thorn-trees
   For pleasure here and there.
Is any man so daring   45
   To dig one up in spite,
He shall find the thornies set
   In his bed at night.

Up the airy mountain,
   Down the rushy glen,   50
We daren't go a hunting
   For fear of little men;
Wee folk, good folk,
   Trooping all together;
Green jacket, red cap,   55
   And white owl's feather!

Lady Alice

I

Now what doth Lady Alice so late on the turret stair,
Without a lamp to light her, but the diamond in her
    hair;
When every arching passage overflows with shallow
    gloom,
And dreams float through the castle, into every silent
    room?

5   She trembles at her footsteps, although they fall so light;
Through the turret loopholes she sees the wild
    mid-night;
Broken vapours streaming across the stormy sky;
Down the empty corridors the blast doth moan and cry.

She steals along a gallery; she pauses by a door
10   And fast her tears are dropping down upon the oaken
    floor;
And thrice she seems returning – but thrice she turns
    again: –
Now heavy lie the cloud of sleep on that old father's
    brain!

Oh, well it were that *never* shouldst thou waken from
    thy sleep!
For wherefore should they waken, who waken but to
    weep?
15   No more, no more beside thy bed doth Peace a vigil
    keep,
But Woe, – a lion that awaits thy rousing for its leap.

II

An afternoon of April, no sun appears on high,
But a moist and yellow lustre fills the deepness of the
    sky:

And through the castle-gateway, left empty and forlorn,
Along the leafless avenue an honour'd bier is borne.

They stop. The long line closes up like some gigantic   5
  worm;
A shape is standing in the path, a wan and ghost-like
  form,
Which gazes fixedly; nor moves, nor utters any sound;
Then, like a statue built of snow, sinks down upon the
  ground.

And though her clothes are ragged, and though her feet
  are bare,
And though all wild and tangled falls her heavy silk-   10
  brown hair;
Though from her eyes the brightness, from her cheeks
  the bloom is fled,
They know their Lady Alice, the darling of the dead.

With silence, in her own old room the fainting form
  they lay,
Where all things stand unalter'd since the night she fled
  away:
But who – but who shall bring to life her father from   15
  the clay?
But who shall give her back again her heart of a
  former day?

The Maids of Elfen-Mere

'Twas when the spinning-room was here,
There came Three Damsels clothed in white,
With their spindles every night;
Two and one, and Three fair Maidens,
Spinning to a pulsing cadence,   5
Singing songs of Elfen-Mere;
Till the eleventh hour was toll'd,

Then departed through the wold.
  Years ago, and years ago;
    And the tall reeds sigh as the wind doth blow.

Three white Lilies, calm and clear,
And they were loved by every one;
Most of all, the Pastor's Son,
Listening to their gentle singing,
Felt his heart go from him, clinging
Round these Maids of Elfen-Mere;
Sued each night to make them stay,
Sadden'd when they went away.
  Years ago, and years ago;
    And the tall reeds sigh as the wind doth blow.

Hands that shook with love and fear
Dared put back the village clock, –
Flew the spindle, turn'd the rock,
Flow'd the song with subtle rounding,
Till the false 'eleven' was sounding;
Then these Maids of Elfen-Mere
Swiftly, softly, left the room,
Like three doves on snowy plume.
  Years ago, and years ago;
    And the tall reeds sigh as the wind doth blow.

One that night who wander'd near
Heard lamentings by the shore,
Saw at dawn three stains of gore
In the waters fade and dwindle.
Nevermore with song and spindle
Saw we Maids of Elfen-Mere.
The Pastor's Son did pine and die;
Because true love should never lie.
  Years ago, and years ego;
    And the tall reeds sigh as the wind doth blow.

Three Sisters of Haworth

Three sisters, Charlotte, Emily, and Anne,
Afar in Yorkshire wolds they live together;
Names that I keep like any sacristan;
The human registry of souls as pure
As sky in hermit waters on a moor,   5
Those liquid islands of dark seas of heather;
Voices that reach my solitude from theirs;
Hands that I kiss a thousand miles away,
And send a thousand greetings of my own –
But these, alas! only the west wind bears.   10
Nay, they have vanish'd. Hills and vales are lone
Where Earth once knew them. What is now to say?
Three strangers dead – 'tis little to endure:
Great crowds of strangers vanish every day.
Yet will I see those gravestones if I may.   15

Express
(From Liverpool, Southwards)

We move in elephantine row,
    The faces of our friends retire,
The roof withdraws, and curtsying flow
    The message-bearing lines of wire;
        With doubling, redoubling beat,   5
        Smoother we run and more fleet.

By flow'r-knots, shrubs, and slopes of grass,
    Cut walls of rock with ivy-stains,
Thro' winking arches swift we pass,
    And flying, meet the flying trains,   10
        Whirr – whirr – gone!
        And still we hurry on;

By orchards, kine in pleasant leas,
　　A hamlet-lane, a spire, a pond,
Long hedgerows, counter-changing trees,
　　With blue and steady hills beyond;
　　　　(House, platform, post,
　　　　Flash – and are lost!)

Smooth-edged canals, and mills on brooks;
　　Old farmsteads, busier than they seem,
Rose-crusted or of graver looks,
　　Rich with old tile and motley beam;
　　　　Clay-cutting, slope, and ridge,
　　　　The hollow rumbling bridge.

Grey vapour-surges, whirl'd in the wind
　　Of roaring tunnels, dark and long,
Then sky and landscape unconfined,
　　Then streets again where workers throng
　　　　Come – go. The whistle shrill
　　　　Controls us to its will.

Broad vents, and chimneys tall as masts,
　　With heavy flags of streaming smoke;
Brick mazes, fiery furnace-blasts,
　　Walls, waggons, gritty heaps of coke;
　　　　Through these our ponderous rank
　　　　Glides in with hiss and clank.

So have we sped our wondrous course
　　Amid a peaceful busy land,
Subdued by long and painful force
　　Of planning head and plodding hand.
　　　　How much by labour can
　　　　The feeble race of man!

Vivant!

No need, I hope, to doubt my loyalty;
From childhood I was fond of Royalty;
To Kings extravagantly dutiful,
To Queens yet more, if young and beautiful.

How rich their robes! What crowns they all had   5
    too!
And yet how friendly to a small lad too!
At glorious banquets highly gracing him,
Beside the lovely Princess placing him.

Their kingdoms' names I did not care about;
They lay in Fairyland or thereabout;   10
Their date, though, to forget were crime indeed, –
Exactly, 'Once upon a time' indeed.

And still they reign o'er folk contented, there:
I hope to have my son presented there –
At every joyous court in Fairyland,   15
Its Cave-Land, Forest-Land, and Airy-Land.

So down with democratic mania!
Long live great Oberon and Titania,
Imperial Rulers of those regions! – he
Be shot who wavers in allegiancy!   20

And bless all Monarchs in alliance with them,
Who've no enchanters, dragons, giants with them,
To keep sweet ladies under lock and key,
And answer challenges in mocking key!

JAMES COLLINSON

From *The Child Jesus*
A Record Typical of the Five Sorrowful Mysteries

'O all ye that pass by the way, attend and see if there be any
sorrow like to my sorrow' – Lamentations 1:12

I
THE AGONY IN THE GARDEN

Joseph, a carpenter of Nazareth,
And his wife Mary had an only child,
Jesus: One holy from his mother's womb.
Both parents loved him: Mary's heart alone
Beat with his blood, and, by her love and his,
She knew that God was with her, and she strove
Meekly to do the work appointed her;
To cherish him with undivided care
Who deigned to call her mother, and who loved
From her the name of son. And Mary gave
Her heart to him, and feared not; yet she seemed
To hold as sacred that he said or did;
And, unlike other women, never spake
His words of innocence again; but all
Were humbly treasured in her memory
With the first secret of his birth. So strong
Grew her affection, as the child increased
In wisdom and in stature with his years,
That many mothers wondered, saying: 'These
Our little ones claim in our hearts a place
The next to God; but Mary's tenderness
Grows almost into reverence for her child.
Is he not of herself? I' the temple when
Kneeling to pray, on him she bends her eyes,
As though God only heard her prayer through him.
Is he to be a prophet? Nay, we know
That out of Galilee no prophet comes.'

But all their children made the boy their friend.

Three cottages that overlooked the sea
Stood side by side eastward of Nazareth.   30
Behind them rose a sheltering range of cliffs,
Purple and yellow, verdure-spotted, red,
Layer upon layer built up against the sky.
In front a row of sloping meadows lay,
Parted by narrow streams, that rose above,   35
Leaped from the rocks, and cut the sands below
Into deep channels widening to the sea.

Within the humblest of these three abodes
Dwelt Joseph, his wife Mary, and their child.
A honeysuckle and a moss-rose grew,   40
With many blossoms, on their cottage front;
And o'er the gable warmed by the South
A sunny grape vine broadened shady leaves
Which gave its tendrils shelter, as they hung
Trembling upon the bloom of purple fruit.   45
And, like the wreathed shadows and deep glows
Which the sun spreads from some old oriel
Upon the marble Altar and the gold
Of God's own Tabernacle, where he dwells
For ever, so the blossoms and the vine,   50
On Jesus' home climbing above the roof,
Traced intricate their windings all about
The yellow thatch, and part concealed the nests
Whence noisy close-housed sparrows peeped unseen.
And Joseph had a little dove-cote placed   55
Between the gable-window and the eaves,
Where two white turtle doves (a gift of love
From Mary's kinsman Zachary to her child)
Cooed pleasantly; and broke upon the ear
The ever dying sound of falling waves.   60

And so it came to pass, one Summer morn,
The mother dove first brought her fledgeling out

To see the sun. It was her only one,
And she had breasted it through three long weeks
With patient instinct till it broke the shell;
And she had nursed it with all tender care,
Another three, and watched the white down grow
Into full feather, till it left her nest.
And now it stood outside its narrow home,
With tremulous wings let loose and blinking eyes;
While, hovering near, the old dove often tried
By many lures to tempt it to the ground,
That they might feed from Jesus' hand, who stood
Watching them from below. The timid bird
At last took heart, and, stretching out its wings,
Brushed the light vine-leaves as it fluttered down.
Just then a hawk rose from a tree, and thrice
Wheeled in the air, and poised his aim to drop
On the young dove, whose quivering plumage swelled
About the sunken talons as it died.
Then the hawk fixed his round eye on the child
Shook from his beak the stained down, screamed, and
     flapped
His broad arched wings, and, darting to a cleft
I' the rocks, there sullenly devoured his prey.
And Jesus heard the mother's anguished cry,
Weak like the distant sob of some lost child,
Who in his terror runs from path to path,
Doubtful alike of all; so did the dove,
As though death-stricken, beat about the air;
Till, settling on the vine, she drooped her head
Deep in her ruffled feathers. She sat there,
Brooding upon her loss, and did not move
All through that day.

                              And the child Jesus wept,
And, sitting by her, covered up his face:
Until a cloud, alone between the earth
And sun, passed with its shadow over him.

Then Jesus for a moment looked above;
And a few drops of rain fell on his brow,
Sad, as with broken hints of a lost dream,   100
Or dim foreboding of some future ill.

Now, from a garden near, a fair-haired girl
Came, carrying a handful of choice flowers,
Which in her lap she sorted orderly,
As little children do at Easter-time   105
To have all seemly when their Lord shall rise.
Then Jesus' covered face she gently raised,
Placed in his hand the flowers, and kissed his
     cheek,
And tried with soothing words to comfort him;
He from his eyes spoke thanks.   110

           But still the tears,
Fast trickling down his face, drop upon drop,
Fell to the ground. That sad look left him not
Till night brought sleep, and sleep closed o'er
     his woe.

THOMAS WOOLNER

My Beautiful Lady

I love my lady; she is very fair;
Her brow is white, and bound by simple hair:
   Her spirit sits aloof, and high,
   Altho' it looks thro' her soft eye
5   Sweetly and tenderly.

As a young forest, when the wind drives thro',
My life is stirred when she breaks on my view.
   Altho' her beauty has such power,
   Her soul is like the simple flower
10   Trembling beneath a shower.

As bliss of saints, when dreaming of large wings,
The bloom around her fancied presence flings,
   I feast and wile her absence, by
   Pressing her choice hand passionately –
15   Imagining her sigh.

My lady's voice, altho' so very mild,
Maketh me feel as strong wine would a child;
   My lady's touch, however slight,
   Moves all my senses with its might,
20   Like to a sudden flight.

A hawk poised high in air, whose nerved wing-tips
Tremble with might suppressed, before he dips, –
   In vigilance, not more intense
   Than I; when her word's gentle sense
25   Makes full-eyed my suspense.

Her mention of a thing – august or poor,
Makes it seem nobler than it was before:
   As where the sun strikes, life will gush,
   And what is pale receive a flush,
30   Rich hues – a richer blush.

My lady's name, if I hear strangers use, –
Not meaning her – seems like a lax misuse.
    I love none but my lady's name;
    Rose, Maud, or Grace, are all the same,
    So blank, so very tame.   35

My lady walks as I have seen a swan
Swim thro' the water just where the sun shone.
    There ends of willow branches ride,
    Quivering with the current's glide,
    By the deep river-side.   40

Whene'er she moves there are fresh beauties stirred;
As the sunned bosom of a humming-bird
    At each pant shows some fiery hue,
    Burns gold, intensest green or blue:
    The same, yet ever new.   45

What time she walketh under flowering May,
I am quite sure the scented blossoms say,
    'O lady with the sunlit hair!
    'Stay, and drink our odorous air –
    'The incense that we bear: 50

'Your beauty, lady, we would ever shade;
'Being near you, our sweetness might not fade.'
    If trees could be broken-hearted,
    I am sure that the green sap smarted,
    When my lady parted.   55

This is why I thought weeds were beautiful; –
Because one day I saw my lady pull
    Some weeds up near a little brook,
    Which home most carefully she took,
    Then shut them in a book.   60

A deer when startled by the stealthy ounce, –
A bird escaping from the falcon's trounce,
    Feels his heart swell as mine, when she
    Stands statelier, expecting me,
65   Than tall white lilies be.

The first white flutter of her robe to trace,
Where binds and perfumed jasmine interlace,
    Expands my gaze triumphantly:
    Even such his gaze, who sees on high
70   His flag, for victory.

We wander forth unconsciously, because
The azure beauty of the evening draws:
    When sober hues pervade the ground,
    And life in one vast hush seems drowned,
75   Air stirs so little sound.

We thread a copse where frequent bramble spray
With loose obtrusion from the side roots stray,
    (Forcing sweet pauses on our walk):
    I'll lift one with my foot, and talk
80   About its leaves and stalk.

Or may be that the prickles of some stem
Will hold a prisoner her long garment's hem;
    To disentangle it I kneel,
    Oft wounding more than I can heal;
85   It makes her laugh, my zeal.

Then on before a thin-legged robin hops,
Or leaping on a twig, he pertly stops,
    Speaking a few clear notes, till nigh
    We draw, when quickly he will fly
90   Into a bush close by.

A flock of goldfinches may stop their flight,
And wheeling round a birchen tree alight
 Deep in its glittering leaves, until
 They see us, when their swift rise will
 Startle a sudden thrill.   95

I recollect my lady in a wood,
Keeping her breath and peering – (firm she stood
 Her slim shape balanced on tiptoe –)
 Into a nest which lay below,
 Leaves shadowing her brow.   100

I recollect my lady asking me,
What that sharp tapping in the wood might be?
 I told her blackbirds made it, which,
 For slimy morsels they count rich,
 Cracked the snail's curling niche: 105

She made no answer. When we reached the stone
Where the shell fragments on the grass were strewn,
 Close to the margin of a rill;
 'The air,' she said, 'seems damp and chill,
 'We'll go home if you will.'   110

'Make not my pathway dull so,' I cried,
'See how those vast cloudpiles in sun-glow dyed,
 'Roll out their splendour: while the breeze
 'Lifts gold from leaf to leaf, as these
 'Ash saplings move at ease.'   115

Piercing the silence in our ears, a bird
Threw some notes up just then, and quickly stirred
 The covert birds that startled, sent
 Their music thro' the air; leaves lent
 Their rustling and blent,   120

Until the whole of the blue warmth was filled
So much with sun and sound, that the air thrilled.
    She gleamed, wrapt in the dying day's
    Glory: altho' she spoke no praise,
125   I saw much in her gaze.

Then, flushed with resolution, I told all; –
The mighty love I bore her, – how would pall
    My very breath of life, if she
    For ever breathed not hers with me; –
130   Could I a cherub be,

How, idly hoping to enrich her grace,
I would snatch jewels from the orbs of space; –
    Then back thro' the vague distance beat,
    Glowing with joy her smile to meet,
135   And heap them round her feet.

Her waist shook to my arm. She bowed her head,
Silent, with hands clasped and arms straightened:
    (Just then we both heard a church bell)
    O God! It is not right to tell:
140   But I remember well

Each breast swelled with its pleasure, and her whole
Bosom grew heavy with love; the swift roll
    Of new sensations dimmed her eyes,
    Half closing them in ecstacies,
145   Turned full against the skies.

The rest is gone; it seemed a whirling round –
No pressure of my feet upon the ground:
    But even when parted from her, bright
    Showed all; yea, to my throbbing sight
150   The dark was starred with light.

Of My Lady in Death

All seems a painted show. I look
    Up thro' the bloom that's shed
    By leaves above my head,
And feel the earnest life forsook
    All being, when she died: –   5
    My heart halts, hot and dried
As the parched course where once a brook
    Thro' fresh growth used to flow, –
    Because her past is now
No more than stories in a printed book.   10

The grass has grown above that breast,
    Now cold and sadly still,
    My happy face felt thrill: –
Her mouth's mere tones so much expressed!
    Those lips are now close set, –   15
    Lips which my own have met;
Her eyelids by the earth are pressed;
    Damp earth weighs on her eyes;
    Damp earth shuts out the skies.
My lady rests her heavy, heavy rest.   20

To see her slim perfection sweep,
    Trembling impatiently,
    With eager gaze at me!
Her feet spared little things that creep: –
    'We've no more right,' she'd say,   25
    'In this the earth than they.'
Some remember it but to weep.
    Her hand's slight weight was such,
    Care lightened with its touch;
My lady sleeps her heavy, heavy sleep.   30

My day-dreams hovered round her brow;
    Now o'er its perfect forms
    Go softly real worms.
Stern death, it was a cruel blow,
    To cut that sweet girl's life
    Sharply, as with a knife.
Cursed life that lets me live and grow,
    Just as a poisonous root,
    From which rank blossoms shoot;
My lady's laid so very, very low.

Dread power, grief cries aloud, 'unjust,' –
    To let her young life play
    Its easy, natural way;
Then, with an unexpected thrust,
    Strike out the life you lent,
    Just when her feelings blent
With those around whom she saw trust
    Her willing power to bless,
    For their whole happiness;
My lady moulders into common dust.

Small birds twitter and peck the weeds
    That wave above her head,
    Shading her lowly bed:
Their brisk wings burst light globes of seeds,
    Scattering the downy pride
    Of dandelions, wide:
Speargrass stoops with watery beads:
    The weight from its fine tips
    Occasionally drips:
The bee drops in the mallow-bloom, and feeds.

About her window, at the dawn,
    From the vine's crooked boughs
    Birds chirruped an arouse:
Flies, buzzing, strengthened with the morn; –
    She'll not hear them again

    At random strike the pane:
No more upon the close-cut lawn,
    Her garment's sun-white hem
    Bend the prim daisy's stem,
In walking forth to view what flowers are born.   70

No more she'll watch the dark-green rings
    Stained quaintly on the lea,
    To image fairy glee;
While thro' dry grass a faint breeze sings,
    And swarms of insects revel   75
    Along the sultry level: –
No more will watch their brilliant wings,
    Now lightly dip, now soar,
    Then sink, and rise once more.
My lady's death makes dear these trivial things.   80

Within a huge tree's steady shade,
    When resting from our walk,
    How pleasant was her talk!
Elegant deer leaped o'er the glade,
    Or stood with wide bright eyes,   85
    Staring a short surprise:
Outside the shadow cows were laid,
    Chewing with drowsy eye
    Their cuds complacently:
Dim for sunshine drew near a milking-maid.   90

Rooks cawed and laboured thro' the heat;
    Each wing-flap seemed to make
    Their weary bodies ache:
The swallows, tho' so very fleet,
    Made breathless pauses there   95
    At something in the air: –
All disappeared: our pulses beat
    Distincter throbs: then each
    Turned and kissed, without speech, –
She trembling, from her mouth down to her feet.   100

My head sank on her bosom's heave,
    So close to the soft skin
    I heard the life within.
My forehead felt her coolly breathe,
105   As with her breath it rose:
    To perfect my repose
Her two arms clasped my neck. The eve
    Spread silently around,
    A hush along the ground,
110 And all sound with the sunlight seemed to leave.

By my still gaze she must have known
    The mighty bliss that filled
    My whole soul, for she thrilled,
Drooping her face, flushed, on my own;
115   I felt that it was such
    By its light warmth of touch,
My lady was with me alone:
    That vague sensation brought
    More real joy than thought.
120 I am without her now, truly alone.

We had no heed of time: the cause
    Was that our minds were quite
    Absorbed in our delight,
Silently blessed. Such stillness awes,
125   And stops with doubt, the breath,
    Like the mute doom of death.
I felt Time's instantaneous pause;
    An instant, on my eye
    Flashed all Eternity: –
130 I started, as if clutched by wild beasts' claws,

Awakened from some dizzy swoon:
    I felt strange vacant fears,
    With singings in my ears,
And wondered that the pallid moon

Swung round the dome of night   135
With such tremendous might.
A sweetness, like the air of June,
Next paled me with suspense,
A weight of clinging sense –
Some hidden evil would burst on me soon.   140

My lady's love has passed away,
To know that it is so
To me is living woe.
That body lies in cold decay,
Which held the vital soul   145
When she was my life's soul.
Bitter mockery it was to say –
'Our souls are as the same:'
My words now sting like shame;
Her spirit went, and mine did not obey.   150

It was as if a fiery dart
Passed seething thro' my brain
When I beheld her lain
There whence in life she did not part.
Her beauty by degrees,   155
Sank, sharpened with disease:
The heavy sinking at her heart
Sucked hollows in her cheek,
And made her eyelids weak,
Tho' oft they'd open wide with sudden start.   160

The deathly power in silence drew
My lady's life away.
I watched, dumb with dismay,
The shock of thrills that quivered thro'
And tightened every limb: 165
For grief my eyes grew dim;

More near, more near, the moment grew.
    O horrible suspense!
    O giddy impotence!
170   I saw her fingers lax, and change their hue.

Her gaze, grown large with fate, was cast
    Where my mute agonies
    Made more sad her sad eyes:
Her breath caught with short plucks and fast: –
175   Then one hot choking strain.
    She never breathed again:
I had the look which was her last:
    Even after breath was gone,
    Her love one moment shone, –
180   Then slowly closed, and hope for ever passed.

Silence seemed to start in space
    When first the bell's harsh toll
    Rang for my lady's soul.
Vitality was hell; her grace
185   The shadow of a dream:
    Things then did scarcely seem:
Oblivion's stroke fell like a mace:
    As a tree that's just hewn
    I dropped, in a dead swoon,
190   And lay a long time cold upon my face.

Earth had one quarter turned before
    My miserable fate
    Pressed on with its whole weight.
My sense came back; and, shivering o'er,
195   I felt a pain to bear
    The sun's keen cruel glare;
It seemed not warm as heretofore.
    Oh, never more its rays
    Will satisfy my gaze.
200   No more; no more; oh, never any more.

O When and Where

All knowledge hath taught me,
All sorrow hath brought me,
   Are smothered sighs
   That pleasure lies,
Like the last gleam of evening's ray,   5
So far and far away, – far away.

Under the cold moist herbs
No wind the calm disturbs.
   O when and where?
   Nor here nor there.   10
Grass cools my face, grief heats my heart.
Will this life I swoon with never part?

Emblems

I lay through one long afternoon,
   Vacantly plucking the grass.
I lay on my back, with steadfast gaze
   Watching the cloud-shapes pass;
Until the evening's chilly damps   5
   Rose from the hollows below,
   Where the cold marsh-reeds grow.

I saw the sun sink down behind
   The high point of a mountain;
Its last light lingered on the weeds   10
   That choked a shattered fountain,
Where lay a rotting bird, whose plumes
   Had beat the air in soaring.
   On these things I was poring: –

15 The sun seemed like my sense of life,
        Now weak, that was so strong;
    The fountain – that continual pulse
        Which throbbed with human song:
    The bird lay dead as that wild hope
20   Which nerved my thoughts when young.
        These symbols had a tongue,

    And told the dreary lengths of years
        I must drag my weight with me;
    Or be like a mastless ship stuck fast
25   On a deep, stagnant sea.
    A man on a dangerous height alone,
        If suddenly struck blind,
        Will never his home path find.

    When divers plunge for ocean's pearls,
30   And chance to strike a rock,
    Who plunged with greatest force below
        Receives the heaviest shock.
    With nostrils wide and breath drawn in,
        I rushed resolved on the race;
35   Then, stumbling, fell in the chase.

    Yet with time's cycles forests swell
        Where stretched a desert plain:
    Time's cycles make the mountains rise
        Where heaved the restless main:
40 On swamps where moped the lonely stork,
        In the silent lapse of time
        Stands a city in its prime.

I thought: then saw the broadening shade
  Grow slowly over the mound,
That reached with one long level slope   45
  Down to a rich vineyard ground:
The air about lay still and hushed,
  As if in serious thought;
  But I scarcely heeded aught,

Till I heard, hard by, a thrush break forth,   50
  Shouting with his whole voice,
So that he made the distant air
  And the things around rejoice,
My soul gushed, for the sound awoke
  Memories of early joy: 55
  I sobbed like a chidden boy.

JOHN TUPPER

A Sketch from Nature

The air blows pure, for twenty miles,
    Over this vast countrié:
Over hill and wood and vale, it goeth,
    Over steeple, and stack, and tree:
5 And there's not a bird on the wind but knoweth
    How sweet these meadows be.

The swallows are flying beside the wood,
    And the corbies are hoarsely crying;
And the sun at the end of the earth hath stood,
10 And, thorough the hedge and over the road,
    On the grassy slope is lying:
And the sheep are taking their supper-food
    While yet the rays are dying.

Sleepy shadows are filling the furrows,
15   And giant-long shadows the trees are making;
And velvet soft are the woodland tufts,
And misty-grey the low-down crofts;
But the aspens there have gold-green tops,
    And the gold-green tops are shaking:
20 The spires are white in the sun's last light; –
And yet a moment ere he drops,
Gazes the sun on the golden slopes.

Two sheep, afar from fold,
    Are on the hill-side straying,
25 With backs all silver, breasts all gold:
    The merle is something saying,
Something very very sweet: –
    'The day – the day – the day is done:'
There answereth a single bleat –
30 The air is cold, the sky is dimming,
And clouds are long like fishes swimming.

Viola and Olivia

When Viola, a servant of the Duke,
Of him she loved the page, went, sent by him,
To tell Olivia that great love which shook
His breast and stopt his tongue; was it a whim,
Or jealousy or fear that she must look   5
  Upon the face of that Olivia?

'Tis hard to say if it were whim or fear
Or jealousy, but it was natural,
As natural as what came next, the near
Intelligence of hearts: Olivia   10
Loveth, her eye abused by a thin wall
  Of custom, but her spirit's eyes were clear.

Clear? we have oft been curious to know
The after-fortunes of those lovers dear;
Having a steady faith some deed must show   15
That they were married souls – unmarried here –
Having an inward faith that love, called so
In verity, is of the spirit, clear
Of earth and dress and sex – it may be near
  What Viola returned Olivia?   20

A Quiet Evening

From mere *ennui* the very cat
Walked out – it was so precious flat.
Due on the sofa Gabriel sat,
And next to him was Stephens found;
I think, but am not certain, that   5
The fender William's legs were round.

However, all was drowsy, mild,
And nothing like to break the charm,
Though John essayed in some alarm
To read his latest muse-born child;
Then Gabriel moved his active arm,
And some believe that Stephens smiled.

But certain 'tis that Aleck, who
Had watched that arm, as anglers do
Their quiet float, an hour or two,
Was pleased to find it move at last.
He therefore filled his pipe anew,
And doubled the mundungus blast.

The poem yet went on and on:
The poet kept his eyes upon
The paper till the piece was done;
And then the coke-fire's roof fell in.
Another accident, which one
Should mention, William scorched his shin.

And nothing more till supper time:
Except that Gabriel read a rhyme
Of Hell and Heaven and ghosts and crime
That gave the room a kind of chill,
And rapture followed – so sublime
That forty minutes all was still.

Till all the solemn company
Went down to supper – verily
The supper went off quietly.
Trying to talk was all in vain:
And then we went up silently
Into the lonesome room again.

Oh was it quiet? I can swear
I heard the separate gas lights flare,
The creak of the vibrating chair

The balanced Aleck swung upon: 40
The balanced Aleck swinging there
Knew it, and so went swinging on.

Six men, each seated in his seat,
With body, arms, and legs complete –
A passive mass of flesh, alack!   45
That none but human cattle make!
The wonder was that they could meet
So silent and so long awake.

But Gabriel coiled himself, at last,
Upon the sofa – Stephens cast   50
His weary arms out, William past
A thoughtful hand across his eyes,
And George has blown a fainter blast
To listen till the snores arise.

And somewhat quickly they arose –   55
He could distinguish Gabriel's nose
From William's mouth in sweet repose,
Whose measured murmurs now began;
While John L. Tupper, half in dose,
Was crooning as he only can.   60

And Stephens – no, he took to flight
Before he slept. Then Aleck's sight
Denied his pipe was yet alight;
He put it down and grimly stared,
Then crammed it to the muzzle tight,   65
And listened – that was all he dared.

For not a waking P.R.B.
Was left; a blinding mystery
Of smoke was over all the three
Enduring souls that kept awake.   70
They listened – 'twas the harmony
Of cats! – or there was some mistake.

Then looking on the garden plot
Without, they verified the not
Unwelcome fact: the cats had got
Convivial, sure enough; and we
Could recognize friend Thomas hot
In mirth-like Burns 'among the three.'

But if the cats held conference,
What then? We might not make pretence
To such – witness the prudent sense
Of Stephens getting up to go.
I'd give my cat the preference,
Who left us somewhat sooner, though.

WALTER HOWELL
DEVERELL

The Sight Beyond

I

Though we may brood with keenest subtlety,
   Sending our reason forth, like Noah's dove,
   To know why we are here to die, hate, love,
With Hope to lead and help our eyes to see
5 Through labour daily in dim mystery,
   Like those who in dense theatre and hall,
   When fire breaks out or weight-strained rafters fall,
Towards some egress struggle doubtfully;
Though we through silent midnight may address
10 The mind to many a speculative page,
Yearning to solve our wrongs and wretchedness,
Yet duty and wise passiveness are won, –
   (So it hath been and is from age to age) –
Though we be blind, by doubting not the sun.

II

Bear on to death serenely, day by day,
   Midst losses, gains, toil, and monotony,
   The ignorance of social apathy,
And artifice which men to men display:
5 Like one who tramps a long and lonely way
   Under the constant rain's inclemency,
   With vast clouds drifting in obscurity,
And sudden lightnings in the welkin grey.
To-morrow may be bright with healthy pleasure,
10 Banishing discontents and vain defiance:
The pearly clouds will pass to a slow measure,
   Wayfarers walk the dusty road in joyance,
   The wide heaths spread far in the sun's alliance,
Among the furze inviting us to leisure.

III

Vanity, say they, quoting him of old.
　　Yet, if full knowledge lifted us serene
　　To look beyond mortality's stern screen,
A reconciling vision could be told,
Brighter than western clouds or shapes of gold   5
　　That change in amber fires, – or the demesne
　　Of ever mystic sleep. Mists intervene,
Which then would melt, to show our eyesight bold
From God a perfect chain throughout the skies,
　　Like Jacob's ladder light with winged men.   10
And as this world, all notched to terrene eyes
　　With Alpine ranges, smoothes to higher ken,
So death and sin and social miseries;
　　By God fixed as His bow o'er moor and fen.

A Modern Idyl

'Pride clings to age, for few and withered powers,
　　Which fall on youth in pleasures manifold,
Like some bright dancer with a crowd of flowers
　　And scented presents more than she can hold:

'Or as it were a child beneath a tree,   5
　　Who in his healthy joy holds hand and cap
Beneath the shaken boughs, and eagerly
　　Expects the fruit to fall into his lap.'

So thought I while my cousin sat alone,
Moving with many leaves in under tone,   10
And, sheened as snow lit by a pale moonlight,
Her childish dress struck clearly on the sight:
That, as the lilies growing by her side
Casting their silver radiance forth with pride,
She seemed to dart an arrowy halo round,   15
Brightening the spring time trees, brightening the
　　　　ground;

And beauty, like keen lustre from a star,
Glorified all the garden near and far.
The sunlight smote the grey and mossy wall
20 Where, 'mid the leaves, the peaches one and all,
Most like twin cherubim entranced above,
Leaned their soft cheeks together, pressed in love.

As the child sat, the tendrils shook round her;
And, blended tenderly in middle air,
25 Gleamed the long orchard through the ivied gate:
And slanting sunbeams made the heart elate,
Startling it into gladness like the sound, –
Which echo childlike mimicks faintly round
Blending it with the lull of some far flood, –
30 Of one long shout heard in a quiet wood.
A gurgling laugh far off the fountain sent,
As if the mermaid shape that in it bent
Spoke with subdued and faintest melody:
And birds sang their whole hearts spontaneously.

35 When from your books released, pass here your hours,
Dear child, the sweet companion of these flowers,
These poplars, scented shrubs, and blossomed boughs
Of fruit-trees, where the noisy sparrows house,
Shaking from off the leaves the beaded dew.
40 Now while the air is warm, the heavens blue,
Give full abandonment to all your gay
Swift childlike impulses in rompish play; –
The while your sisters in shrill laughter shout,
Whirling above the leaves and round about, –
45 Until at length it drops behind the wall, –
With awkward jerks, the particoloured ball:
Winning a smile even from the stooping age
Of that old matron leaning on her page,
Who in the orchard takes a stroll or two,
50 Watching you closely yet unseen by you.

Then, tired of gambols, turn into the dark
Fir-skirted margins of your father's park;
And watch the moving shadows, as you pass,
Trace their dim network on the tufted grass,
And how on birch-trunks smooth and branches   55
   old,
The velvet moss bursts out in green and gold,
Like the rich lustre full and manifold
On breasts of birds that star the curtained gloom
From their glass cases in the drawing room.
Mark the spring leafage bend its tender spray   60
Gracefully on the sky's aërial grey;
And listen how the birds so voluble
Sing joyful pæans winding to a swell,
And how the wind, fitful and mournful, grieves
In gusty whirls among the dry red leaves;   65
And watch the minnows in the water cool,
And floating insects wrinkling all the pool.

So in your ramblings bend your earnest eyes.
  High thoughts and feelings will come unto you, –
  Gladness will fall upon your heart like dew, –   70
Because you love the earth and love the skies.

Fair pearl, the pride of all our family:
  Girt with the plentitude of joys so strong,
  Fashion and custom dull can do no wrong:
Nestling your young face thus on Nature's knee.   75

GEORGE MEREDITH

From *Modern Love*

I

By this he knew she wept with waking eyes:
That, at his hand's light quiver by her head,
The strange low sobs that shook their common bed
Were called into her with a sharp surprise,
5   And strangled mute, like little gaping snakes,
Dreadfully venomous to him. She lay
Stone-still, and the long darkness flowed away
With muffled pulses. Then, as midnight makes
Her giant heart of Memory and Tears
10   Drink the pale drug of silence, and so beat
Sleep's heavy measure, they from head to feet
Were moveless, looking through their dead black years,
By vain regret scrawled over the blank wall.
Like sculptured effigies they might be seen
15   Upon their marriage-tomb, the sword between;
Each wishing for the sword that severs all.

II

It ended, and the morrow brought the task.
Her eyes were guilty gates, that let him in
By shutting all too zealous for their sin:
Each sucked a secret, and each wore a mask.
5   But, oh, the bitter taste her beauty had!
He sickened as at breath of poison-flowers:
A languid humour stole among the hours,
And if their smiles encountered, he went mad,
And raged deep inward, till the light was brown
10   Before his vision, and the world, forgot,
Looked wicked as some old dull murder-spot.
A star with lurid beams, she seemed to crown
The pit of infamy: and then again
He fainted on his vengefulness, and strove
15   To ape the magnanimity of love,
And smote himself, a shuddering heap of pain.

VI

It chanced his lips did meet her forehead cool.
She had no blush, but slanted down her eye.
Shamed nature, then, confesses love can die:
And most she punishes the tender fool
Who will believe what honours her the most!   5
Dead! is it dead? She has a pulse, and flow
Of tears, the price of blood-drops, as I know,
For whom the midnight sobs around Love's ghost,
Since then I heard her, and so will sob on.
The love is here; it has but changed its aim.   10
O bitter barren woman! what's the name?
The name, the name, the new name thou hast won?
Behold me striking the world's coward stroke!
That will I not do, though the sting is dire.
– Beneath the surface this, while by the fire   15
They sat, she laughing at a quiet joke.

VII

She issues radiant from her dressing-room,
Like one prepared to scale an upper sphere:
– By stirring up a lower, much I fear!
How deftly that oiled barber lays his bloom!
That long-shanked dapper Cupid with frisked curls   5
Can make known women torturingly fair;
The gold-eyed serpent dwelling in rich hair
Awakes beneath his magic whisks and twirls.
His art can take the eyes from out my head,
Until I see with eyes of other men;   10
While deeper knowledge crouches in its den,
And sends a spark up: – is it true we are wed?
Yea! filthiness of body is most vile,
But faithlessness of heart I do hold worse.
The former, it were not so great a curse   15
To read on the steel-mirror of her smile.

IX

He felt the wild beast in him betweenwhiles
So masterfully rude, that he would grieve
To see the helpless delicate thing receive
His guardianship through certain dark defiles.
Had he not teeth to rend, and hunger too?
But still he spared her. Once: 'Have you no fear?'
He said: 'twas dusk; she in his grasp; none near.
She laughed: 'No, surely; am I not with you?'
And uttering that soft starry 'you,' she leaned
Her gentle body near him, looking up;
And from her eyes, as from a poison-cup,
He drank until the flittering eyelids screened.
Devilish malignant witch! and oh, young beam
Of heaven's circle-glory! Here thy shape
To squeeze like an intoxicating grape –
I might, and yet thou goest safe, supreme.

XI

Out in the yellow meadows, where the bee
Hums by us with the honey of the Spring,
And showers of sweet notes from the larks on wing,
Are dropping like a noon-dew, wander we.
Or is it now? or was it then? for now,
As then, the larks from running rings pour showers;
The golden foot of May is on the flowers,
And friendly shadows dance upon her brow.
What's this, when Nature swears there is no change
To challenge eyesight? Now, as then, the grace
Of heaven seems holding earth in its embrace.
Nor eyes, nor heart, has she to feel it strange?
Look, woman, in the West. There wilt thou see
An amber cradle near the sun's decline:
Within it, featured even in death divine,
Is lying a dead infant, slain by thee.

XVI

In our old shipwrecked days there was an hour,
When in the firelight steadily aglow,
Joined slackly, we beheld the red chasm grow
Among the clicking coals. Our library-bower
That eve was left to us: and hushed we sat   5
As lovers to whom Time is whispering.
From sudden-opened doors we heard them sing:
The nodding elders mixed good wine with chat.
Well knew we that Life's greatest treasure lay
With us, and of it was our talk. 'Ah, yes!   10
Love dies!' I said: I never thought it less.
She yearned to me that sentence to unsay.
Then when the fire domed blackening, I found
Her cheek was salt against my kiss, and swift
Up the sharp scale of sobs her breast did lift: –   15
Now am I haunted by that taste! that sound!

XVII

At dinner, she is hostess, I am host.
Went the feast ever cheerfuller? She keeps
The Topic over intellectual deeps
In buoyancy afloat. They see no ghost.
With sparkling surface-eyes we ply the ball: 5
It is in truth a most contagious game:
HIDING THE SKELETON, shall be its name.
Such play as this the devils might appal!
But here's the greater wonder; in that we,
Enamoured of an acting nought can tire,   10
Each other, like true hypocrites, admire;
Warm-lighted looks, Love's ephemerioe,
Shoot gaily o'er the dishes and the wine.
We waken envy of our happy lot.
Fast, sweet, and golden, shows the marriage-knot.   15
Dear guests, you now have seen Love's corpse-light
    shine.

XXI

We three are on the cedar-shadowed lawn;
My friend being third. He who at love once laughed
Is in the weak rib by a fatal shaft
Struck through, and tells his passion's bashful dawn
5 And radiant culmination, glorious crown,
When 'this' she said: went 'thus': most wondrous she.
Our eyes grow white, encountering: that we are three,
Forgetful; then together we look down.
But he demands our blessing; is convinced
10 That words of wedded lovers must bring good.
We question; if we dare! or if we should!
And pat him, with light laugh. We have not winced.
Next, she has fallen. Fainting points the sign
To happy things in wedlock. When she wakes,
15 She looks the star that thro' the cedar shakes:
Her lost moist hand clings mortally to mine.

XXVI

Love ere he bleeds, an eagle in high skies,
Has earth beneath his wings: from reddened eve
He views the rosy dawn. In vain they weave
The fatal web below while far he flies.
5 But when the arrow strikes him, there's a change.
He moves but in the track of his spent pain,
Whose red drops are the links of a harsh chain,
Binding him to the ground, with narrow range.
A subtle serpent then has Love become.
10 I had the eagle in my bosom erst:
Henceforward with the serpent I am cursed.
I can interpret where the mouth is dumb.
Speak, and I see the side-lie of a truth.
Perchance my heart may pardon you this deed:
15 But be no coward: – you that made Love bleed,
You must bear all the venom of his tooth!

XXIX

Am I failing? For no longer can I cast
A glory round about this head of gold.
Glory she wears, but springing from the mould;
Not like the consecration of the Past!
Is my soul beggared? Something more than earth   5
I cry for still: I cannot be at peace
In having Love upon a mortal lease.
I cannot take the woman at her worth!
Where is the ancient wealth wherewith I clothed
Our human nakedness, and could endow   10
With spiritual splendour a white brow
That else had grinned at me the fact I loathed?
A kiss is but a kiss now! and no wave
Of a great flood that whirls me to the sea.
But, as you will! we'll sit contentedly,   15
And eat our pot of honey on the grave.

XXXVII

Along the garden terrace, under which
A purple valley (lighted at its edge
By smoky torch-flame on the long cloud-ledge
Whereunder dropped the chariot) glimmers rich,
A quiet company we pace, and wait   5
The dinner-bell in prae-digestive calm.
So sweet up violet banks the Southern balm
Breathes round, we care not if the bell be late:
Though here and there grey seniors question Time
In irritable coughings. With slow foot   10
The low rosed moon, the face of Music mute,
Begins among her silent bars to climb.
As in and out, in silvery dusk, we thread,
I hear the laugh of Madam, and discern
My Lady's heel before me at each turn.   15
Our tragedy, is it alive or dead?

XXXIX

She yields: my Lady in her noblest mood
Has yielded: she, my golden-crownëd rose!
The bride of every sense! more sweet than those
Who breathe the violet breath of maidenhood.
5   O visage of still music in the sky!
Soft moon! I feel thy song, my fairest friend!
True harmony within can apprehend
Dumb harmony without. And hark! 'tis nigh!
Belief has struck the note of sound: a gleam
10 Of living silver shows me where she shook
Her long white fingers down the shadowy brook,
That sings her song, half waking, half in dream.
What two come here to mar this heavenly tune?
A man is one: the woman bears my name,
15 And honour. Their hands touch! Am I still tame?
God, what a dancing spectre seems the moon!

XLV

It is the season of the sweet wild rose,
My Lady's emblem in the heart of me!
So golden-crownëd shines she gloriously,
And with that softest dream of blood she glows:
5   Mild as an evening heaven round Hesper bright!
I pluck the flower, and smell it, and revive
The time when in her eyes I stood alive.
I seem to look upon it out of Night.
Here's Madam, stepping hastily. Her whims
10 Bid her demand the flower, which I let drop.
As I proceed, I feel her sharply stop,
And crush it under heel with trembling limbs.
She joins me in a cat-like way, and talks
Of company, and even condescends
15 To utter laughing scandal of old friends.
These are the summer days, and these our walks.

DANTE GABRIEL ROSSETTI

The Blessed Damozel

The blessed damozel leaned out
   From the gold bar of Heaven;
Her eyes were deeper than the depth
   Of waters stilled at even;
She had three lilies in her hand,
   And the stars in her hair were seven.

Her robe, ungirt from clasp to hem,
   No wrought flowers did adorn,
But a white rose of Mary's gift,
   For service meetly worn;
Her hair that lay along her back
   Was yellow like ripe corn.

Herseemed she scarce had been a day
   One of God's choristers;
The wonder was not yet quite gone
   From that still look of hers;
Albeit, to them she left, her day
   Had counted as ten years.

(To one, it is ten years of years.
   . . . Yet now, and in this place,
Surely she leaned o'er me – her hair
   Fell all about my face . . .
Nothing: the autumn-fall of leaves.
   The whole year sets apace.)

It was the rampart of God's house
   That she was standing on;
By God built over the sheer depth
   The which is Space begun;
So high, that looking downward thence
   She scarce could see the sun.

It lies in Heaven, across the flood
   Of ether, as a bridge.
Beneath, the tides of day and night
   With flame and darkness ridge
The void, as low as where this earth   35
   Spins like a fretful midge.

Around her, lovers, newly met
   'Mid deathless love's acclaims,
Spoke evermore among themselves
   Their heart-remembered names;   40
And the souls mounting up to God
   Went by her like thin flames.

And still she bowed herself and stooped
   Out of the circling charm;
Until her bosom must have made   45
   The bar she leaned on warm,
And the lilies lay as if asleep
   Along her bended arm.

From the fixed place of Heaven she saw
   Time like a pulse shake fierce   50
Through all the worlds. Her gaze still strove
   Within the gulf to pierce
Its path; and now she spoke as when
   The stars sang in their spheres.

The sun was gone now; the curled moon   55
   Was like a little feather
Fluttering far down the gulf; and now
   She spoke through the still weather.
Her voice was like the voice the stars
   Had when they sang together.   60

(Ah sweet! Even now, in that bird's song,
   Strove not her accents there,
Fain to be hearkened? When those bells

    Possessed the mid-day air,
Strove not her steps to reach my side
    Down all the echoing stair?)

'I wish that he were come to me,
    For he will come,' she said.
'Have I not prayed in Heaven? – on earth,
    Lord, Lord, has he not pray'd?
Are not two prayers a perfect strength?
    And shall I feel afraid?

'When round his head the aureole clings,
    And he is clothed in white,
I'll take his hand and go with him
    To the deep wells of light;
As unto a stream we will step down,
    And bathe there in God's sight.

'We two will stand beside that shrine,
    Occult, withheld, untrod,
Whose lamps are stirred continually
    With prayer sent up to God;
And see our old prayers, granted, melt
    Each like a little cloud.

'We two will lie i' the shadow of
    That living mystic tree
Within whose secret growth the Dove
    Is sometimes felt to be,
While every leaf that His plumes touch
    Saith His Name audibly.

And I myself will teach to him,
    I myself, lying so,
The songs I sing here; which his voice
    Shall pause in, hushed and slow,
And find some knowledge at each pause,
    Or some new thing to know.'

(Alas! We two, we two, thou say'st!
    Yea, one wast thou with me
That once of old. But shall God lift
    To endless unity   100
The soul whose likeness with thy soul
    Was but its love for thee?)

'We two,' she said, 'will seek the groves
    Where the lady Mary is,
With her five handmaidens, whose names   105
    Are five sweet symphonies,
Cecily, Gertrude, Magdalen,
    Margaret and Rosalys.

'Circlewise sit they, with bound locks
    And foreheads garlanded;   110
Into the fine cloth white like flame
    Weaving the golden thread,
To fashion the birth-robes for them
    Who are just born, being dead.

'He shall fear, haply, and be dumb: 115
    Then will I lay my cheek
To his, and tell about our love,
    Not once abashed or weak:
And the dear Mother will approve
    My pride, and let me speak.   120

'Herself shall bring us, hand in hand,
    To him round whom all souls
Kneel, the clear-ranged unnumbered heads
    Bowed with their aureoles:
And angels meeting us shall sing   125
    To their citherns and citoles.

'There will I ask of Christ the Lord
    Thus much for him and me: –
Only to live as once on earth

130   With Love, – only to be,
     As then awhile, for ever now
         Together, I and he.'

     She gazed and listened and then said,
         Less sad of speech than mild, –
135 'All this is when he comes.' She ceased.
         The light thrilled towards her, fill'd
     With angels in strong level flight.
         Her eyes prayed, and she smil'd.

     (I saw her smile.) But soon their path
140   Was vague in distant spheres:
     And then she cast her arms along
         The golden barriers,
     And laid her face between her hands,
         And wept. (I heard her tears.)

The Card-Dealer

     Could you not drink her gaze like wine?
         Yet though its splendour swoon
     Into the silence languidly
         As a tune into a tune,
5   Those eyes unravel the coiled night
         And know the stars at noon.

     The gold that's heaped beside her hand,
         In truth rich prize it were;
     And rich the dreams that wreathe her brows
10   With magic stillness there;
     And he were rich who should unwind
         That woven golden hair.

     Around her, where she sits, the dance
         Now breathes its eager heat;
15   And not more lightly or more true

Fall there the dancers' feet
Than fall her cards on the bright board
As 'twere an heart that beat.

Her fingers let them softly through,
    Smooth polished silent things;
And each one as it falls reflects
    In swift light-shadowings,
Blood-red and purple, green and blue,
    The great eyes of her rings.

Whom plays she with? With thee, who lov'st
    Those gems upon her hand;
With me, who search her secret brows;
    With all men, bless'd or bann'd.
We play together, she and we,
    Within a vain strange land:

A land without any order, –
    Day even as night, (one saith,) –
Where who lieth down ariseth not
    Nor the sleeper awakeneth;
A land of darkness as darkness itself
    And of the shadow of death.

What be her cards, you ask? Even these: –
    The heart, that doth but crave
More, having fed; the diamond,
    Skilled to make base seem brave;
The club, for smiting in the dark;
    The spade, to dig a grave.

And do you ask what game she plays?
    With me 'tis lost or won;
With thee it is playing still; with him
    It is not well begun;
But 'tis a game she plays with all
    Beneath the sway o' the sun.

Thou seest the card that falls, – she knows
    The card that followeth:
Her game in thy tongue is called Life,
    As ebbs thy daily breath:
When she shall speak, thou'lt learn her tongue
    And know she calls it Death.

The Burden of Nineveh

In our Museum galleries
To-day I lingered o'er the prize
Dead Greece vouchsafes to living eyes, –
Her Art for ever in fresh wise
    From hour to hour rejoicing me.
Sighing I turned at last to win
Once more the London dirt and din;
And as I made the swing-door spin
And issued, they were hoisting in
    A wingèd beast from Nineveh.

A human face the creature wore,
And hoofs behind and hoofs before,
And flanks with dark runes fretted o'er.
'Twas bull, 'twas mitred Minotaur,
    A dead disbowelled mystery:
The mummy of a buried faith
Stark from the charnel without scathe,
Its wings stood for the light to bathe, –
Such fossil cerements as might swathe
    The very corpse of Nineveh.

The print of its first rush-wrapping,
Wound ere it dried, still ribbed the thing.
What song did the brown maidens sing,
From purple mouths alternating,
    When that was woven languidly?

What vows, what rites, what prayers preferr'd,
What songs has the strange image heard?
In what blind vigil stood interr'd
For ages, till an English word
    Broke silence first at Nineveh?   30

Oh when upon each sculptured court,
Where even the wind might not resort, –
O'er which Time passed, of like import
With the wild Arab boys at sport, –
    A living face looked in to see: –   35
O seemed it not – the spell once broke –
As though the carven warriors woke,
As though the shaft the string forsook,
The cymbals clashed, the chariots shook,
    And there was life in Nineveh?   40

On London stones our sun anew
The beast's recovered shadow threw.
(No shade that plague of darkness knew,
No light, no shade, while older grew
    By ages the old earth and sea.)   45
Lo thou! could all thy priests have shown
Such proof to make thy godhead known?
From their dead Past thou liv'st alone;
And still thy shadow is thine own,
    Even as of yore in Nineveh.   50

That day whereof we keep record,
When near thy city-gates the Lord
Sheltered His Jonah with a gourd,
This sun, (I said) here present, pour'd
    Even thus this shadow that I see.   55
This shadow has been shed the same
From sun and moon, – from lamps which came
For prayer, – from fifteen days of flame,
The last, while smouldered to a name
    Sardanapalus' Nineveh.   60

Within thy shadow, haply, once
Sennacherib has knelt, whose sons
Smote him between the altar-stones:
Or pale Semiramis her zones
65   Of gold, her incense brought to thee,
In love for grace, in war for aid: . . .
Ay, and who else? . . . till 'neath thy shade
Within his trenches newly made
Last year the Christian knelt and pray'd –
70   Not to thy strength – in Nineveh.*

Now, thou poor god, within this hall
Where the blank windows blind the wall
From pedestal to pedestal,
The kind of light shall on thee fall
75   Which London takes the day to be:
While school-foundations in the act
Of holiday, three files compact,
Shall learn to view thee as a fact
Connected with that zealous tract:
80   'ROME, – Babylon and Nineveh.'

Deemed they of this, those worshippers,
When, in some mythic chain of verse
Which man shall not again rehearse,
The faces of thy ministers
85   Yearned pale with bitter ecstasy?
Greece, Egypt, Rome, – did any god
Before whose feet men knelt unshod
Deem that in this unblest abode
Another scarce more unknown god
90   Should house with him, from Nineveh?

---

*   During the excavations, the Tiyari workmen held their services in the shad-
ow of the great bulls (Layard's *Nineveh*, ch. ix).

Ah! in what quarries lay the stone
From which this pillared pile has grown,
Unto man's need how long unknown,
Since those thy temples, court and cone
    Rose far in desert history?   95
Ah! what is here that does not lie
All strange to thine awakened eye?
Ah! what is here can testify
(Save that dumb presence of the sky)
    Unto thy day and Nineveh?   100

Why, of those mummies in the room
Above, there might indeed have come
One out of Egypt to thy home,
An alien. Nay, but were not some
    Of these thine own 'antiquity?'   105
And now, – they and their gods and thou
All relics here together, – now
Whose profit? whether bull or cow,
Isis or Ibis, who or how,
    Whether of Thebes or Nineveh?   110

The consecrated metals found,
And ivory tablets, underground,
Winged teraphim and creatures crown'd,
When air and daylight filled the mound,
    Fell into dust immediately.   115
And even as these, the images
Of awe and worship, – even as these, –
So, smitten with the sun's increase,
Her glory mouldered and did cease
    From immemorial Nineveh.   120

The day her builders made their halt,
Those cities of the lake of salt
Stood firmly 'stablished without fault,
Made proud with pillars of basalt,
    With sardonyx and porphyry.   125

The day that Jonah bore abroad
To Nineveh the voice of God,
A brackish lake lay in his road,
Where erst Pride fixed her sure abode,
130   As then in royal Nineveh.

The day when he, Pride's lord and Man's,
Showed all the kingdoms at a glance
To Him before whose countenance
The years recede, the years advance,
135   And said, Fall down and worship me: –
'Mid all the pomp beneath that look,
Then stirred there, haply, some rebuke,
Where to the wind the Salt Pools shook,
And in those tracts, of life forsook,
140   That knew thee not, O Nineveh!

Delicate harlot! On thy throne
Thou with a world beneath thee prone
In state for ages sat'st alone;
And needs were years and lustres flown
145   Ere strength of man could vanquish thee:
Whom even thy victor foes must bring,
Still royal, among maids that sing
As with doves' voices, taboring
Upon their breasts, unto the King, –
150   A kingly conquest, Nineveh!

. . . Here woke my thought. The wind's slow sway
Had waxed; and like the human play
Of scorn that smiling spreads away,
The sunshine shivered off the day:
155   The callous wind, it seemed to me,
Swept up the shadow from the ground:
And pale as whom the Fates astound,
The god forlorn stood winged and crown'd:
Within I knew the cry lay bound.
160   Of the dumb soul of Nineveh.

And as I turned, my sense half shut
Still saw the crowds of kerb and rut
Go past as marshalled to the strut
Of ranks in gypsum quaintly cut.
    It seemed in one same pageantry   165
They followed forms which had been erst;
To pass, till on my sight should burst
That future of the best or worst
When some may question which was first,
    Of London or of Nineveh.   170

For as that Bull-god once did stand
And watched the burial-clouds of sand,
Till these at last without a hand
Rose o'er his eyes, another land,
    And blinded him with destiny: –   175
So may he stand again; till now,
In ships of unknown sail and prow,
Some tribe of the Australian plough
Bear him afar, – a relic now
    Of London, not of Nineveh!   180

Or it may chance indeed that when
Man's age is hoary among men, –
His centuries threescore and ten, –
His furthest childhood shall seem then
    More clear than later times may be: 185
Who, finding in this desert place
This form, shall hold us for some race
That walked not in Christ's lowly ways,
But bowed its pride and vowed its praise
    Unto the God of Nineveh.   190

The smile rose first, – anon drew nigh
The thought: . . . Those heavy wings spread high
So sure of flight, which do not fly;
That set gaze never on the sky;
    Those scriptured flanks it cannot see;   195

     Its crown, a brow-contracting load;
     Its planted feet which trust the sod: . . .
     (So grew the image as I trod:)
     O Nineveh, was this thy God, –
200   Thine also, mighty Nineveh?

Jenny

'Vengeance of Jenny's case! Fie on her! Never name her, child!'
– Mrs Quickly

     Lazy laughing languid Jenny,
     Fond of a kiss and fond of a guinea,
     Whose head upon my knee to-night
     Rests for a while, as if grown light
5   With all our dances and the sound
     To which the wild tunes spun you round:
     Fair Jenny mine, the thoughtless queen
     Of kisses which the blush between
     Could hardly make much daintier;
10   Whose eyes are as blue skies, whose hair
     Is countless gold incomparable:
     Fresh flower, scarce touched with signs that tell
     Of Love's exuberant hotbed: – Nay,
     Poor flower left torn since yesterday
15   Until to-morrow leave you bare;
     Poor handful of bright spring-water
     Flung in the whirlpool's shrieking face;
     Poor shameful Jenny, full of grace
     Thus with your head upon my knee; –
20   Whose person or whose purse may be
     The lodestar of your reverie?

     This room of yours, my Jenny, looks
     A change from mine so full of books,
     Whose serried ranks hold fast, forsooth,
25   So many captive hours of youth, –

The hours they thieve from day and night
To make one's cherished work come right,
And leave it wrong for all their theft,
Even as to-night my work was left:
Until I vowed that since my brain   30
And eyes of dancing seemed so fain,
My feet should have some dancing too: –
And thus it was I met with you.
Well, I suppose 'twas hard to part,
For here I am. And now, sweetheart,   35
You seem too tired to get to bed.

It was a careless life I led
When rooms like this were scarce so strange
Not long ago. What breeds the change, –
The many aims or the few years?   40
Because to-night it all appears
Something I do not know again.

The cloud's not danced out of my brain, –
The cloud that made it turn and swim
While hour by hour the books grew dim.   45
Why, Jenny, as I watch you there, –
For all your wealth of loosened hair,
Your silk ungirdled and unlac'd
And warm sweets open to the waist,
All golden in the lamplight's gleam, –   50
You know not what a book you seem,
Half-read by lightning in a dream!
How should you know, my Jenny? Nay,
And I should be ashamed to say: –
Poor beauty, so well worth a kiss!   55
But while my thought runs on like this
With wasteful whims more than enough,
I wonder what you're thinking of.

If of myself you think at all,
What is the thought? – conjectural
On sorry matters best unsolved? –
Or inly is each grace revolved
To fit me with a lure? – or (sad
To think!) perhaps you're merely glad
That I'm not drunk or ruffianly
And let you rest upon my knee.

For sometimes, were the truth confess'd,
You're thankful for a little rest, –
Glad from the crush to rest within,
From the heart-sickness and the din
Where envy's voice at virtue's pitch
Mocks you because your gown is rich;
And from the pale girl's dumb rebuke,
Whose ill-clad grace and toil-worn look
Proclaim the strength that keeps her weak
And other nights than yours bespeak;
And from the wise unchildish elf,
To schoolmate lesser than himself
Pointing you out, what thing you are: –
Yes, from the daily jeer and jar,
From shame and shame's outbraving too,
Is rest not sometimes sweet to you? –
But most from the hatefulness of man
Who spares not to end what he began,
Whose acts are ill and his speech ill,
Who, having used you at his will,
Thrusts you aside, as when I dine
I serve the dishes and the wine.

Well, handsome Jenny mine, sit up,
I've filled our glasses, let us sup,
And do not let me think of you,
Lest shame of yours suffice for two.
What, still so tired? Well, well then, keep
Your head there, so you do not sleep;

But that the weariness may pass   95
And leave you merry, take this glass.
Ah! lazy lily hand, more bless'd
If ne'er in rings it had been dress'd
Nor ever by a glove conceal'd!

Behold the lilies of the field,   100
They toil not neither do they spin;
(So doth the ancient text begin, –
Not of such rest as one of these
Can share.) Another rest and ease
Along each summer-sated path   105
From its new lord the garden hath,
Than that whose spring in blessings ran
Which praised the bounteous husbandman,
Ere yet, in days of hankering breath,
The lilies sickened unto death.   110

What, Jenny, are your lilies dead?
Aye, and the snow-white leaves are spread
Like winter on the garden-bed.
But you had roses left in May, –
They were not gone too. Jenny, nay,   115
But must your roses die, and those
Their purfled buds that should unclose?
Even so; the leaves are curled apart,
Still red as from the broken heart,
And here's the naked stem of thorns.   120

Nay, nay, mere words. Here nothing warns
As yet of winter. Sickness here
Or want alone could waken fear, –
Nothing but passion wrings a tear.
Except when there may rise unsought   125
Haply at times a passing thought
Of the old days which seem to be
Much older than any history
That is written in any book;

130   When she would lie in fields and look
        Along the ground through the blown grass,
        And wonder where the city was,
        Far out of sight, whose broil and bale
        They told her then for a child's tale.

135   Jenny, you know the city now.
        A child can tell the tale there, how
        Some things which are not yet enroll'd
        In market-lists are bought and sold
        Even till the early Sunday light,
140   When Saturday night is market-night
        Everywhere, be it dry or wet,
        And market-night in the Haymarket.
        Our learned London children know,
        Poor Jenny, all your pride and woe;
145   Have seen your lifted silken skirt
        Advertise dainties through the dirt;
        Have seen your coach-wheels splash rebuke
        On virtue; and have learned your look
        When, wealth and health slipped past, you stare
150   Along the streets alone, and there,
        Round the long park, across the bridge,
        The cold lamps at the pavement's edge
        Wind on together and apart,
        A fiery serpent for your heart.

155   Let the thoughts pass, an empty cloud!
        Suppose I were to think aloud, –
        What if to her all this were said?
        Why, as a volume seldom read
        Being opened halfway shuts again,
160   So might the pages of her brain
        Be parted at such words, and thence
        Close back upon the dusty sense.
        For is there hue or shape defin'd
        In Jenny's desecrated mind,

Where all contagious currents meet, 165
A Lethe of the middle street?
Nay, it reflects not any face,
Nor sound is in its sluggish pace,
But as they coil those eddies clot,
And night and day remember not. 170

Why, Jenny, you're asleep at last! –
Asleep, poor Jenny, hard and fast, –
So young and soft and tired; so fair,
With chin thus nestled in your hair,
Mouth quiet, eyelids almost blue 175
As if some sky of dreams shone through!

Just as another woman sleeps!
Enough to throw one's thoughts in heaps
Of doubt and horror, – what to say
Or think, – this awful secret sway, 180
The potter's power over the clay!
Of the same lump (it has been said)
For honour and dishonour made,
Two sister vessels. Here is one.

My cousin Nell is fond of fun, 185
And fond of dress, and change, and praise,
So mere a woman in her ways:
And if her sweet eyes rich in youth
Are like her lips that tell the truth,
My cousin Nell is fond of love. 190
And she's the girl I'm proudest of.
Who does not prize her, guard her well?
The love of change, in cousin Nell,
Shall find the best and hold it dear:
The unconquered mirth turn quieter 195
Not through her own, through others' woe:
The conscious pride of beauty glow
Beside another's pride in her,
One little part of all they share.

200   For Love himself shall ripen these
       In a kind soil to just increase
       Through years of fertilizing peace.

           Of the same lump (as it is said)
       For honour and dishonour made,
205   Two sister vessels. Here is one.

           It makes a goblin of the sun.

           So pure, – so fall'n! How dare to think
       Of the first common kindred link?
       Yet, Jenny, till the world shall burn
210   It seems that all things take their turn;
       And who shall say but this fair tree
       May need, in changes that may be,
       Your children's children's charity?
       Scorned then, no doubt, as you are scorn'd!
215   Shall no man hold his pride forewarn'd
       Till in the end, the Day of Days,
       At Judgment, one of his own race,
       As frail and lost as you, shall rise, –
       His daughter, with his mother's eyes?

220   How Jenny's clock ticks on the shelf!
       Might not the dial scorn itself
       That has such hours to register?
       Yet as to me, even so to her
       Are golden sun and silver moon,
225   In daily largesse of earth's boon,
       Counted for life-coins to one tune.
       And if, as blindfold fates are toss'd,
       Through some one man this life be lost,
       Shall soul not somehow pay for soul?

230   Fair shines the gilded aureole
       In which our highest painters place
       Some living woman's simple face.

And the stilled features thus descried
As Jenny's long throat droops aside, –
The shadows where the cheeks are thin,   235
And pure wide curve from ear to chin, –
With Raffael's, Leonardo's hand
To show them to men's souls, might stand,
Whole ages long, the whole world through,
For preachings of what God can do.   240
What has man done here? How atone,
Great God, for this which man has done?
And for the body and soul which by
Man's pitiless doom must now comply
With lifelong hell, what lullaby   245
Of sweet forgetful second birth
Remains? All dark. No sign on earth
What measure of God's rest endows
The many mansions of his house.

If but a woman's heart might see   250
Such erring heart unerringly
For once! But that can never be.

Like a rose shut in a book
In which pure women may not look,
For its base pages claim control   255
To crush the flower within the soul;
Where through each dead rose-leaf that clings,
Pale as transparent psyche-wings,
To the vile text, are traced such things
As might make lady's cheek indeed   260
More than a living rose to read;
So nought save foolish foulness may
Watch with hard eyes the sure decay;
And so the life-blood of this rose,
Puddled with shameful knowledge, flows   265
Through leaves no chaste hand may unclose:
Yet still it keeps such faded show
Of when 'twas gathered long ago,

That the crushed petals' lovely grain,
270 The sweetness of the sanguine stain,
Seen of a woman's eyes, must make
Her pitiful heart, so prone to ache,
Love roses better for its sake: –
Only that this can never be: –
275 Even so unto her sex is she.

Yet, Jenny, looking long at you,
The woman almost fades from view.
A cipher of man's changeless sum
Of lust, past, present, and to come,
280 Is left. A riddle that one shrinks
To challenge from the scornful sphinx.

Like a toad within a stone
Seated while Time crumbles on;
Which sits there since the earth was curs'd
285 For Man's transgression at the first;
Which, living through all centuries,
Not once has seen the sun arise;
Whose life, to its cold circle charmed,
The earth's whole summers have not warmed;
290 Which always – whitherso the stone
Be flung – sits there, deaf, blind, alone; –
Aye, and shall not be driven out
Till that which shuts him round about
Break at the very Master's stroke,
295 And the dust thereof vanish as smoke,
And the seed of Man vanish as dust: –
Even so within this world is Lust.

Come, come, what use in thoughts like this?
Poor little Jenny, good to kiss, –
300 You'd not believe by what strange roads
Thought travels, when your beauty goads
A man to-night to think of toads!
Jenny, wake up . . . Why, there's the dawn!

And there's an early wagon drawn
To market, and some sheep that jog   305
Bleating before a barking dog;
And the old streets come peering through
Another night that London knew;
And all as ghostlike as the lamps.

So on the wings of day decamps   310
My last night's frolic. Glooms begin
To shiver off as lights creep in
Past the gauze curtains half drawn-to,
And the lamp's doubled shade grows blue, –
Your lamp, my Jenny, kept alight,   315
Like a wise virgin's, all one night!
And in the alcove coolly spread
Glimmers with dawn your empty bed;
And yonder your fair face I see
Reflected lying on my knee,   320
Where teems with first foreshadowings
Your pier-glass scrawled with diamond rings:
And on your bosom all night worn
Yesterday's rose now droops forlorn
But dies not yet this summer morn.   325

And now without, as if some word
Had called upon them that they heard,
The London sparrows far and nigh
Clamour together suddenly;
And Jenny's cage-bird grown awake   330
Here in their song his part must take,
Because here too the day doth break.

And somehow in myself the dawn
Among stirred clouds and veils withdrawn
Strikes greyly on her. Let her sleep.   335
But will it wake her if I heap
These cushions thus beneath her head
Where my knee was? No, – there's your bed,

My Jenny, while you dream. And there
I lay among your golden hair
Perhaps the subject of your dreams,
These golden coins.

                                    For still one deems
That Jenny's flattering sleep confers
New magic on the magic purse, –
Grim web, how clogged with shrivelled flies!
Between the threads fine fumes arise
And shape their pictures in the brain.
There roll no streets in glare and rain,
Nor flagrant man-swine whets his tusk;
But delicately sighs in musk
The homage of the dim boudoir;
Or like a palpitating star
Thrilled into song, the opera-night
Breathes faint in the quick pulse of light;
Or at the carriage-window shine
Rich wares for choice; or, free to dine,
Whirls through its hour of health (divine
For her) the concourse of the Park.
And though in the discounted dark
Her functions there and here are one,
Beneath the lamps and in the sun
There reigns at least the acknowledged belle
Apparelled beyond parallel.
Ah Jenny, yes, we know your dreams.

For even the Paphian Venus seems
A goddess o'er the realms of love,
When silver-shrined in shadowy grove:
Aye, or let offerings nicely plac'd
But hide Priapus to the waist,
And whoso looks on him shall see
An eligible deity.

Why, Jenny, waking here alone
May help you to remember one,
Though all the memory's long outworn   375
Of many a double-pillowed morn.
I think I see you when you wake,
And rub your eyes for me, and shake
My gold, in rising, from your hair,
A Danaë for a moment there.   380

Jenny, my love rang true! for still
Love at first sight is vague, until
That tinkling makes him audible.

And must I mock you to the last,
Ashamed of my own shame, – aghast   385
Because some thoughts not born amiss
Rose at a poor fair face like this?
Well, of such thoughts so much I know:
In my life, as in hers, they show,
By a far gleam which I may near,   390
A dark path I can strive to clear.

Only one kiss. Goodbye, my dear.

The Portrait

This is her picture as she was:
    It seems a thing to wonder on,
As though mine image in the glass
    Should tarry when myself am gone
I gaze until she seems to stir, –   5
Until mine eyes almost aver
    That now, even now, the sweet lips part
    To breathe the words of the sweet heart: –
And yet the earth is over her.

Alas! even such the thin-drawn ray
 That makes the prison-depths more rude, –
The drip of water night and day
 Giving a tongue to solitude.
Yet only this, of love's whole prize,
Remains; save what in mournful guise
 Takes counsel with my soul alone, –
 Save what is secret and unknown,
Below the earth, above the skies.

In painting her I shrined her face
 Mid mystic trees, where light falls in
Hardly at all; a covert place
 Where you might think to find a din
Of doubtful talk, and a live flame
Wandering, and many a shape whose name
 Not itself knoweth, and old dew,
 And your own footsteps meeting you,
And all things going as they came.

A deep dim wood; and there she stands
 As in that wood that day: for so
Was the still movement of her hands
 And such the pure line's gracious flow.
And passing fair the type must seem,
Unknown the presence and the dream.
 'Tis she: though of herself, alas!
 Less than her shadow on the grass
Or than her image in the stream.

That day we met there, I and she
 One with the other all alone;
And we were blithe; yet memory
 Saddens those hours, as when the moon
Looks upon daylight. And with her
I stooped to drink the spring-water,

Athirst where other waters sprang;
    And where the echo is, she sang, –
My soul another echo there.   45

But when that hour my soul won strength
    For words whose silence wastes and kills,
Dull raindrops smote us, and at length
    Thundered the heat within the hills.
That eve I spoke those words again   50
Beside the pelted window-pane;
    And there she hearkened what I said,
    With under-glances that surveyed
The empty pastures blind with rain.

Next day the memories of these things,   55
    Like leaves through which a bird has flown,
Still vibrated with Love's warm wings;
    Till I must make them all my own
And paint this picture. So, 'twixt ease
Of talk and sweet long silences,   60
    She stood among the plants in bloom
    At windows of a summer room,
To feign the shadow of the trees.

And as I wrought, while all above
    And all around was fragrant air,   65
In the sick burthen of my love
    It seemed each sun-thrilled blossom there
Beat like a heart among the leaves.
O heart that never beats nor heaves,
    In that one darkness lying still,   70
    What now to thee my love's great will
Or the fine web the sunshine weaves?

For now doth daylight disavow
    Those days, – nought left to see or hear.
Only in solemn whispers now   75
    At night-time these things reach mine ear;

When the leaf-shadows at a breath
Shrink in the road, and all the heath,
   Forest and water, far and wide,
    In limpid starlight glorified,
Lie like the mystery of death.

Last night at last I could have slept,
   And yet delayed my sleep till dawn,
Still wandering. Then it was I wept:
   For unawares I came upon
Those glades where once she walked with me:
And as I stood there suddenly,
   All wan with traversing the night,
   Upon the desolate verge of light
Yearned loud the iron-bosomed sea.

Even so, where Heaven holds breath and hears
   The beating heart of Love's own breast, –
Where round the secret of all spheres
   All angels lay their wings to rest, –
How shall my soul stand rapt and awed,
When, by the new birth borne abroad
   Throughout the music of the suns,
   It enters in her soul at once
And knows the silence there for God!

Here with her face doth memory sit
   Meanwhile, and wait the day's decline,
Till other eyes shall look from it,
   Eyes of the spirit's Palestine,
Even than the old gaze tenderer:
While hopes and aims long lost with her
   Stand round her image side by side,
   Like tombs of pilgrims that have died
About the Holy Sepulchre.

Nuptial Sleep

At length their long kiss severed, with sweet smart:
   And as the last slow sudden drops are shed
   From sparkling eaves when all the storm has fled,
So singly flagged the pulses of each heart.
Their bosoms sundered, with the opening start   5
   Of married flowers to either side outspread
   From the knit stem; yet still their mouths, burnt red,
Fawned on each other where they lay apart.

Sleep sank them lower than the tide of dreams,
   And their dreams watched them sink, and slid   10
     away.
Slowly their souls swam up again, through gleams
   Of watered light and dull drowned waifs of day;
Till from some wonder of new woods and streams
   He woke, and wondered more: for there she lay.

The Woodspurge

The wind flapped loose, the wind was still,
Shaken out dead from tree and hill:
I had walked on at the wind's will, –
I sat now, for the wind was still.

Between my knees my forehead was, –   5
My lips, drawn in, said not Alas!
My hair was over in the grass,
My naked ears heard the day pass.

My eyes, wide open, had the run
Of some ten weeds to fix upon;   10
Among those few, out of the sun,
The woodspurge flowered, three cups in one.

From perfect grief there need not be
Wisdom or even memory:
One thing then learnt remains to me, –
The woodspurge has a cup of three.

The Honeysuckle

I plucked a honeysuckle where
    The hedge on high is quick with thorn,
    And climbing for the prize, was torn,
And fouled my feet in quag-water;
    And by the thorns and by the wind
    The blossom that I took was thinn'd,
And yet I found it sweet and fair.

Thence to a richer growth I came,
    Where, nursed in mellow intercourse,
    The honeysuckles sprang by scores,
Not harried like my single stem,
    All virgin lamps of scent and dew.
    So from my hand that first I threw,
Yet plucked not any more of them.

The Sea-Limits

Consider the sea's listless chime:
    Time's self it is, made audible, –
    The murmur of the earth's own shell.
Secret continuance sublime
    Is the sea's end: our sight may pass
    No furlong further. Since time was,
This sound hath told the lapse of time.

No quiet, which is death's, – it hath
   The mournfulness of ancient life,
   Enduring always at dull strife.   10
As the world's heart of rest and wrath,
   Its painful pulse is in the sands.
   Last utterly, the whole sky stands,
Grey and not known, along its path.

Listen alone beside the sea,   15
   Listen alone among the woods;
   Those voices of twin solitudes
Shall have one sound alike to thee:
   Hark where the murmurs of thronged men
   Surge and sink back and surge again, –   20
Still the one voice of wave and tree.

Gather a shell from the strown beach
   And listen at its lips: they sigh
   The same desire and mystery,
The echo of the whole sea's speech.   25
   And all mankind is thus at heart
   Not anything but what thou art:
And Earth, Sea, Man, are all in each.

For 'The Wine of Circe' by Edward Burne-Jones

Dusk-haired and gold-robed o'er the golden wine
   She stoops, wherein, distilled of death and shame,
   Sink the black drops; while, lit with fragrant flame,
Round her spread board the golden sunflowers shine.
Doth Helios here with Hecatè combine   5
   (O Circe, thou their votaress?) to proclaim
   For these thy guests all rapture in Love's name,
Till pitiless Night give Day the countersign?

Lords of their hour, they come. And by her knee
10   Those cowering beasts, their equals heretofore,
Wait; who with them in new equality
      To-night shall echo back the sea's dull roar
      With a vain wail from passion's tide-strown shore
Where the dishevelled seaweed hates the sea.

Mary's Girlhood
(For a Picture)

This is that blessed Mary, pre-elect
      God's Virgin. Gone is a great while, and she
      Dwelt young in Nazareth of Galilee.
Unto God's will she brought devout respect,
5   Profound simplicity of intellect,
      And supreme patience. From her mother's knee
      Faithful and hopeful; wise in charity;
Strong in grave peace; in pity circumspect.

So held she through her girlhood; as it were
10   An angel-watered lily, that near God
      Grows and is quiet. Till, one dawn at home,
She woke in her white bed, and had no fear
      At all, – yet wept till sunshine, and felt awed:
      Because the fulness of the time was come.

On the 'Vita Nuova' of Dante

As he that loves oft looks on the dear form
      And guesses how it grew to womanhood,
      And gladly would have watched the beauties bud
And the mild fire of precious life wax warm: –
5   So I, long bound within the threefold charm
      Of Dante's love sublimed to heavenly mood,
      Had marvelled, touching his Beatitude,
How grew such presence from man's shameful swarm.

At length within this book I found portrayed
   Newborn that Paradisal Love of his,   10
And simple like a child; with whose clear aid
   I understood. To such a child as this,
Christ, charging well his chosen ones, forbade
   Offence: 'for lo! of such my kingdom is.'

Beauty and the Bird

She fluted with her mouth as when one sips,
   And gently waved her golden head, inclin'd
   Outside his cage close to the window-blind;
Till her fond bird, with little turns and dips,
Piped low to her of sweet companionships.   5
   And when he made an end, some seed took she
   And fed him from her tongue, which rosily
Peeped as a piercing bud between her lips.

And like the child in Chaucer, on whose tongue
   The Blessed Mary laid, when he was dead,   10
A grain, – who straightway praised her name in song:
   Even so, when she, a little lightly red,
Now turned on me and laughed, I heard the throng
   Of inner voices praise her golden head.

A Match with the Moon

Weary already, weary miles to-night
   I walked for bed: and so, to get some ease,
   I dogged the flying moon with similes.
And like a wisp she doubled on my sight
In ponds; and caught in tree-tops like a kite;   5
   And in a globe of film all liquorish
   Swam full-faced like a silly silver fish; –
Last like a bubble shot the welkin's height

Where my road turned, and got behind me, and sent
10   My wizened shadow craning round at me,
    And jeered, 'So, step the measure, – one two three!' –
And if I faced on her, looked innocent.
    But just at parting, halfway down a dell,
    She kissed me for good-night. So you'll not tell.

John Keats

The weltering London ways where children weep
    And girls whom none call maidens laugh, – strange
        road
    Miring his outward steps, who inly trode
5   The bright Castalian brink and Latmos' steep: –
Even such his life's cross-paths; till deathly deep
    He toiled through sands of Lethe; and long pain,
    Weary with labour spurned and love found vain,
In dead Rome's sheltering shadow wrapped his sleep.

10   O pang-dowered Poet, whose reverberant lips
And heart-strung lyre awoke the Moon's eclipse, –
    Thou whom the daisies glory in growing o'er, –
Their fragrance clings around thy name, not writ
But rumour'd in water, while the fame of it
15   Along Time's flood goes echoing evermore.

Words on the Window-Pane*

Did she in summer write it, or in spring,
    Or with this wail of autumn at her ears,
    Or in some winter left among old years
Scratched it through tettered cark? A certain thing
5   That round her heart the frost was hardening,

* For a woman's fragmentary inscription.

Not to be thawed of tears, which on this pane
   Channelled the rime, perchance, in fevered rain,
For false man's sake and love's most bitter sting.

Howbeit, between this last word and the next
Unwritten, subtly seasoned was the smart,   10
   And here at least the grace to weep: if she,
Rather, midway in her disconsolate text,
Rebelled not, loathing from the trodden heart
   That thing which she had found man's love to be.

Astarte Syriaca
(For a Picture)

Mystery: lo! betwixt the sun and moon
   Astarte of the Syrians: Venus Queen
   Ere Aphrodite was. In silver sheen
Her twofold girdle clasps the infinite boon
Of bliss whereof the heaven and earth commune: 5
   And from her neck's inclining flower-stem lean
   Love-freighted lips and absolute eyes that wean
The pulse of hearts to the spheres' dominant tune.

Torch-bearing, her sweet ministers compel
   All thrones of light beyond the sky and sea   10
   The witnesses of Beauty's face to be:
That face, of Love's all-penetrative spell
Amulet, talisman, and oracle, –
   Betwixt the sun and moon a mystery.

FROM *THE HOUSE OF LIFE*

A Sonnet is a moment's monument, –
   Memorial from the Soul's eternity
   To one dead deathless hour. Look that it be,
Whether for lustral rite or dire portent,
Of its own arduous fulness reverent:
   Carve it in ivory or in ebony,
   As Day or Night may rule; and let Time see
Its flowering crest impearled and orient.

A Sonnet is a coin: its face reveals
   The soul, – its converse, to what Power 'tis due: –
Whether for tribute to the august appeals
   Of Life, or dower in Love's high retinue,
It serve; or, 'mid the dark wharf's cavernous breath,
In Charon's palm it pay the toll to Death.

V
Heart's Hope

By what word's power, the key of paths untrod,
   Shall I the difficult deeps of Love explore,
   Till parted waves of Song yield up the shore
Even as that sea which Israel crossed dryshod?
For lo! in some poor rhythmic period,
   Lady, I fain would tell how evermore
   Thy soul I know not from thy body, nor
Thee from myself, neither our love from God.

Yea, in God's name, and Love's, and thine, would I
   Draw from one loving heart such evidence
As to all hearts all things shall signify;

Tender as dawn's first hill-fire, and intense
As instantaneous penetrating sense,
In Spring's birth-hour, of other Springs gone by.

VI
The Kiss

What smouldering senses in death's sick delay
    Or seizure of malign vicissitude
    Can rob this body of honour, or denude
This soul of wedding-raiment worn to-day?
For lo! even now my lady's lips did play   5
    With these my lips such consonant interlude
    As laurelled Orpheus longed for when he wooed
The half-drawn hungering face with that last lay.

I was a child beneath her touch, – a man
    When breast to breast we clung, even I and   10
        she, –
    A spirit when her spirit looked through me, –
A god when all our life-breath met to fan
Our life-blood, till love's emulous ardours ran,
    Fire within fire, desire in deity.

X
The Portrait

O Lord of all compassionate control,
    O Love! let this my lady's picture glow
    Under my hand to praise her name, and show
Even of her inner self the perfect whole:
That he who seeks her beauty's furthest goal,   5
    Beyond the light that the sweet glances throw
    And refluent wave of the sweet smile, may know
The very sky and sea-line of her soul.

Lo! it is done. Above the enthroning throat
    The mouth's mould testifies of voice and kiss,
    The shadowed eyes remember and foresee.
Her face is made her shrine. Let all men note
    That in all years (O Love, thy gift is this!)
    They that would look on her must come to me.

XI
The Love-Letter

Warmed by her hand and shadowed by her hair
    As close she leaned and poured her heart through thee,
    Whereof the articulate throbs accompany
The smooth black stream that makes thy whiteness fair, –
Sweet fluttering sheet, even of her breath aware, –
    Oh let thy silent song disclose to me
    That soul wherewith her lips and eyes agree
Like married music in Love's answering air.

Fain had I watched her when, at some fond thought,
    Her bosom to the writing closelier press'd,
    And her breast's secrets peered into her breast;
When, through eyes raised an instant, her soul sought
My soul, and from the sudden confluence caught
    The words that made her love the loveliest.

XVIII
Genius in Beauty

Beauty like hers is genius. Not the call
    Of Homer's or of Dante's heart sublime, –
    Not Michael's hand furrowing the zones of time, –
Is more with compassed mysteries musical;

Nay, not in Spring's or Summer's sweet footfall   5
    More gathered gifts exuberant Life bequeathes
    Than doth this sovereign face, whose love-spell breathes
Even from its shadowed contour on the wall.

As many men are poets in their youth,
    But for one sweet-strung soul the wires prolong   10
    Even through all change the indomitable song;
So in likewise the envenomed years, whose tooth
Rends shallower grace with ruin void of ruth,
    Upon this beauty's power shall wreak no wrong.

XIX
Silent Noon

Your hands lie open in the long fresh grass, –
    The finger-points look through like rosy blooms:
    Your eyes smile peace. The pasture gleams and glooms
'Neath billowing skies that scatter and amass.
All round our nest, far as the eye can pass,   5
    Are golden kingcup-fields with silver edge
    Where the cow-parsley skirts the hawthorn-hedge.
'Tis visible silence, still as the hour-glass.

Deep in the sun-searched growths the dragon-fly
Hangs like a blue thread loosened from the sky: –   10
    So this wing'd hour is dropt to us from above.
Oh! clasp we to our hearts, for deathless dower,
This close-companioned inarticulate hour
    When twofold silence was the song of love.

XXV
Winged Hours

Each hour until we meet is as a bird
   That wings from far his gradual way along
   The rustling covert of my soul, – his song
Still loudlier trilled through leaves more deeply stirr'd:
But at the hour of meeting, a clear word
   Is every note he sings, in Love's own tongue;
   Yet, Love, thou know'st the sweet strain suffers wrong,
Full oft through our contending joys unheard.

What of that hour at last, when for her sake
   No wing may fly to me nor song may flow;
   When, wandering round my life unleaved, I know
The bloodied feathers scattered in the brake,
   And think how she, far from me, with like eyes
Sees through the untuneful bough the wingless skies?

XXVII
Heart's Compass

Sometimes thou seem'st not as thyself alone,
   But as the meaning of all things that are;
   A breathless wonder, shadowing forth afar
Some heavenly solstice hushed and halcyon;
Whose unstirred lips are music's visible tone;
   Whose eyes the sun-gate of the soul unbar,
   Being of its furthest fires oracular; –
The evident heart of all life sown and mown.

Even such Love is; and is not thy name Love?
   Yea, by thy hand the Love-god rends apart
   All gathering clouds of Night's ambiguous art;

Flings them far down, and sets thine eyes above;
And simply, as some gage of flower or glove,
   Stakes with a smile the world against thy heart.

XXIX
The Moonstar

Lady, I thank thee for thy loveliness,
   Because my lady is more lovely still.
   Glorying I gaze, and yield with glad goodwill
To thee thy tribute; by whose sweet-spun dress
Of delicate life Love labours to assess   5
   My lady's absolute queendom; saying, 'Lo!
   How high this beauty is, which yet doth show
But as that beauty's sovereign votaress.'

Lady, I saw thee with her, side by side;
   And as, when night's fair fires their queen   10
     surround,
An emulous star too near the moon will ride, –
   Even so thy rays within her luminous bound
   Were traced no more; and by the light so drown'd,
Lady, not thou but she was glorified.

XL
Severed Selves

Two separate divided silences,
   Which, brought together, would find loving voice;
   Two glances which together would rejoice
In love, now lost like stars beyond dark trees;
Two hands apart whose touch alone gives ease;   5
   Two bosoms which, heart-shrined with mutual flame,
   Would, meeting in one clasp, be made the same;
Two souls, the shores wave-mocked of sundering seas: –

Such are we now. Ah! may our hope forecast
10   Indeed one hour again, when on this stream
    Of darkened love once more the light shall gleam? –
An hour how slow to come, how quickly past, –
Which blooms and fades, and only leaves at last,
    Faint as shed flowers, the attenuated dream.

XLIX, L, LI, LII
Willowwood

I

I sat with Love upon a woodside well,
    Leaning across the water, I and he;
    Nor ever did he speak nor looked at me,
But touched his lute wherein was audible
5   The certain secret thing he had to tell:
    Only our mirrored eyes met silently
    In the low wave; and that sound came to be
The passionate voice I knew; and my tears fell.

And at their fall, his eyes beneath grew hers;
10   And with his foot and with his wing-feathers
    He swept the spring that watered my heart's drouth.
Then the dark ripples spread to waving hair,
And as I stooped, her own lips rising there
    Bubbled with brimming kisses at my mouth.

II

And now Love sang: but his was such a song,
    So meshed with half-remembrance hard to free,
    As souls disused in death's sterility
May sing when the new birthday tarries long.
5   And I was made aware of a dumb throng
    That stood aloof, one form by every tree,
    All mournful forms, for each was I or she,
The shades of those our days that had no tongue.

They looked on us, and knew us and were known;
  While fast together, alive from the abyss,   10
  Clung the soul-wrung implacable close kiss;
And pity of self through all made broken moan
Which said, 'For once, for once, for once alone!'
  And still Love sang, and what he sang was this: –

III

'O ye, all ye that walk in Willowwood,
  That walk with hollow faces burning white;
What fathom-depth of soul-struck widowhood,
  What long, what longer hours, one lifelong night,
Ere ye again, who so in vain have wooed   5
  Your last hope lost, who so in vain invite
Your lips to that their unforgotten food,
  Ere ye, ere ye again shall see the light!

Alas! the bitter banks in Willowwood,
  With tear-spurge wan, with blood-wort burning red: 10
Alas! if ever such a pillow could
  Steep deep the soul in sleep till she were dead, –
Better all life forget her than this thing,
That Willowwood should hold her wandering!'

IV

So sang he: and as meeting rose and rose
  Together cling through the wind's wellaway
  Nor change at once, yet near the end of day
The leaves drop loosened where the heart-stain glows, –
So when the song died did the kiss unclose;   5
  And her face fell back drowned, and was as grey
  As its grey eyes; and if it ever may
Meet mine again I know not if Love knows.

Only I know that I leaned low and drank
A long draught from the water where she sank,   10
  Her breath and all her tears and all her soul:

And as I leaned, I know I felt Love's face
Pressed on my neck with moan of pity and grace,
    Till both our heads were in his aureole.

LIII
Without Her

What of her glass without her? The blank grey
    There where the pool is blind of the moon's face.
    Her dress without her? The tossed empty space
Of cloud-rack whence the moon has passed away.
Her paths without her? Day's appointed sway
    Usurped by desolate night. Her pillowed place
    Without her? Tears, ah me! for love's good grace,
And cold forgetfulness of night or day.

What of the heart without her? Nay, poor heart,
    Of thee what word remains ere speech be still?
    A wayfarer by barren ways and chill,
Steep ways and weary, without her thou art,
Where the long cloud, the long wood's counterpart,
    Sheds doubled darkness up the labouring hill.

LXIII
Inclusiveness

The changing guests, each in a different mood,
    Sit at the roadside table and arise:
    And every life among them in likewise
Is a soul's board set daily with new food.
What man has bent o'er his son's sleep, to brood
    How that face shall watch his when cold it lies? –
    Or thought, as his own mother kissed his eyes,
Of what her kiss was when his father wooed?

5
10
5

May not this ancient room thou sit'st in dwell
  In separate living souls for joy or pain?   10
  Nay, all its corners may be painted plain
Where Heaven shows pictures of some life spent well;
  And may be stamped, a memory all in vain,
Upon the sight of lidless eyes in Hell.

LXIX
Autumn Idleness

This sunlight shames November where he grieves
  In dead red leaves, and will not let him shun
  The day, though bough with bough be over-run.
But with a blessing every glade receives
High salutation; while from hillock-eaves   5
  The deer gaze calling, dappled white and dun,
  As if, being foresters of old, the sun
Had marked them with the shade of forest-leaves.

Here dawn to-day unveiled her magic glass;
  Here noon now gives the thirst and takes the   10
    dew;
Till eve bring rest when other good things pass.
  And here the lost hours the lost hours renew
While I still lead my shadow o'er the grass,
  Nor know, for longing, that which I should do.

LXXVIII
Body's Beauty

Of Adam's first wife, Lilith, it is told
  (The witch he loved before the gift of Eve,)
  That, ere the snake's, her sweet tongue could
    deceive,

And her enchanted hair was the first gold.
And still she sits, young while the earth is old,
    And, subtly of herself contemplative,
    Draws men to watch the bright web she can weave,
Till heart and body and life are in its hold.

The rose and poppy are her flowers; for where
    Is he not found, O Lilith, whom shed scent
And soft-shed kisses and soft sleep shall snare?
    Lo! as that youth's eyes burned at thine, so went
    Thy spell through him, and left his straight neck bent
And round his heart one strangling golden hair.

LXXXIII
Barren Spring

Once more the changed year's turning wheel returns:
    And as a girl sails balanced in the wind,
    And now before and now again behind
Stoops as it swoops, with cheek that laughs and burns, –
So Spring comes merry towards me here, but earns
    No answering smile from me, whose life is twin'd
    With the dead boughs that winter still must bind,
And whom to-day the Spring no more concerns.

Behold, this crocus is a withering flame;
    This snowdrop, snow; this apple-blossom's part
    To breed the fruit that breeds the serpent's art.
Nay, for these Spring-flowers, turn thy face from them,
Nor stay till on the year's last lily-stem
    The white cup shrivels round the golden heart.

LXXXV
Vain Virtues

What is the sorriest thing that enters Hell?
　　None of the sins, – but this and that fair deed
　　Which a soul's sin at length could supersede.
These yet are virgins, whom death's timely knell
Might once have sainted; whom the fiends compel　　　5
　　Together now, in snake-bound shuddering sheaves
　　Of anguish, while the pit's pollution leaves
Their refuse maidenhood abominable.

Night sucks them down, the tribute of the pit,
　　Whose names, half entered in the book of Life,　　　10
　　　Were God's desire at noon. And as their hair
And eyes sink last, the Torturer deigns no whit
　　To gaze, but, yearning, waits his destined wife,
　　　The Sin still blithe on earth that sent them there.

LXXXVI
Lost Days

The lost days of my life until to-day,
　　What were they, could I see them on the street
　　Lie as they fell? Would they be ears of wheat
Sown once for food but trodden into clay?
Or golden coins squandered and still to pay?　　　5
　　Or drops of blood dabbling the guilty feet?
　　Or such spilt water as in dreams must cheat
The undying throats of Hell, athirst alway?

I do not see them here; but after death
10   God knows I know the faces I shall see,
Each one a murdered self, with low last breath.
    'I am thyself, – what hast thou done to me?'
'And I – and I – thyself,' (lo! each one saith,)
    'And thou thyself to all eternity!'

XCV
The Vase of Life

Around the vase of Life at your slow pace
    He has not crept, but turned it with his hands,
    And all its sides already understands.
There, girt, one breathes alert for some great race;
5   Whose road runs far by sands and fruitful space;
        Who laughs, yet through the jolly throng has pass'd;
        Who weeps, nor stays for weeping; who at last,
A youth, stands somewhere crowned, with silent face.

And he has filled this vase with wine for blood,
10   With blood for tears, with spice for burning vow,
            With watered flowers for buried love most fit;
And would have cast it shattered to the flood,
        Yet in Fate's name has kept it whole; which now
        Stands empty till his ashes fall in it.

XCVII
A Superscription

Look in my face; my name is Might-have-been;
    I am also called No-more, Too-late, Farewell;
    Unto thine ear I hold the dead-sea shell
Cast up thy Life's foam-fretted feet between;
5   Unto thine eyes the glass where that is seen

Which had Life's form and Love's, but by my spell
  Is now a shaken shadow intolerable,
Of ultimate things unuttered the frail screen.

Mark me, how still I am! But should there dart
  One moment through thy soul the soft surprise   10
  Of that winged Peace which lulls the breath of sigh, –
Then shalt thou see me smile, and turn apart
Thy visage to mine ambush at thy heart
  Sleepless with cold commemorative eyes.

CI
The One Hope

When vain desire at last and vain regret
  Go hand in hand to death, and all is vain,
  What shall assuage the unforgotten pain
And teach the unforgetful to forget?
Shall Peace be still a sunk stream long unmet, –   5
  Or may the soul at once in a green plain
  Stoop through the spray of some sweet life-fountain
And cull the dew-drenched flowering amulet?

Ah! when the wan soul in that golden air
  Between the scriptured petals softly blown   10
  Peers breathless for the gift of grace unknown, –
Ah! let none other alien spell soe'er
But only the one Hope's one name be there, –
  Not less nor more, but even that word alone.

To the P.R.B.

Woolner and Stephens, Collinson, Millais,
  And my first brother, each and every one,
  What portion is theirs now beneath the sun
Which, even as here, in England makes to-day?
5 For most of them life runs not the same way
  Always, but leaves the thought at loss: I know
  Merely that Woolner keeps not even the show
Of work, nor is enough awake for play.
Meanwhile Hunt and myself race at full speed
10 Along the Louvre, and yawn from school to school,
  Wishing worn-out those masters known as old.
And no man asks of Browning; though indeed
  (As the book travels with me) any fool
  Who would might hear Sordello's story told.

St Wagnes' Eve

The hop-shop is shut up: the night doth wear.
  Here, early, Collinson this evening fell
  'Into the gulfs of sleep'; and Deverell
Has turned upon the pivot of his chair
5 The whole of this night long; and Hancock there
  Has laboured to repeat, in accents screechy,
  'Guardami ben, ben son, ben son Beatrice';
And Bernhard Smith still beamed, serene and square.
By eight, the coffee was all drunk. At nine
10 We gave the cat some milk. Our talk did shelve,
  Ere ten, to gasps and stupor. Helpless grief
Made, towards eleven, my inmost spirit pine,
  Knowing North's hour. And Hancock, hard on twelve,
  Showed an engraving of his bas-relief.

NONSENSE VERSES

There's an infantine Artist named Hughes –
Him and his the R.A.'s did refuse:
    At length, though, among
    The lot, one was hung –
But it was himself in a noose.   5

There is a young Artist named Jones
Whose conduct no genius atones:
    His behaviour in life
    Is a pang to the wife
And a plague to the neighbours of Jones.   5

There is a young Painter called Jones
(A cheer here, and hisses, and groans):
    The state of his mind
    Is a shame to mankind,
But a matter of triumph to Jones.   5

There's a combative Artist named Whistler
Who is, like his own hog-hairs, a bristler:
    A tube of white lead
    And a punch on the head
Offer varied attractions to Whistler.   5

A Historical Painter named Brown
Was in manners and language a clown:
    At epochs of victual
    Both *pudden* and *kittle*
Were expressions familiar to Brown.   5

There was a young rascal called Nolly
Whose habits though dirty were jolly;
    And when this book comes
    To be marked with his thumbs
5 You may know that its owner is Nolly.

There's a Scotch correspondent named Scott
Thinks a penny for postage a lot:
    Books, verses, and letters,
    Too good for his betters,
5 Cannot screw out an answer from Scott.

There once was a painter named Scott
Who seemed to have hair, but had not.
    He seemed too to have sense:
    'Twas an equal pretence
5 On the part of the painter named Scott.

There's the Irishman Arthur O'Shaughnessy –
On the chessboard of poets a pawn is he:
    Though a bishop or king
    Would be rather the thing
5 To the fancy of Arthur O'Shaughnessy.

There is a poor sneak called Rossetti:
As a painter with many kicks met he –
    With more as a man –
    But sometimes he ran,
5 And that saved the rear of Rossetti.

As a critic, the Poet Buchanan
Thinks Pseudo much safer than Anon.
    Into Maitland he shrunk,
    But the smell of the skunk
Guides the shuddering nose to Buchanan.   5

ELIZABETH SIDDAL

True Love

Farewell, Earl Richard,
　　Tender and brave;
Kneeling I kiss
　　The dust from thy grave.

Pray for me, Richard,
　　Lying alone,
With hands pleading earnestly,
　　All in white stone.

Soon must I leave thee
　　This sweet summer tide;
That other is waiting
　　To claim his pale bride.

Soon I'll return to thee,
　　Hopeful and brave,
When the dead leaves
　　Blow over thy grave.

Then shall they find me
　　Close at thy head,
Watching or fainting,
　　Sleeping or dead.

Dead Love

Oh never weep for love that's dead,
　　Since love is seldom true,
But changes his fashion from blue to red,
　　From brightest red to blue,
And love was born to an early death
　　And is so seldom true.

Then harbour no smile on your loving face
   To win the deepest sigh;
The fairest words on truest lips
   Pass off and surely die;   10
And you will stand alone, my dear,
   When wintry winds draw nigh.

Sweet, never weep for what cannot be,
   For this God has not given:
If the merest dream of love were true,   15
   Then, sweet, we should be in heaven;
And this is only earth, my dear,
   Where true love is not given.

Shepherd Turned Sailor

Now Christ thee save, thou bonny Shepherd,
   Sailing on the sea;
Ten thousand souls are sailing there
   But I belong to thee.
If thou art lost then all is lost   5
   And all is dead to me.

My love should have a grey head-stone
   And green moss at his feet,
And clinging grass above his breast
   Whereon his lambs could bleat;   10
And I should know the span of earth
   Where one day I might sleep.

Gone

To touch the glove upon her tender hand,
   To watch the jewel sparkle in her ring,
Lifted my heart into a sudden song,
   As when the wild birds sing.

5   To track her shadow on the sunny grass,
          To break her pathway through the darkened wood,
      Filled all my life with trembling and tears
          And silence where I stood.

      I watch the shadows gather round my heart,
10   I live to know that she is gone –
      Gone, gone for ever, like the tender dove
          That left the ark alone.

Speechless

      Many a mile o'er land and sea
      Unsummoned my Love returned to me;
      I remember not the words he said,
      But only the trees mourning overhead.
5   And he came ready to take and bear
      The cross I had carried for many a year:
      But my words came slowly one by one
      From frozen lips that were still and dumb.
      How sounded my words so still and slow
10   To the great strong heart that loved me so?
      Ah I remember, my God, so well,
      How my brain lay dumb in a frozen spell;
      And I leaned away from my lover's face
      To watch the dead leaves that were running a race.
15   I felt the spell that held my breath,
      Bending me down to a living death –
      As if hope lay buried when he had come
      Who knew my sorrows all and some.

The Lust of the Eyes

I care not for my Lady's soul,
    Though I worship before her smile:
I care not where be my Lady's goal
    When her beauty shall lose its wile.

Low sit I down at my Lady's feet,   5
    Gazing through her wild eyes,
Smiling to think how my love will fleet
    When their starlike beauty dies.

I care not if my Lady pray
    To our Father which is in Heaven;   10
But for joy my heart's quick pulses play,
    For to me her love is given.

Then who shall close my Lady's eyes,
    And who shall fold her hands?
Will any hearken if she cries   15
    Up to the unknown lands?

Worn Out

Thy strong arms are around me, love,
    My head is on thy breast:
Though words of comfort come from thee,
    My soul is not at rest:

For I am but a startled thing,   5
    Nor can I ever be
Aught save a bird whose broken wing
    Must fly away from thee.

I cannot give to thee the love
    I gave so long ago –
The love that turned and struck me down
    Amid the blinding snow.

I can but give a sinking heart
    And weary eyes of pain,
A faded mouth that cannot smile
    And may not laugh again.

Yet keep thine arms around me, love,
    Until I drop to sleep:
Then leave me – saying no good-bye,
    Lest I might fall and weep.

At Last

O mother, open the window wide
    And let the daylight in;
The hills grow darker to my sight,
    And thoughts begin to swim.

And, mother dear, take my young son
    (Since I was born of thee),
And care for all his little ways,
    And nurse him on thy knee.

And, mother, wash my pale, pale hands,
    And then bind up my feet;
My body may no longer rest
    Out of its winding-sheet.

And, mother dear, take a sapling twig
    And green grass newly mown,
And lay them on my empty bed,
    That my sorrow be not known.

And, mother, find three berries red
   And pluck them from the stalk,
And burn them at the first cockcrow,
   That my spirit may not walk.   20

And, mother dear, break a willow wand,
   And if the sap be even,
Then save it for my lover's sake,
   And he'll know my soul's in heaven.

And, mother, when the big tears fall   25
   (And fall, God knows, they may),
Tell him I died of my great love,
   And my dying heart was gay.

And, mother dear, when the sun has set,
   And the pale church grass waves,   30
Then carry me through the dim twilight
   And hide me among the graves.

Early Death

Oh grieve not with thy bitter tears
   The life that passes fast:
The gates of heaven will open wide,
   And take me in at last.

Then sit down meekly at my side,   5
   And watch my young life flee:
Then solemn peace of holy death
   Come quickly unto thee.

But, true love, seek me in the throng
   Of spirits floating past;   10
And I will take thee by the hands,
   And know thee mine at last.

He and She and Angels Three

Ruthless hands have torn her
  From one that loved her well;
Angels have upborne her,
  Christ her grief to tell.

5   She shall stand to listen,
  She shall stand and sing,
Till three winged angels
  Her lover's soul shall bring.

He and she and the angels three
10   Before God's face shall stand:
There they shall pray among themselves,
  And sing at His right hand.

A Silent Wood

O silent wood, I enter thee
With a heart so full of misery –
For all the voices from the trees
And the ferns that cling about my knees.

5   In thy darkest shadow let me sit
When the grey owls about thee flit:
There I will ask of thee a boon,
That I may not faint or die or swoon.

Gazing through the gloom like one
10   Whose life and hopes are also done,
Frozen like a thing of stone,
I sit in thy shadow – but not alone.

Can God bring back the day when we two stood
Beneath the clinging trees in that dark wood?

Love and Hate

Ope not thy lips, thou foolish one,
    Nor turn to me thy face:
The blasts of heaven shall strike me down
    Ere I will give thee grace.

Take thou thy shadow from my path,   5
    Nor turn to me and pray:
The wild, wild winds thy dirge may sing
    Ere I will bid thee stay.

Lift up thy false brow from the dust,
    Nor wild thine hands entwine   10
Among the golden summer-leaves
    To mock the gay sunshine.

And turn away thy false dark eyes,
    Nor gaze into my face:
Great love I bore thee; now great hate   15
    Sits grimly in its place.

All changes pass me like a dream,
    I neither sing nor pray;
And thou art like the poisonous tree
    That stole my life away.   20

The Passing of Love

O God, forgive me that I merged
    My life into a dream of love!
Will tears of anguish never wash
    The poison from my blood?

Love kept my heart in a song of joy,
  My pulses quivered to the tune;
The coldest blasts of winter blew
    Upon me like sweet airs in June.

Love floated on the mists of morn,
  And rested on the sunset's rays;
He calmed the thunder of the storm,
  And lighted all my ways.

Love held me joyful through the day,
  And dreaming ever through the night:
No evil thing could come to me,
  My spirit was so light.

Oh Heaven help my foolish heart
  Which heeded not the passing time
That dragged my idol from its place
    And shattered all its shrine!

Lord, May I Come?

Life and night are falling from me,
Death and day are opening on me.
Wherever my footsteps come and go
Life is a stony way of woe.
    Lord, have I long to go?
Hollow hearts are ever near me,
Soulless eyes have ceased to cheer me:
    Lord, may I come to Thee?

Life and youth and summer weather
To my heart no joy can gather:
Lord, lift me from life's stony way.
Loved eyes, long closed in death, watch o'er me –
Holy Death is waiting for me –
    Lord may I come to-day?

My outward life feels sad and still,   15
Like lilies in a frozen rill.
I am gazing upwards to the sun,
Lord, Lord, remembering my lost one.
    O Lord, remember me!
How is it in the unknown land?   20
Do the dead wander hand in hand?
Do we clasp dead hands, and quiver
With an endless joy for ever?
Is the air filled with the sound
Of spirits circling round and round?   25
Are there lakes, of endless song,
To rest our tirèd eyes upon?
Do tall white angels gaze and wend
Along the banks where lilies bend?
Lord, we know not how this may be;   30
Good Lord, we put our faith in Thee –
    O God, remember me.

A Year and a Day

Slow days have passed that make a year,
    Slow hours that make a day,
Since I could take my first dear love,
    And kiss him the old way:
Yet the green leaves touch me on the cheek,   5
    Dear Christ, this month of May

I lie among the tall green grass
    That bends above my head,
And covers up my wasted face,
    And folds me in its bed   10
Tenderly and lovingly
    Like grass above the dead.

Dim phantoms of an unknown ill
  Float through my tiring brain;
15 The unformed visions of my life
    Pass by in ghostly train;
Some pause to touch me on the cheek,
  Some scatter tears like rain.

The river ever running down
20   Between its grassy bed,
The voices of a thousand birds
  That clang above my head,
Shall bring to me a sadder dream
  When this sad dream is dead.

25 A silence falls upon my heart,
  And hushes all its pain
I stretch my hands in the long grass,
  And fall to sleep again,
There to lie empty of all love,
30   Like beaten corn of grain.

WILLIAM MICHAEL ROSSETTI

Her First Season

He gazed her over, from her eyebrows down
   Even to her feet: he gazed so with the good
   Undoubting faith of fools, much as who should
Accost God for a comrade. In the brown
     Of all her curls he seemed to think the town
   Would make an acquisition; but her hood
   Was not the newest fashion, and his brood
Of lady-friends might scarce approve her gown.
If I did smile, 'twas faintly; for my cheeks
   Burned, thinking she'd be shown up to be sold,
   And cried about, in the thick jostling run
Of the loud world, till all the weary weeks
   Should bring her back to herself and to the old
   Familiar face of nature and the sun.

'Jesus Wept'

Mary rose up, as one in sleep might rise,
   And went to meet her brother's Friend: and they
   Who tarried with her said: 'she goes to pray
And weep where her dead brother's body lies.'
So, with their wringing of hands and with sighs,
   They stood before Him in the public way.
   'Had'st Thou been with him, Lord, upon that day,
He had not died,' she said, drooping her eyes.
Mary and Martha with bowed faces kept
   Holding His garments, one on each side. – 'Where
    Have ye laid him?' He asked. 'Lord, come and see.' –
   The sound of grieving voices heavily
And universally was round Him there,
A sound that smote His spirit. Jesus wept.

The Evil Under the Sun

How long, oh Lord? – The voice is sounding still,
  Not only heard beneath the altar stone,
  Not heard of John Evangelist alone
In Patmos. It doth cry aloud and will
Between the earth's end and earth's end, until   5
  The day of the great reckoning, bone for bone,
  And blood for righteous blood, and groan for groan:
Then shall it cease on the air with a sudden thrill;
Not slowly growing fainter if the rod
  Strikes one or two amid the evil throng,   10
  Or one oppressor's hand is stayed and numbs, –
  Not till the vengeance that is coming comes:
For shall all hear the voice excepting God?
  Or God not listen, hearing? – Lord, how long?

Dedication
(To the Memory of Dante Gabriel Rossetti)

Brother, my brother, in the churchyard mould
Where canopied by fame thou liest asleep
In that inscrutable unuttered deep
Which Death has channelled from the years of old,
While day and night, procession multifold,   5
Finite in infinite, their vigil keep,
And men, ere yet the sickle reaps them, reap
Harvest of grain and their own deeds untold:
Gabriel, accept what verse may dedicate –
A brother's heart deep-dinted with the pang   10
Of one remembered mortal Easter-day.
Silent the lips which might have answered yea –
Lips out of which the laden spirit rang
Reverberant echoes – Love and Change and Fate.

Mary Shelley

Daughter of her who never quailing led
In the forlorn hope of the women's cause;
Daughter of him who reasoned out the laws
Of Justice in the State's firm balance weighed;
Heart-mate and wife of one who, burning red
With world-embracing love, for ever draws
Into his orbit the thrilled globe, and awes
With visioned poesy each highest head
Of song for aye; – White Mary, with the voice
The sweetest ever heard, rejoin him now,
In the long thirtieth year of severance.
With drowning Harriet's and drowned Shelley's brow,
Thine own has passed the gate of deathly trance:
He dies not, neither diest thou, his choice.

CHRISTINA GEORGINA ROSSETTI

Dream Land

Where sunless rivers weep
Their waves into the deep,
She sleeps a charmèd sleep:
    Awake her not.
Led by a single star,
She came from very far
To seek where shadows are
    Her pleasant lot.

She left the rosy morn,
She left the fields of corn,
For twilight cold and lorn
    And water springs.
Through sleep, as through a veil,
She sees the sky look pale,
And hears the nightingale
    That sadly sings.

Rest, rest, a perfect rest
Shed over brow and breast;
Her face is toward the west,
    The purple land.
She cannot see the grain
Ripening on hill and plain;
She cannot feel the rain
    Upon her hand.

Rest, rest, for evermore
Upon a mossy shore;
Rest, rest at the heart's core
    Till time shall cease:
Sleep that no pain shall wake,
Night that no morn shall break
Till joy shall overtake
    Her perfect peace.

An End

Love, strong as Death, is dead
Come, let us make his bed
Among the dying flowers:
A green turf at his head;
And a stone at his feet,   5
Whereon we may sit
In the quiet evening hours.

He was born in the Spring,
And died before the harvesting:
On the last warm summer day   10
He left us; he would not stay
For Autumn twilight cold and grey.
Sit we by his grave, and sing
He is gone away.

To few chords and sad and low   15
Sing we so:
Be our eyes fixed on the grass
Shadow-veiled as the years pass,
While we think of all that was
In the long ago.   20

A Pause of Thought

I looked for that which is not, nor can be,
    And hope deferred made my heart sick in truth:
    But years must pass before a hope of youth
        Is resigned utterly.

I watched and waited with a steadfast will: 5
    And though the object seemed to flee away
    That I so longed for, ever day by day
        I watched and waited still.

Sometimes I said: This thing shall be no more;
10   My expectation wearies and shall cease;
I will resign it now and be at peace:
Yet never gave it o'er.

Sometimes I said: It is an empty name
I long for; to a name why should I give
15   The peace of all the days I have to live? –
Yet gave it all the same.

Alas, thou foolish one! alike unfit
For healthy joy and salutary pain:
Thou knowest the chase useless, and again
20   Turnest to follow it.

Sweet Death

The sweetest blossoms die.
And so it was that, going day by day
Unto the Church to praise and pray,
And crossing the green churchyard thoughtfully,
5   I saw how on the graves the flowers
Shed their fresh leaves in showers,
And how their perfume rose up to the sky
Before it passed away.

The youngest blossoms die.
10   They die and fall and nourish the rich earth
From which they lately had their birth;
Sweet life, but sweeter death that passeth by
And is as though it had not been: –
All colours turn to green;
15   The bright hues vanish and the odours fly,
The grass hath lasting worth.

And youth and beauty die.
   So be it, O my God, Thou God of truth:
   Better than beauty and than youth
Are Saints and Angels, a glad company;   20
   And Thou, O Lord, our Rest and Ease,
   Art better far than these.
Why should we shrink from our full harvest? why
   Prefer to glean with Ruth?

Goblin Market

   Morning and evening
   Maids heard the goblins cry:
   'Come buy our orchard fruits,
   Come buy, come buy:
   Apples and quinces,   5
   Lemons and oranges,
   Plump unpecked cherries,
   Melons and raspberries,
   Bloom-down-cheeked peaches,
   Swart-headed mulberries,   10
   Wild free-born cranberries,
   Crab-apples, dewberries,
   Pine-apples, blackberries,
   Apricots, strawberries; –
   All ripe together   15
   In summer weather, –
   Morns that pass by,
   Fair eves that fly;
   Come buy, come buy:
   Our grapes fresh from the vine,   20
   Pomegranates full and fine.
   Dates and sharp bullaces,
   Rare pears and greengages,
   Damsons and bilberries,

25   Taste them and try:
      Currants and gooseberries,
      Bright-fire-like barberries,
      Figs to fill your mouth,
      Citrons from the South,
30   Sweet to tongue and sound to eye;
      Come buy, come buy.'

         Evening by evening
      Among the brookside rushes,
      Laura bowed her head to hear,
35   Lizzie veiled her blushes:
      Crouching close together
      In the cooling weather,
      With clasping arms and cautioning lips,
      With tingling cheeks and finger tips.
40   'Lie close,' Laura said,
      Pricking up her golden head:
      'We must not look at goblin men,
      We must not buy their fruits:
      Who knows upon what soil they fed
45   Their hungry thirsty roots?'
      'Come buy,' call the goblins
      Hobbling down the glen.
      'Oh,' cried Lizzie, 'Laura, Laura,
      You should not peep at goblin men.'
50   Lizzie covered up her eyes,
      Covered close lest they should look;
      Laura reared her glossy head,
      And whispered like the restless brook:
      'Look, Lizzie, look, Lizzie,
55   Down the glen tramp little men.
      One hauls a basket,
      One bears a plate,
      One lugs a golden dish
      Of many pounds weight.
60   How fair the vine must grow

Whose grapes are so luscious;
How warm the wind must blow
Through those fruit bushes.'
'No,' said Lizzie: 'No, no, no;
Their offers should not charm us,   65
Their evil gifts would harm us.'
She thrust a dimpled finger
In each ear, shut eyes and ran:
Curious Laura chose to linger
Wondering at each merchant man.   70
One had a cat's face,
One whisked a tail,
One tramped at a rat's pace,
One crawled like a snail,
One like a wombat prowled obtuse and   75
    furry,
One like a ratel tumbled hurry skurry.
She heard a voice like voice of doves
Cooing all together:
They sounded kind and full of loves
In the pleasant weather.   80

Laura stretched her gleaming neck
Like a rush-imbedded swan,
Like a lily from the beck,
Like a moonlit poplar branch,
Like a vessel at the launch   85
When its last restraint is gone.

Backwards up the mossy glen
Turned and trooped the goblin men,
With their shrill repeated cry,
'Come buy, come buy.'   90
When they reached where Laura was
They stood stock still upon the moss,
Leering at each other,
Brother with queer brother;
Signalling each other,   95

Brother with sly brother.
One set his basket down,
One reared his plate;
One began to weave a crown
Of tendrils, leaves and rough nuts brown
(Men sell not such in any town);
One heaved the golden weight
Of dish and fruit to offer her:
'Come buy, come buy,' was still their cry.
Laura stared but did not stir,
Longed but had no money:
The whisk-tailed merchant bade her taste
In tones as smooth as honey,
The cat-faced purr'd,
The rat-paced spoke a word
Of welcome, and the snail-paced even was heard;
One parrot-voiced and jolly
Cried 'Pretty Goblin' still for 'Pretty Polly;' –
One whistled like a bird.

    But sweet-tooth Laura spoke in haste:
'Good folk, I have no coin;
To take were to purloin:
I have no copper in my purse,
I have no silver either,
And all my gold is on the furze
That shakes in windy weather
Above the rusty heather.'
'You have much gold upon your head,'
They answered all together:
'Buy from us with a golden curl.'
She clipped a precious golden lock,
She dropped a tear more rare than pearl,
Then sucked their fruit globes fair or red:
Sweeter than honey from the rock,
Stronger than man-rejoicing wine,

Clearer than water flowed that juice;
She never tasted such before,
How should it cloy with length of use?
She sucked and sucked and sucked the more
Fruits which that unknown orchard bore;   135
She sucked until her lips were sore;
Then flung the emptied rinds away
But gathered up one kernel-stone,
And knew not was it night or day
As she turned home alone.   140

    Lizzie met her at the gate
Full of wise upbraidings:
'Dear, you should not stay so late,
Twilight is not good for maidens;
Should not loiter in the glen   145
In the haunts of goblin men.
Do you not remember Jeanie,
How she met them in the moonlight,
Took their gifts both choice and many,
Ate their fruits and wore their flowers   150
Plucked from bowers
Where summer ripens at all hours?
But ever in the noonlight
She pined and pined away;
Sought them by night and day,   155
Found them no more but dwindled and grew grey;
Then fell with the first snow,
While to this day no grass will grow
Where she lies low:
I planted daisies there a year ago   160
That never blow.
You should not loiter so.'
'Nay, hush,' said Laura:
'Nay, hush, my sister:
I ate and ate my fill,   165
Yet my mouth waters still;
To-morrow night I will

Buy more:' and kissed her:
'Have done with sorrow;
170 I'll bring you plums to-morrow
Fresh on their mother twigs,
Cherries worth getting;
You cannot think what figs
My teeth have met in,
175 What melons icy-cold
Piled on a dish of gold
Too huge for me to hold,
What peaches with a velvet nap,
Pellucid grapes without one seed:
180 Odorous indeed must be the mead
Whereon they grow, and pure the wave they drink
With lilies at the brink,
And sugar-sweet their sap.'

Golden head by golden head,
185 Like two pigeons in one nest
Folded in each other's wings,
They lay down in their curtained bed:
Like two blossoms on one stem,
Like two flakes of new-fall'n snow,
190 Like two wands of ivory
Tipped with gold for awful kings.
Moon and stars gazed in at them,
Wind sang to them lullaby,
Lumbering owls forbore to fly,
195 Not a bat flapped to and fro
Round their rest:
Cheek to cheek and breast to breast
Locked together in one nest.

Early in the morning
200 When the first cock crowed his warning,
Neat like bees, as sweet and busy,
Laura rose with Lizzie:

Fetched in honey, milked the cows,
Aired and set to rights the house,
Kneaded cakes of whitest wheat,   205
Cakes for dainty mouths to eat,
Next churned butter, whipped up cream,
Fed their poultry, sat and sewed;
Talked as modest maidens should:
Lizzie with an open heart,   210
Laura in an absent dream,
One content, one sick in part;
One warbling for the mere bright day's delight,
One longing for the night.

   At length slow evening came: 215
They went with pitchers to the reedy brook;
Lizzie most placid in her look,
Laura most like a leaping flame.
They drew the gurgling water from its deep;
Lizzie plucked purple and rich golden flags,   220
Then turning homewards said: 'The sunset flushes
Those furthest loftiest crags;
Come, Laura, not another maiden lags,
No wilful squirrel wags,
The beasts and birds are fast asleep.'   225
But Laura loitered still among the rushes
And said the bank was steep.

   And said the hour was early still,
The dew not fall'n, the wind not chill:
Listening ever, but not catching   230
The customary cry,
'Come buy, come buy,'
With its iterated jingle
Of sugar-baited words:
Not for all her watching   235
Once discerning even one goblin
Racing, whisking, tumbling, hobbling;

Let alone the herds
That used to tramp along the glen,
In groups or single,
Of brisk fruit-merchant men.

Till Lizzie urged, 'O Laura, come;
I hear the fruit-call but I dare not look:
You should not loiter longer at this brook
Come with me home.
The stars rise, the moon bends her arc,
Each glowworm winks her spark,
Let us get home before the night grows dark:
For clouds may gather
Though this is summer weather,
Put out the lights and drench us through;
Then if we lost our way what should we do?'

Laura turned cold as stone
To find her sister heard that cry alone,
That goblin cry,
'Come buy our fruits, come buy.'
Must she then buy no more such dainty fruits?
Must she no more that succous pasture find,
Gone deaf and blind?
Her tree of life drooped from the root:
She said not one word in her heart's sore ache;
But peering thro' the dimness, nought discerning,
Trudged home, her pitcher dripping all the way;
So crept to bed, and lay
Silent till Lizzie slept;
Then sat up in a passionate yearning,
And gnashed her teeth for baulked desire, and wept
As if her heart would break.

Day after day, night after night,
Laura kept watch in vain
In sullen silence of exceeding pain.
She never caught again the goblin cry:

'Come buy, come buy;' –
She never spied the goblin men
Hawking their fruits along the glen: 275
But when the noon waxed bright
Her hair grew thin and grey;
She dwindled, as the fair full moon doth turn
To swift decay and burn
Her fire away.   280

One day remembering her kernel-stone
She set it by a wall that faced the south;
Dewed it with tears, hoped for a root,
Watched for a waxing shoot,
But there came none;   285
It never saw the sun,
It never felt the trickling moisture run:
While with sunk eyes and faded mouth
She dreamed of melons, as a traveller sees
False waves in desert drouth   290
With shade of leaf-crowned trees,
And burns the thirstier in the sandful breeze.

She no more swept the house,
Tended the fowls or cows,
Fetched honey, kneaded cakes of wheat,   295
Brought water from the brook:
But sat down listless in the chimney-nook
And would not eat.

Tender Lizzie could not bear
To watch her sister's cankerous care   300
Yet not to share.
She night and morning
Caught the goblins' cry:
'Come buy our orchard fruits,
Come buy, come buy:' –   305
Beside the brook, along the glen,
She heard the tramp of goblin men,

The voice and stir
Poor Laura could not hear;
310   Longed to buy fruit to comfort her,
But feared to pay too dear.
She thought of Jeanie in her grave,
Who should have been a bride;
But who for joys brides hope to have
315   Fell sick and died
In her gay prime,
In earliest Winter time,
With the first glazing rime,
With the first snow-fall of crisp Winter time.

320   Till Laura dwindling
Seemed knocking at Death's door:
Then Lizzie weighed no more
Better and worse;
But put a silver penny in her purse,
325   Kissed Laura, crossed the heath with clumps of furze
At twilight, halted by the brook:
And for the first time in her life
Began to listen and look.

           Laughed every goblin
330   When they spied her peeping:
Came towards her hobbling,
Flying, running, leaping,
Puffing and blowing,
Chuckling, clapping, crowing,
335   Clucking and gobbling,
Mopping and mowing,
Full of airs and graces,
Pulling wry faces,
Demure grimaces,
340   Cat-like and rat-like,
Ratel- and wombat-like,
Snail-paced in a hurry,
Parrot-voiced and whistler,

Helter skelter, hurry skurry,
Chattering like magpies,   345
Fluttering like pigeons,
Gliding like fishes, –
Hugged her and kissed her,
Squeezed and caressed her:
Stretched up their dishes,   350
Panniers, and plates:
'Look at our apples
Russet and dun,
Bob at our cherries,
Bite at our peaches,   355
Citrons and dates,
Grapes for the asking,
Pears red with basking
Out in the sun,
Plums on their twigs;   360
Pluck them and suck them.
Pomegranates, figs.' –

'Good folk,' said Lizzie,
Mindful of Jeanie:
'Give me much and many;' –   365
Held out her apron,
Tossed them her penny.
'Nay, take a seat with us,
Honour and eat with us,'
They answered grinning: 370
'Our feast is but beginning.
Night yet is early,
Warm and dew-pearly,
Wakeful and starry:
Such fruits as these   375
No man can carry;
Half their bloom would fly,
Half their dew would dry,
Half their flavour would pass by.
Sit down and feast with us,   380

Be welcome guest with us,
Cheer you and rest with us.' –
'Thank you,' said Lizzie: 'But one waits
At home alone for me:
So without further parleying,
If you will not sell me any
Of your fruits though much and many,
Give me back my silver penny
I tossed you for a fee.' –
They began to scratch their pates,
No longer wagging, purring,
But visibly demurring,
Grunting and snarling.
One called her proud,
Cross-grained, uncivil;
Their tones waxed loud,
Their looks were evil.
Lashing their tails
They trod and hustled her,
Elbowed and jostled her,
Clawed with their nails,
Barking, mewing, hissing, mocking,
Tore her gown and soiled her stocking,
Twitched her hair out by the roots,
Stamped upon her tender feet,
Held her hands and squeezed their fruits
Against her mouth to make her eat.

White and golden Lizzie stood,
Like a lily in a flood, –
Like a rock of blue-veined stone
Lashed by tides obstreperously, –
Like a beacon left alone
In a hoary roaring sea,
Sending up a golden fire, –
Like a fruit-crowned orange-tree
White with blossoms honey-sweet
Sore beset by wasp and bee, –

Like a royal virgin town
Topped with gilded dome and spire
Close beleaguered by a fleet   420
Mad to tug her standard down.

    One may lead a horse to water,
Twenty cannot make him drink.
Though the goblins cuffed and caught her,
Coaxed and fought her,   425
Bullied and besought her,
Scratched her, pinched her black as ink,
Kicked and knocked her,
Mauled and mocked her,
Lizzie uttered not a word;   430
Would not open lip from lip
Lest they should cram a mouthful in:
But laughed in heart to feel the drip
Of juice that syrupped all her face,
And lodged in dimples of her chin,   435
And streaked her neck which quaked like curd.
At last the evil people
Worn out by her resistance
Flung back her penny, kicked their fruit
Along whichever road they took,   440
Not leaving root or stone or shoot;
Some writhed into the ground,
Some dived into the brook
With ring and ripple,
Some scudded on the gale without a sound,   445
Some vanished in the distance.

    In a smart, ache, tingle,
Lizzie went her way;
Knew not was it night or day;
Sprang up the bank, tore thro' the furze,   450
Threaded copse and dingle,
And heard her penny jingle
Bouncing in her purse, –

Its bounce was music to her ear.
455   She ran and ran
As if she feared some goblin man
Dogged her with gibe or curse
Or something worse:
But not one goblin skurried after,
460   Nor was she pricked by fear;
The kind heart made her windy-paced
That urged her home quite out of breath with haste
And inward laughter.

465   She cried 'Laura,' up the garden,
'Did you miss me?
Come and kiss me.
Never mind my bruises,
Hug me, kiss me, suck my juices
470   Squeezed from goblin fruits for you,
Goblin pulp and goblin dew.
Eat me, drink me, love me;
Laura, make much of me:
For your sake I have braved the glen
475   And had to do with goblin merchant men.'

        Laura started from her chair,
Flung her arms up in the air,
Clutched her hair:
'Lizzie, Lizzie, have you tasted
480   For my sake the fruit forbidden?
Must your light like mine be hidden,
Your young life like mine be wasted,
Undone in mine undoing
And ruined in my ruin,
485   Thirsty, cankered, goblin-ridden?' –
She clung about her sister,
Kissed and kissed and kissed her:
Tears once again
Refreshed her shrunken eyes,
490   Dropping like rain

After long sultry drouth;
Shaking with aguish fear, and pain,
She kissed and kissed her with a hungry mouth.

    Her lips began to scorch,
That juice was wormwood to her tongue,   495
She loathed the feast:
Writhing as one possessed she leaped and sung,
Rent all her robe, and wrung
Her hands in lamentable haste,
And beat her breast.   500
Her locks streamed like the torch
Borne by a racer at full speed,
Or like the mane of horses in their flight,
Or like an eagle when she stems the light
Straight toward the sun,   505
Or like a caged thing freed,
Or like a flying flag when armies run.

    Swift fire spread through her veins, knocked at
        her heart,
Met the fire smouldering there
And overbore its lesser flame;   510
She gorged on bitterness without a name:
Ah! fool, to choose such part
Of soul-consuming care!
Sense failed in the mortal strife:
Like the watch-tower of a town   515
Which an earthquake shatters down,
Like a lightning-stricken mast,
Like a wind-uprooted tree
Spun about,
Like a foam-topped waterspout   520
Cast down headlong in the sea,
She fell at last;
Pleasure past and anguish past,
Is it death or is it life?

525   Life out of death.
         That night long Lizzie watched by her,
         Counted her pulse's flagging stir,
         Felt for her breath,
         Held water to her lips, and cooled her face
530   With tears and fanning leaves:
         But when the first birds chirped about their eaves,
         And early reapers plodded to the place
         Of golden sheaves,
         And dew-wet grass
535   Bowed in the morning winds so brisk to pass,
         And new buds with new day
         Opened of cup-like lilies on the stream,
         Laura awoke as from a dream,
         Laughed in the innocent old way,
540   Hugged Lizzie but not twice or thrice;
         Her gleaming locks showed not one thread of grey,
         Her breath was sweet as May
         And light danced in her eyes.

         Days, weeks, months, years,
545   Afterwards, when both were wives
         With children of their own;
         Their mother-hearts beset with fears,
         Their lives bound up in tender lives;
         Laura would call the little ones
550   And tell them of her early prime,
         Those pleasant days long gone
         Of not-returning time:
         Would talk about the haunted glen,
         The wicked, quaint fruit-merchant men,
555   Their fruits like honey to the throat
         But poison in the blood;
         (Men sell not such in any town:)
         Would tell them how her sister stood
         In deadly peril to do her good,
560   And win the fiery antidote:
         Then joining hands to little hands

Would bid them cling together,
'For there is no friend like a sister
In calm or stormy weather;
To cheer one on the tedious way,   565
To fetch one if one goes astray,
To lift one if one totters down,
To strengthen whilst one stands.'

A Birthday

My heart is like a singing bird
   Whose nest is in a watered shoot;
My heart is like an appletree
   Whose boughs are bent with thickset fruit;
My heart is like a rainbow shell   5
   That paddles in a halcyon sea;
My heart is gladder than all these
   Because my love is come to me.

Raise me a dais of silk and down;
   Hang it with vair and purple dyes;   10
Carve it in doves, and pomegranates,
   And peacocks with a hundred eyes;
Work it in gold and silver grapes,
   In leaves, and silver fleurs-de-lys;
Because the birthday of my life   15
   Is come, my love is come to me.

After Death
Sonnet

The curtains were half drawn, the floor was swept
   And strewn with rushes, rosemary and may
   Lay thick upon the bed on which I lay,
Where through the lattice ivy-shadows crept.
He leaned above me, thinking that I slept   5

And could not hear him; but I heard him say:
'Poor child, poor child:' and as he turned away
Came a deep silence, and I knew he wept.
He did not touch the shroud, or raise the fold
That hid my face, or take my hand in his,
Or ruffle the smooth pillows for my head:
He did not love me living; but once dead
He pitied me; and very sweet it is
To know he still is warm though I am cold.

My Dream

Hear now a curious dream I dreamed last night,
Each word whereof is weighed and sifted truth.

I stood beside Euphrates while it swelled
Like overflowing Jordan in its youth:
It waxed and coloured sensibly to sight;
Till out of myriad pregnant waves there welled
Young crocodiles, a gaunt blunt-featured crew,
Fresh-hatched perhaps and daubed with birthday dew.
The rest if I should tell, I fear my friend
My closest friend would deem the facts untrue;
And therefore it were wisely left untold;
Yet if you will, why hear it to the end.

Each crocodile was girt with massive gold
And polished stones that with their wearers grew:
But one there was who waxed beyond the rest,
Wore kinglier girdle and a kingly crown,
Whilst crowns and orbs and sceptres starred his breast.
All gleamed compact and green with scale on scale,
But special burnishment adorned his mail
And special terror weighed upon his frown;
His punier brethren quaked before his tail,
Broad as a rafter, potent as a flail.

So he grew lord and master of his kin:
But who shall tell the tale of all their woes?
An execrable appetite arose,   25
He battened on them, crunched, and sucked them in.
He knew no law, he feared no binding law,
But ground them with inexorable jaw:
The luscious fat distilled upon his chin,
Exuded from his nostrils and his eyes,   30
While still like hungry death he fed his maw;
Till every minor crocodile being dead
And buried too, himself gorged to the full,
He slept with breath oppressed and unstrung claw.
Oh marvel passing strange which next I saw: 35
In sleep he dwindled to the common size,
And all the empire faded from his coat.
Then from far off a wingèd vessel came,
Swift as a swallow, subtle as a flame:
I know not what it bore of freight or host,   40
But white it was as an avenging ghost.
It levelled strong Euphrates in its course;
Supreme yet weightless as an idle mote
It seemed to tame the waters without force
Till not a murmur swelled or billow beat: 45
Lo, as the purple shadow swept the sands,
The prudent crocodile rose on his feet
And shed appropriate tears and wrung his hands.

   What can it mean? you ask. I answer not
For meaning, but myself must echo, What?   50
And tell it as I saw it on the spot.

The World
Sonnet

By day she wooes me, soft, exceeding fair:
   But all night as the moon so changeth she;
   Loathsome and foul with hideous leprosy

And subtle serpents gliding in her hair.
By day she wooes me to the outer air,
   Ripe fruits, sweet flowers, and full satiety:
   But through the night, a beast she grins at me,
A very monster void of love and prayer.
By day she stands a lie: by night she stands
   In all the naked horror of the truth
With pushing horns and clawed and clutching hands.
Is this a friend indeed; that I should sell
   My soul to her, give her my life and youth,
Till my feet, cloven too, take hold on hell?

From *The Prince's Progress*

'Too late for love, too late for joy,
   Too late, too late!
You loitered on the road too long,
   You trifled at the gate:
The enchanted dove upon her branch
   Died without a mate;
The enchanted princess in her tower
   Slept, died, behind the grate;
Her heart was starving all this while
     You made it wait.

'Ten years ago, five years ago,
   One year ago,
Even then you had arrived in time,
   Though somewhat slow;
Then you had known her living face
   Which now you cannot know:
The frozen fountain would have leaped,
   The buds gone on to blow,
The warm south wind would have awaked
     To melt the snow.

Is she fair now as she lies?
   Once she was fair;
Meet queen for any kingly king,
   With gold-dust on her hair.
Now these are poppies in her locks,   25
   White poppies she must wear;
Must wear a veil to shroud her face
   And the want graven there:
Or is the hunger fed at length,
     Cast off the care?   30

'We never saw her with a smile
   Or with a frown;
Her bed seemed never soft to her,
   Though tossed of down;
She little heeded what she wore,   35
   Kirtle, or wreath, or gown;
We think her white brows often ached
   Beneath her crown,
Till silvery hairs showed in her locks
   That used to be so brown.   40

'We never heard her speak in haste:
   Her tones were sweet,
And modulated just so much
   As it was meet:
Her heart sat silent through the noise   45
   And concourse of the street.
There was no hurry in her hands,
   No hurry in her feet;
There was no bliss drew nigh to her,
   That she might run to greet.   50

'You should have wept her yesterday,
   Wasting upon her bed:
But wherefore should you weep to-day
   That she is dead?
Lo, we who love weep not to-day,   55

But crown her royal head.
Let be these poppies that we strew,
　　Your roses are too red:
Let be these poppies, not for you
60　　　Cut down and spread.'

The Queen of Hearts

How comes it, Flora, that, whenever we
Play cards together, you invariably,
　　However the pack parts,
　　Still hold the Queen of Hearts?

5　　I've scanned you with a scrutinizing gaze,
Resolved to fathom these your secret ways:
　　But, sift them as I will,
　　Your ways are secret still.

I cut and shuffle; shuffle, cut, again;
10　But all my cutting, shuffling, proves in vain:
　　Vain hope, vain forethought too;
　　That Queen still falls to you.

I dropped her once, prepense; but, ere the deal
Was dealt, your instinct seemed her loss to feel:
15　　'There should be one card more,'
　　You said, and searched the floor.

I cheated once; I made a private notch
In Heart-Queen's back, and kept a lynx-eyed watch;
　　Yet such another back
20　　Deceived me in the pack;

The Queen of Clubs assumed by arts unknown
An imitative dint that seemed my own;
　　This notch, not of my doing,
　　Misled me to my ruin.

It baffles me to puzzle out the clue,   25
  Which must be skill, or craft, or luck in you:
    Unless, indeed, it be
    Natural affinity.

From *Monna Innominata*
A Sonnet of Sonnets

Beatrice, immortalized by 'altissimo poeta . . . cotanto amante'; Laura, celebrated by a great though an inferior bard, – have alike paid the exceptional penalty of exceptional honour, and have come down to us resplendent with charms, but (at least, to my apprehension) scant of attractiveness.

These heroines of world-wide fame were preceded by a bevy of unnamed ladies 'donne innominate' sung by a school of less conspicuous poets; and in that land and that period which gave simultaneous birth to Catholics, to Albigenses, and to Troubadours, one can imagine many a lady as sharing her lover's poetic aptitude, while the barrier between them might be one held sacred by both, yet not such as to render mutual love incompatible with mutual honour.

Had such a lady spoken for herself, the portrait left us might have appeared more tender, if less dignified, than any drawn even by a devoted friend. Or had the Great Poetess of our own day and nation only been unhappy instead of happy, her circumstances would have invited her to bequeath to us, in lieu of the 'Portuguese Sonnets,' an inimitable 'donna innominata' drawn not from fancy but from feeling, and worthy to occupy a niche beside Beatrice and Laura.

I

'Lo dì che han detto a' dolci amici addio' – Dante
'Amor, con quanto sforzo oggi mi vinci!' – Petrarca

Come back to me, who wait and watch for you: –
    Or come not yet, for it is over then,
    And long it is before you come again,
So far between my pleasures are and few.
While, when you come not, what I do I do
    Thinking 'Now when he comes,' my sweetest 'when:'
    For one man is my world of all the men
This wide world holds; O love, my world is you.
Howbeit, to meet you grows almost a pang
    Because the pang of parting comes so soon;
    My hope hangs waning, waxing, like a moon
        Between the heavenly days on which we meet:
Ah me, but where are now the songs I sang
        When life was sweet because you called them sweet?

4

'Poca favilla gran fiamma seconda' – Dante
'Ogni altra cosa, ogni pensier va fore,
    E sol ivi con voi rimansi amore' – Petrarca

I loved you first: but afterwards your love
    Outsoaring mine, sang such a loftier song
As drowned the friendly cooings of my dove.
    Which owes the other most? my love was long,
    And yours one moment seemed to wax more strong;
I loved and guessed at you, you construed me
And loved me for what might or might not be –
    Nay, weights and measures do us both a wrong.
For verily love knows not 'mine' or 'thine;'
    With separate 'I' and 'thou' free love has done,
    For one is both and both are one in love:
Rich love knows nought of 'thine that is not mine;'
        Both have the strength and both the length thereof,
    Both of us, of the love which makes us one.

7

'Qui primavera sempre ed ogni frutto' – Dante
'Ragionando con meco ed io con lui' – Petrarca

'Love me, for I love you' – and answer me,
  'Love me, for I love you' – so shall we stand
  As happy equals in the flowering land
Of love, that knows not a dividing sea.
Love builds the house on rock and not on sand,   5
  Love laughs what while the winds rave desperately;
And who hath found love's citadel unmanned?
  And who hath held in bonds love's liberty?
My heart's a coward though my words are brave –
  We meet so seldom, yet we surely part   10
  So often; there's a problem for your art!
    Still I find comfort in his Book, who saith,
Though jealousy be cruel as the grave,
  And death be strong, yet love is strong as death.

8

'Come dicesse a Dio: D'altro non calme' – Dante
'Spero trovar pietà non che perdono' – Petrarca

'I, if I perish, perish' – Esther spake:
  And bride of life or death she made her fair
  In all the lustre of her perfumed hair
And smiles that kindle longing but to slake.
She put on pomp of loveliness, to take   5
  Her husband through his eyes at unaware;
  She spread abroad her beauty for a snare,
Harmless as doves and subtle as a snake.
She trapped him with one mesh of silken hair,
  She vanquished him by wisdom of her wit,   10
    And built her people's house that it should
      stand: –
    If I might take my life so in my hand,
And for my love to Love put up my prayer,
  And for love's sake by Love be granted it!

I I
'Vien dietro a me e lascia dir le genti' – Dante
'Contando i casi della vita nostra' – Petrarca

Many in aftertimes will say of you
    'He loved her' – while of me what will they say?
    Not that I loved you more than just in play,
For fashion's sake as idle women do.
Even let them prate; who know not what we knew
    Of love and parting in exceeding pain,
    Of parting hopeless here to meet again,
Hopeless on earth, and heaven is out of view.
But by my heart of love laid bare to you,
    My love that you can make not void nor vain,
Love that foregoes you but to claim anew
        Beyond this passage of the gate of death,
    I charge you at the Judgment make it plain
        My love of you was life and not a breath.

I 4
'E la Sua Volontade è nostra pace' – Dante
'Sol con questi pensier, con altre chiome' – Petrarca

Youth gone, and beauty gone if ever there
    Dwelt beauty in so poor a face as this;
    Youth gone and beauty, what remains of bliss?
I will not bind fresh roses in my hair,
To shame a cheek at best but little fair, –
    Leave youth his roses, who can bear a thorn, –
I will not seek for blossoms anywhere,
    Except such common flowers as blow with corn.
Youth gone and beauty gone, what doth remain?
    The longing of a heart pent up forlorn,
        A silent heart whose silence loves and longs;
        The silence of a heart which sang its songs
    While youth and beauty made a summer morn,
Silence of love that cannot sing again.

Babylon the Great

Foul is she and ill-favoured, set askew:
  Gaze not upon her till thou dream her fair,
  Lest she should mesh thee in her wanton hair,
Adept in arts grown old yet ever new.
Her heart lusts not for love, but thro' and thro'   5
  For blood, as spotted panther lusts in lair;
  No wine is in her cup, but filth is there
Unutterable, with plagues hid out of view.
Gaze not upon her; for her dancing whirl
  Turns giddy the fixed gazer presently: 10
  Gaze not upon her, lest thou be as she
    When at the far end of her long desire
Her scarlet vest and gold and gem and pearl
    And she amid her pomp are set on fire.

On Keats

A garden in a garden: a green spot
  Where all is green: most fitting slumber-place
  For the strong man grown weary of a race
Soon over. Unto him a goodly lot
Hath fallen in fertile ground; there thorns are not,   5
  But his own daisies; silence, full of grace,
  Surely hath shed a quiet on his face;
His earth is but sweet leaves that fall and rot.
What was his record of himself, ere he
  Went from us? 'Here lies one whose name   10
    was writ
  In water.' While the chilly shadows flit
  Of sweet St Agnes' Eve, while basil springs –
  His name, in every humble heart that sings,
Shall be a fountain of love, verily.

Portraits

An easy lazy length of limb,
   Dark eyes and features from the South,
A short-legged meditative pipe
   Set in a supercilious mouth:
Ink and a pen and papers laid
   Down on a table for the night,
Beside a semi-dozing man
   Who wakes to go to bed by light.

A pair of brothers brotherly,
   Unlike and yet how much the same
In heart and high-toned intellect,
   In face and bearing, hope and aim:
Friends of the selfsame treasured friends
   And of one home the dear delight,
Beloved of many a loving heart,
   And cherished both in mine, Good-night.

In an Artist's Studio

One face looks out from all his canvases,
   One selfsame figure sits or walks or leans:
   We found her hidden just behind those screens,
That mirror gave back all her loveliness.
A queen in opal or in ruby dress,
   A nameless girl in freshest summer-greens,
   A saint, an angel – every canvas means
The same one meaning, neither more nor less.
He feeds upon her face by day and night,
   And she with true kind eyes looks back on
      him,
Fair as the moon and joyful as the light:

Not wan with waiting, not with sorrow dim;
Not as she is, but was when hope shone bright;
Not as she is, but as she fills his dream.

The P.R.B.

The P.R.B. is in its decadence:
For Woolner in Australia cooks his chops,
And Hunt is yearning for the land of Cheops;
D. G. Rossetti shuns the vulgar optic;
While William M. Rossetti merely lops   5
His B's in English disesteemed as Coptic;
Calm Stephens in the twilight smokes his pipe,
But long the dawning of his public day;
And he at last the champion great Millais,
Attaining academic opulence,   10
Winds up his signature with A.R.A.
So rivers merge in the perpetual sea;
So luscious fruit must fall when over-ripe;
And so the consummated P.R.B.

ARTHUR HUGHES

To a Child
On a Dot

My beloved is taller than I,
   But yet I'm above him;
He's not all himself without me,
   And therefore I love him;
5   He is I, while I am not he,
   But a part if he lets me;
Yet I am but a speck in his eye,
   And he often forgets me.

In a Letter to William Bell Scott at Penkill

Scotus never sends a line,
   Perhaps poor Scotus has no ink,
   Or reads in some wise book I think,
He should not cast his pearls to swine.

5 This was my thought the other day,
   When sick and sore from Fortune's bumps –
   And, fool-like, nursing doleful dumps,
A silly state that does not pay.

But now his letter comes along –
10   To me in Cornwall, weather-bound,
   Wild storm and wind and rain all round –
Clear Penkill sunshine cleaves the throng.

And all my swine run down to sea,
   And drown themselves by Michael's Mount,
15   It does not matter, does not count
One penny, tho' so fat they be.

WILLIAM MORRIS

The Chapel in Lyoness
Sir Ozana le Cure Hardy. Sir Galahad.
Sir Bors de Ganys.

SIR OZANA

All day long and every day,
From Christmas-Eve to Whit-Sunday,
Within that Chapel-aisle I lay,
    And no man came a-near.

Naked to the waist was I,
And deep within my breast did lie,
Though no man any blood could spy,
    The truncheon of a spear.

No meat did ever pass my lips.
Those days – (Alas! the sunlight slips
From off the gilded parclose, dips,
    And night comes on apace.)

My arms lay back behind my head;
Over my raised-up knees was spread
A samite cloth of white and red;
    A rose lay on my face.

Many a time I tried to shout;
But as in dream of battle-rout,
My frozen speech would not well out;
    I could not even weep.

With inward sigh I see the sun
Fade off the pillars one by one,
My heart faints when the day is done,
    Because I cannot sleep.

Sometimes strange thoughts pass through my   25
    head;
Not like a tomb is this my bed,
Yet oft I think that I am dead;
  That round my tomb is writ,

'Ozana of the hardy heart,
  Knight of the Table Round,   30
Pray for his soul, lords, of your part;
  A true knight he was found.'
Ah! me, I cannot fathom it. [*He sleeps.*]

SIR GALAHAD

All day long and every day,
Till his madness pass'd away,   35
I watch'd Ozana as he lay
  Within the gilded screen.

All my singing moved him not;
As I sung my heart grew hot,
With the thought of Launcelot   40
  Far away, I ween.

So I went a little space
From out the chapel, bathed my face
In the stream that runs apace
  By the churchyard wall.   45

There I pluck'd a faint wild rose,
Hard by where the linden grows,
Sighing over silver rows
  Of the lilies tall.

I laid the flower across his mouth;   50
The sparkling drops seem'd good for drouth;
He smiled, turn'd round towards the south,
  Held up a golden tress.

The light smote on it from the west:
He drew the covering from his breast,
Against his heart that hair he prest;
    Death him soon will bless.

SIR BORS

I entered by the western door;
    I saw a knight's helm lying there:
I raised my eyes from off the floor,
    And caught the gleaming of his hair.

I stept full softly up to him;
    I laid my chin upon his head;
I felt him smile; my eyes did swim,
    I was so glad he was not dead.

I heard Ozana murmur low,
    'There comes no sleep nor any love.'
But Galahad stoop'd and kiss'd his brow:
    He shiver'd; I saw his pale lips move.

SIR OZANA

There comes no sleep nor any love;
    Ah me! I shiver with delight.
I am so weak I cannot move;
    God move me to thee, dear, to-night!
Christ help! I have but little wit:
My life went wrong; I see it writ,

'Ozana of the hardy heart,
    Knight of the Table Round,
Pray for his soul, lords, on your part;
    A good knight he was found.'
Now I begin to fathom it. [*He dies.*]

SIR BORS

Galahad sits dreamily;
What strange things may his eyes see,
Great blue eyes fix'd full on me?
On his soul, Lord, have mercy.

SIR GALAHAD

Ozana, shall I pray for thee?   85
Her cheek is laid to thine;
No long time hence, also I see
    Thy wasted fingers twine

Within the tresses of her hair
    That shineth gloriously,   90
Thinly outspread in the clear air
    Against the jasper sea.

Riding Together

For many, many days together
    The wind blew steady from the East;
For many days hot grew the weather,
    About the time of our Lady's Feast.

For many days we rode together,   5
    Yet met we neither friend nor foe;
Hotter and clearer grew the weather,
    Steadily did the East wind blow.

We saw the trees in the hot, bright weather,
    Clear-cut, with shadows very black,   10
As freely we rode on together
    With helms unlaced and bridles slack.

And often as we rode together,
   We, looking down the green-bank'd stream,
Saw flowers in the sunny weather,
   And saw the bubble-making bream.

And in the night lay down together,
   And hung above our heads the rood,
Or watch'd night-long in the dewy weather,
   The while the moon did watch the wood.

Our spears stood bright and thick together,
   Straight out the banners stream'd behind,
As we gallop'd on in the sunny weather,
   With faces turn'd towards the wind.

Down sank our threescore spears together,
   As thick we saw the pagans ride;
His eager face in the clear fresh weather,
   Shone out that last time by my side.

Up the sweep of the bridge we dash'd together,
   It rock'd to the crash of the meeting spears,
Down rain'd the buds of the dear spring weather,
   The elm-tree flowers fell like tears.

There, as we roll'd and writhed together,
   I threw my arms above my head,
For close by my side, in the lovely weather,
   I saw him reel and fall back dead.

I and the slayer met together,
   He waited the death-stroke there in his place,
With thoughts of death, in the lovely weather,
   Gapingly mazed at my madden'd face.

Madly I fought as we fought together;
   In vain: the little Christian band
The pagans drown'd, as in stormy weather,
   The river drowns low-lying land.

They bound my blood-stain'd hands together,   45
   They bound his corpse to nod by my side:
Then on we rode, in the bright March weather,
   With clash of cymbals did we ride.

We ride no more, no more together;
   My prison-bars are thick and strong,   50
I take no heed of any weather,
   The sweet Saints grant I live not long.

The Defence of Guenevere

But, knowing now that they would have her speak,
She threw her wet hair backward from her brow,
Her hand close to her mouth touching her cheek,

As though she had had there a shameful blow,
And feeling it shameful to feel ought but shame   5
All through her heart, yet felt her cheek burned so,

She must a little touch it; like one lame
She walked away from Gauwaine, with her head
Still lifted up; and on her cheek of flame

The tears dried quick; she stopped at last and said: 10
'O knights and lords, it seems but little skill
To talk of well-known things past now and dead.

'God wot I ought to say, I have done ill,
And pray you all forgiveness heartily!
Because you must be right such great lords – still   15

'Listen, suppose your time were come to die,
And you were quite alone and very weak;
Yea, laid a dying while very mightily

'The wind was ruffling up the narrow streak
20   Of river through your broad lands running well:
Suppose a hush should come, then some one speak:

'"One of these cloths is heaven, and one is hell,
Now choose one cloth for ever, which they be,
I will not tell you, you must somehow tell

25   '"Of your own strength and mightiness; here, see!"
Yea, yea, my lord, and you to ope your eyes,
At foot of your familiar bed to see

'A great God's angel standing, with such dyes,
Not known on earth, on his great wings, and hands,
30   Held out two ways, light from the inner skies

'Showing him well, and making his commands
Seem to be God's commands, moreover, too,
Holding within his hands the cloths on wands;

'And one of these strange choosing cloths was blue,
35   Wavy and long, and one cut short and red;
No man could tell the better of the two.

'After a shivering half-hour you said,
"God help! heaven's colour, the blue;" and he said,
    "hell."
Perhaps you then would roll upon your bed,

40   'And cry to all good men that loved you well,
"Ah Christ! if only I had known, known, known;"
Launcelot went away, then I could tell,

'Like wisest man how all things would be, moan,
And roll and hurt myself, and long to die,
And yet fear much to die for what was sown.   45

'Nevertheless you, O Sir Gauwaine, lie,
Whatever may have happened through these years,
God knows I speak truth, saying that you lie.'

Her voice was low at first, being full of tears,
But as it cleared, it grew full loud and shrill,   50
Growing a windy shriek in all men's ears,

A ringing in their startled brains, until
She said that Gauwaine lied, then her voice sunk,
And her great eyes began again to fill,

Though still she stood right up, and never shrunk,   55
But spoke on bravely, glorious lady fair!
Whatever tears her full lips may have drunk,

She stood, and seemed to think, and wrung her hair,
Spoke out at last with no more trace of shame,
With passionate twisting of her body there: 60

'It chanced upon a day that Launcelot came
To dwell at Arthur's court: at Christmas-time
This happened; when the heralds sung his name,

'"Son of King Ban of Benwick," seemed to chime
Along with all the bells that rang that day,   65
O'er the white roofs, with little change of rhyme.

'Christmas and whitened winter passed away,
And over me the April sunshine came,
Made very awful with black hail-clouds, yea

70   'And in the Summer I grew white with flame,
       And bowed my head down – Autumn, and the sick
       Sure knowledge things would never be the same,

      'However often Spring might be most thick
       Of blossoms and buds, smote on me, and I grew
75   Careless of most things, let the clock tick, tick,

      'To my unhappy pulse, that beat right through
       My eager body; while I laughed out loud,
       And let my lips curl up at false or true,

      'Seemed cold and shallow without any cloud.
80   Behold my judges, then the cloths were brought:
       While I was dizzied thus, old thoughts would crowd,

      'Belonging to the time ere I was bought
       By Arthur's great name and his little love,
       Must I give up for ever then, I thought,

85   'That which I deemed would ever round me move
       Glorifying all things; for a little word,
       Scarce ever meant at all, must I now prove

      'Stone-cold for ever? Pray you, does the Lord
       Will that all folks should be quite happy and good?
90   I love God now a little, if this cord

      'Were broken, once for all what striving could
       Make me love anything in earth or heaven.
       So day by day it grew, as if one should

      'Slip slowly down some path worn smooth and even,
95   Down to a cool sea on a summer day;
       Yet still in slipping was there some small leaven

'Of stretched hands catching small stones by the way,
Until one surely reached the sea at last,
And felt strange new joy as the worn head lay

'Back, with the hair like sea-weed; yea all past   100
Sweat of the forehead, dryness of the lips,
Washed utterly out by the dear waves o'ercast

'In the lone sea, far off from any ships!
Do I not know now of a day in Spring?
No minute of that wild day ever slips   105

'From out my memory; I hear thrushes sing,
And wheresoever I may be, straightway
Thoughts of it all come up with most fresh sting;

'I was half mad with beauty on that day,
And went without my ladies all alone,   110
In a quiet garden walled round every way;

'I was right joyful of that wall of stone,
That shut the flowers and trees up with the sky,
And trebled all the beauty: to the bone,

'Yea right through to my heart, grown very shy   115
With weary thoughts, it pierced, and made me glad;
Exceedingly glad, and I knew verily,

'A little thing just then had made me mad;
I dared not think, as I was wont to do,
Sometimes, upon my beauty; if I had   120

'Held out my long hand up against the blue,
And, looking on the tenderly darkened fingers,
Thought that by rights one ought to see quite through,

'There, see you, where the soft still light yet lingers,
125   Round by the edges; what should I have done,
If this had joined with yellow spotted singers,

'And startling green drawn upward by the sun?
But shouting, loosed out, see now! all my hair,
And trancedly stood watching the west wind run

130   'With faintest half-heard breathing sound – why there
I lose my head e'en now in doing this;
But shortly listen – in that garden fair

'Came Launcelot walking; this is true, the kiss
Wherewith we kissed in meeting that spring day,
135   I scarce dare talk of the remember'd bliss,

'When both our mouths went wandering in one way,
And aching sorely, met among the leaves;
Our hands being left behind strained far away.

'Never within a yard of my bright sleeves
140   Had Launcelot come before – and now, so nigh!
After that day why is it Guenevere grieves?

'Nevertheless you, O Sir Gauwaine, lie,
Whatever happened on through all those years,
God knows I speak truth, saying that you lie.

145   'Being such a lady could I weep these tears
If this were true? A great queen such as I
Having sinn'd this way, straight her conscience sears;

'And afterwards she liveth hatefully,
Slaying and poisoning, certes never weeps, –
150   Gauwaine be friends now, speak me lovingly.

'Do I not see how God's dear pity creeps
All through your frame, and trembles in your mouth?
Remember in what grave your mother sleeps,

'Buried in some place far down in the south,
Men are forgetting as I speak to you;   155
By her head sever'd in that awful drouth

'Of pity that drew Agravaine's fell blow,
I pray your pity! let me not scream out
For ever after, when the shrill winds blow

'Through half your castle-locks! let me not shout   160
For ever after in the winter night
When you ride out alone! in battle-rout

'Let not my rusting tears make your sword light!
Ah! God of mercy how he turns away!
So, ever must I dress me to the fight,   165

'So – let God's justice work! Gauwaine, I say,
See me hew down your proofs: yea all men know
Even as you said how Mellyagraunce one day,

'One bitter day in *la Fausse Garde*, for so
All good knights held it after, saw –   170
Yea, sirs, by cursed unknightly outrage; though

'You, Gauwaine, held his word without a flaw,
This Mellyagraunce saw blood upon my bed –
Whose blood then pray you? is there any law

'To make a queen say why some spots of red   175
Lie on her coverlet? or will you say,
"Your hands are white, lady, as when you wed,

'"Where did you bleed?" and must I stammer out –
  "Nay,
I blush indeed, fair lord, only to rend
My sleeve up to my shoulder, where there lay

'"A knife-point last night:" so must I defend
The honour of the lady Guenevere?
Not so, fair lords, even if the world should end

'This very day, and you were judges here
Instead of God. Did you see Mellyagraunce
When Launcelot stood by him? what white fear

'Curdled his blood, and how his teeth did dance,
His side sink in? as my knight cried and said,
"Slayer of unarm'd men, here is a chance!

'"Setter of traps, I pray you guard your head,
By God I am so glad to fight with you,
Stripper of ladies, that my hand feels lead

'"For driving weight; hurrah now! draw and do,
For all my wounds are moving in my breast,
And I am getting mad with waiting so."

'He struck his hands together o'er the beast,
Who fell down flat, and grovell'd at his feet,
And groan'd at being slain so young – "at least."

'My knight said, "Rise you, sir, who are so fleet
At catching ladies, half-arm'd will I fight,
My left side all uncovered!" then I weet,

'Up sprang Sir Mellyagraunce with great delight
Upon his knave's face; not until just then
Did I quite hate him, as I saw my knight

'Along the lists look to my stake and pen   205
With such a joyous smile, it made me sigh
From agony beneath my waist-chain, when

'The fight began, and to me they drew nigh;
Ever Sir Launcelot kept him on the right,
And traversed warily, and ever high   210

'And fast leapt caitiff's sword, until my knight
Sudden threw up his sword to his left hand,
Caught it, and swung it; that was all the fight.

'Except a spout of blood on the hot land;
For it was hottest summer; and I know   215
I wonder'd how the fire, while I should stand,

'And burn, against the heat, would quiver so,
Yards above my head; thus these matters went:
Which things were only warnings of the woe

'That fell on me. Yet Mellyagraunce was shent,   220
For Mellyagraunce had fought against the Lord;
Therefore, my lords, take heed lest you be blent

'With all this wickedness; say no rash word
Against me, being so beautiful; my eyes,
Wept all away the grey, may bring some sword   225

'To drown you in your blood; see my breast rise,
Like waves of purple sea, as here I stand;
And how my arms are moved in wonderful wise,

'Yea also at my full heart's strong command,
See through my long throat how the words go up   230
In ripples to my mouth; how in my hand

'The shadow lies like wine within a cup
Of marvellously colour'd gold; yea now
This little wind is rising, look you up,

235   'And wonder how the light is falling so
Within my moving tresses: will you dare,
When you have looked a little on my brow,

'To say this thing is vile? or will you care
For any plausible lies of cunning woof,
240   When you can see my face with no lie there

'For ever? am I not a gracious proof –
"But in your chamber Launcelot was found" –
Is there a good knight then would stand aloof,

'When a queen says with gentle queenly sound:
245   "O true as steel come now and talk with me,
I love to see your step upon the ground

'"Unwavering, also well I love to see
That gracious smile light up your face, and hear
Your wonderful words, that all mean verily

250   '"The thing they seem to mean: good friend, so dear
To me in everything, come here to-night,
Or else the hours will pass most dull and drear;

'"If you come not, I fear this time I might
Get thinking over much of times gone by,
255   When I was young, and green hope was in sight:

'"For no man cares now to know why I sigh;
And no man comes to sing me pleasant songs,
Nor any brings me the sweet flowers that lie

'"So thick in the gardens; therefore one so longs
To see you, Launcelot; that we may be   260
Like children once again, free from all wrongs

'"Just for one night." Did he not come to me?
What thing could keep true Launcelot away
If I said "come?" there was one less than three

'In my quiet room that night, and we were gay;   265
Till sudden I rose up, weak, pale, and sick,
Because a bawling broke our dream up, yea

'I looked at Launcelot's face and could not speak,
For he looked helpless too, for a little while;
Then I remember how I tried to shriek,   270

'And could not, but fell down; from tile to tile
The stones they threw up rattled o'er my head
And made me dizzier; till within a while

'My maids were all about me, and my head
On Launcelot's breast was being soothed away   275
From its white chattering, until Launcelot said –

'By God! I will not tell you more to-day,
Judge any way you will – what matters it?
You know quite well the story of that fray,

'How Launcelot still'd their bawling, the mad fit   280
That caught up Gauwaine – all, all, verily,
But just that which would save me; these things flit.

'Nevertheless you, O Sir Gauwaine, lie,
Whatever may have happen'd these long years,
God knows I speak truth, saying that you lie!   285

'All I have said is truth, by Christ's dear tears.'
She would not speak another word, but stood
Turn'd sideways; listening, like a man who hears

His brother's trumpet sounding through the wood
290   Of his foes' lances. She lean'd eagerly,
And gave a slight spring sometimes, as she could

At last hear something really; joyfully
Her cheek grew crimson, as the headlong speed
Of the roan charger drew all men to see,
295   The knight who came was Launcelot at good need.

The Gilliflower of Gold

A golden gilliflower to-day
I wore upon my helm alway,
And won the prize of this tourney,
   Hah! hah! la belle jaune giroflée.

5   However well Sir Giles might sit,
His sun was weak to wither it,
Lord Miles's blood was dew on it:
   Hah! hah! la belle jaune giroflée.

Although my spear in splinters flew,
10   From John's steel-coat my eye was true;
I wheel'd about, and cried for you,
   Hah! hah! la belle jaune giroflée.

Yea, do not doubt my heart was good,
Though my sword flew like rotten wood,
15   To shout, although I scarcely stood,
   Hah! hah! la belle jaune giroflée.

My hand was steady too, to take
My axe from round my neck, and break

John's steel-coat up for my love's sake.
  Hah! hah! la belle jaune giroflée.   20

When I stood in my tent again,
Arming afresh, I felt a pain
Take hold of me, I was so fain –
  Hah! hah! la belle jaune giroflée.

To hear: '*Honneur aux fils des preux!*'
Right in my ears again, and shew   25
The gilliflower blossom'd new.
  Hah! hah! la belle jaune giroflée.

The Sieur Guillaume against me came,
His tabard bore three points of flame
From a red heart: with little blame –   30
  Hah! hah! la belle jaune giroflée.

Our tough spears crackled up like straw;
He was the first to turn and draw
His sword, that had nor speck nor flaw, –
  Hah! hah! la belle jaune giroflée.   35

But I felt weaker than a maid,
And my brain, dizzied and afraid,
Within my helm a fierce tune play'd, –
  Hah! hah! la belle jaune giroflée.

     40

Until I thought of your dear head,
Bow'd to the gilliflower bed,
The yellow flowers stain'd with red; –
  Hah! hah! la belle jaune giroflée.

Crash! How the swords met, '*giroflée!*'
The fierce tune in my helm would play,   45
'*La belle! la belle! jaune giroflée!*'
  Hah! hah! la belle jaune giroflée.

Once more the great swords met again,
50   'La belle! La belle!' but who fell then
Le Sieur Guillaume, who struck down ten; –
     Hah! hah! la belle jaune giroflée.

And as with mazed and unarm'd face,
Toward my own crown and the Queen's place,
55   They led me at a gentle pace –
     Hah! hah! la belle jaune giroflée.

I almost saw your quiet head
Bow'd o'er the gilliflower bed,
The yellow flowers stain'd with red –
60   Hah! hah! la belle jaune giroflée.

The Judgment of God

'Swerve to the left, son Roger,' he said,
   'When you catch his eyes through the helmet-slit,
Swerve to the left, then out at his head,
   And the Lord God give you joy of it!'

5   The blue owls on my father's hood
     Were a little dimm'd as I turn'd away;
This giving up of blood for blood
     Will finish here somehow to-day.

So – when I walk'd out from the tent,
10   Their howling almost blinded me;
Yet for all that I was not bent
     By any shame. Hard by, the sea

Made a noise like the aspens where
     We did that wrong, but now the place
15   Is very pleasant, and the air
     Blows cool on any passer's face.

And all the wrong is gathered now
    Into the circle of these lists –
Yea, howl out, butchers! tell me how
    His hands were cut off at the wrists;   20

And how Lord Roger bore his face
    A league above his spear-point, high
Above the owls, to that strong place
    Among the waters – yea, yea, cry:

'What a brave champion we have got!   25
    Sir Oliver, the flower of all
The Hainault knights.' The day being hot,
    He sat beneath a broad white pall,

White linen over all his steel;
    What a good knight he look'd! his sword   30
Laid thwart his knees; he liked to feel
    Its steadfast edge clear as his word.

And he look'd solemn; how his love
    Smiled whitely on him, sick with fear!
How all the ladies up above   35
    Twisted their pretty hands! so near

The fighting was – Ellayne! Ellayne!
    They cannot love like you can, who
Would burn your hands off, if that pain
    Could win a kiss – am I not true   40

To you for ever? therefore I
    Do not fear death or anything;
If I should limp home wounded, why,
    While I lay sick you would but sing,

45   And soothe me into quiet sleep.
            If they spat on the recreant knight,
        Threw stones at him, and cursed him deep,
            Why then – what then; your hand would light

        So gently on his drawn-up face,
50   And you would kiss him, and in soft
        Cool scented clothes would lap him, pace
            The quiet room and weep oft, – oft

        Would turn and smile, and brush his cheek
            With your sweet chin and mouth; and in
55   The order'd garden you would seek
            The biggest roses – any sin.

        And these say: 'No more now my knight,
            Or God's knight any longer' – you,
        Being than they so much more white,
60   So much more pure and good and true,

        Will cling to me for ever – there,
            Is not that wrong turn'd right at last
        Through all these years, and I wash'd clean?
            Say, yea, Ellayne; the time is past,

65   Since on that Christmas-day last year
            Up to your feet the fire crept,
        And the smoke through the brown leaves sere
            Blinded your dear eyes that you wept;

        Was it not I that caught you then,
70   And kiss'd you on the saddle-bow?
        Did not the blue owl mark the men
            Whose spears stood like the corn a-row?

This Oliver is a right good knight,
    And must needs beat me, as I fear,
Unless I catch him in the fight,   75
    My father's crafty way – John, here!

Bring up the men from the south gate,
    To help me if I fall or win,
For even if I beat, their hate
    Will grow to more than this mere grin.   80

Spell-Bound

How weary is it none can tell,
    How dismally the days go by!
I hear the tinkling of the bell,
    I see the cross against the sky.

The year wears round to autumn-tide,   5
    Yet comes no reaper to the corn;
The golden land is like a bride
    When first she knows herself forlorn –

She sits and weeps with all her hair
    Laid downward over tender hands;   10
For stained silk she hath no care,
    No care for broken ivory wands;

The silver cups beside her stand;
    The golden stars on the blue roof
Yet glitter, though against her hand   15
    His cold sword presses for a proof

He is not dead, but gone away.
    How many hours did she wait
For me, I wonder? Till the day
    Had faded wholly, and the gate   20

Clanged to behind returning knights?
 I wonder did she raise her head
And go away, fleeing the lights;
 And lay the samite on her bed,

25   The wedding samite strewn with pearls:
 Then sit with hands laid on her knees,
Shuddering at half-heard sound of girls
 That chatter outside in the breeze?

I wonder did her poor heart throb
30   At distant tramp of coming knight?
How often did the choking sob
 Raise up her head and lips? The light,

Did it come on her unawares,
 And drag her sternly down before
35   People who loved her not? in prayers
 Did she say one name and no more?

And once – all songs they ever sung,
 All tales they ever told to me,
This only burden through them rung:
40   *O! golden love that waitest me,*

The days pass on, pass on a pace,
 Sometimes I have a little rest
In fairest dreams, when on thy face
 My lips lie, or thy hands are prest

45   *About my forehead, and thy lips*
 Draw near and nearer to mine own;
But when the vision from me slips,
 In colourless dawn I lie and moan,

And wander forth with fever'd blood,
   That makes me start at little things,   50
The blackbird screaming from the wood,
   The sudden whirr of pheasants' wings.

O! dearest, scarcely seen by me –
   But when that wild time had gone by,
And in these arms I folded thee,   55
   Who ever thought those days could die?

Yet now I wait, and you wait too,
   For what perchance may never come;
You think I have forgotten you,
   That I grew tired and went home.   60

But what if some day as I stood
   Against the wall with strained hands,
And turn'd my face toward the wood,
   Away from all the golden lands;

And saw you come with tired feet,   65
   And pale face thin and wan with care,
And stained raiment no more neat,
   The white dust lying on your hair: –

Then I should say, I could not come;
   This land was my wide prison, dear;   70
I could not choose but go; at home
   There is a wizard whom I fear:

He bound me round with silken chains
   I could not break; he set me here
Above the golden-waving plains,   75
   Where never reaper cometh near.

And you have brought me my good sword,
    Wherewith in happy days of old
I won you well from knight and lord;
    My heart upswells and I grow bold.

But I shall die unless you stand,
    – Half lying now, you are so weak, –
Within my arms, unless your hand
    Pass to and fro across my cheek.

The Blue Closet

THE DAMOZELS

Lady Alice, lady Louise,
Between the wash of the tumbling seas
We are ready to sing, if so ye please;
So lay your long hands on the keys;
                    Sing, '*Laudate pueri.*'

And ever the great bell overhead
Boom'd in the wind a knell for the dead,
Though no one toll'd it, a knell for the dead.

LADY LOUISE

Sister, let the measure swell
Not too loud; for you sing not well
If you drown the faint boom of the bell;
                    He is weary, so am I.

And ever the chevron overhead
Flapp'd on the banner of the dead;
(Was he asleep, or was he dead?)

LADY ALICE

Alice the Queen, and Louise the Queen,
Two damozels wearing purple and green,
Four lone ladies dwelling here
From day to day and year to year;
And there is none to let us go;   20
To break the locks of the doors below,
Or shovel away the heaped-up snow;
And when we die no man will know
That we are dead; but they give us leave,
Once every year on Christmas-eve,   25
To sing in the Closet Blue one song;
And we should be so long, so long,
If we dared, in singing; for dream on dream,
They float on in a happy stream;
Float from the gold strings, float from the keys,   30
Float from the open'd lips of Louise;
But, alas! the sea-salt oozes through
The chinks of the tiles of the Closet Blue;
And ever the great bell overhead
Booms in the wind a knell for the dead,   35
The wind plays on it a knell for the dead.

[*They sing all together.*]
How long ago was it, how long ago,
He came to this tower with hands full of snow?

'Kneel down, O love Louise, kneel down,' he said,   40
And sprinkled the dusty snow over my head.

He watch'd the snow melting, it ran through my
    hair,
Ran over my shoulders, white shoulders and bare.

'I cannot weep for thee, poor love Louise,
For my tears are all hidden deep under the seas;

'In a gold and blue casket she keeps all my tears,
But my eyes are no longer blue, as in old years;

'Yea, they grow grey with time, grow small and dry,
I am so feeble now, would I might die.'

And in truth the great bell overhead
Left off his pealing for the dead,
Perchance, because the wind was dead.

Will he come back again, or is he dead?
O! is he sleeping, my scarf round his head?

Or did they strangle him as he lay there,
With the long scarlet scarf I used to wear?

Only I pray thee, Lord, let him come here!
Both his soul and his body to me are most dear.

Dear Lord, that loves me, I wait to receive
Either body or spirit this wild Christmas-eve.

Through the floor shot up a lily red,
With a patch of earth from the land of the dead,
For he was strong in the land of the dead.

What matter that his cheeks were pale,
    His kind kiss'd lips all grey?
'O, love Louise, have you waited long?'
    'O, my lord Arthur, yea.'

What if his hair that brush'd her cheek
    Was stiff with frozen rime?
His eyes were grown quite blue again,
    As in the happy time.

'O, love Louise, this is the key
  Of the happy golden land!
O, sisters, cross the bridge with me,
  My eyes are full of sand.   75
What matter that I cannot see,
  If ye take me by the hand?'

And ever the great bell overhead,
And the tumbling seas mourn'd for the dead;
For their song ceased, and they were dead.   80

The Tune of Seven Towers

No one goes there now:
  For what is left to fetch away
From the desolate battlements all arow,
  And the lead roof heavy and grey?
'Therefore,' said fair Yoland of the flowers,   5
'This is the tune of Seven Towers.'

No one walks there now;
  Except in the white moonlight
The white ghosts walk in a row;
  If one could see it, an awful sight, –   10
'Listen!' said fair Yoland of the flowers,
'This is the tune of Seven Towers.'

But none can see them now,
  Though they sit by the side of the moat,
Feet half in the water, there in a row,   15
  Long hair in the wind afloat
'Therefore,' said fair Yoland of the flowers,
'This is the tune of Seven Towers.'

If any will go to it now,
  He must go to it all alone,   20

Its gates will not open to any row
    Of glittering spears – will *you* go alone?
'Listen!' said fair Yoland of the flowers,
'This is the tune of Seven Towers.'

25 By my love go there now,
        To fetch me my coif away,
    My coif and my kirtle, with pearls arow,
        Oliver, go to-day!
    'Therefore,' said fair Yoland of the flowers,
30 *'This is the tune of Seven Towers.'*

    I am unhappy now,
        I cannot tell you why;
    If you go, the priests and I in a row
        Will pray that you may not die.
35 *'Listen!,' said fair Yoland of the flowers,*
    'This is the tune of Seven Towers.'

    If you will go for me now,
        I will kiss your mouth at last;
                    [*She sayeth inwardly.*]
    (*The graves stand grey in a row,*)
40   Oliver, hold me fast!
    'Therefore,' said fair Yoland of the flowers,
    'This is the tune of Seven Towers.'

Golden Wings

Midways of a walled garden,
    In the happy poplar land,
    Did an ancient castle stand,
With an old knight for a warden.

Many scarlet bricks there were   5
   In its walls, and old grey stone;
   Over which red apples shone
At the right time of the year.

On the bricks the green moss grew,
   Yellow lichen on the stone,   10
   Over which red apples shone;
Little war that castle knew.

Deep green water fill'd the moat,
   Each side had a red-brick lip,
   Green and mossy with the drip   15
Of dew and rain; there was a boat

Of carven wood, with hangings green
   About the stern; it was great bliss
   For lovers to sit there and kiss
In the hot summer noons, not seen.   20

Across the moat the fresh west wind
   In very little ripples went;
   The way the heavy aspens bent
Towards it, was a thing to mind.

The painted drawbridge over it   25
   Went up and down with gilded chains,
   'Twas pleasant in the summer rains
Within the bridge-house there to sit.

There were five swans that ne'er did eat
   The water-weeds, for ladies came   30
   Each day, and young knights did the same,
And gave them cakes and bread for meat.

They had a house of painted wood,
  A red roof gold-spiked over it,
  Wherein upon their eggs to sit
Week after week; no drop of blood,

Drawn from men's bodies by sword-blows,
  Came ever there, or any tear;
  Most certainly from year to year
'Twas pleasant as a Provence rose.

The banners seem'd quite full of ease,
  That over the turret-roofs hung down;
  The battlements could get no frown
From the flower-moulded cornices.

Who walked in that garden there?
  Miles and Giles and Isabeau,
  Tall Jehane du Castel beau,
Alice of the golden hair,

Big Sir Gervaise, the good knight,
  Fair Ellayne le Violet,
  Mary, Constance fille de fay,
Many dames with footfall light.

Whosoever wander'd there,
  Whether it be dame or knight,
  Half of scarlet, half of white
Their raiment was; of roses fair

Each wore a garland on the head,
  At Ladies' Gard the way was so:
  Fair Jehane du Castel beau
Wore her wreath till it was dead.

Little joy she had of it,
   Of the raiment white and red,
   Or the garland on her head,
She had none with whom to sit

In the carven boat at noon;   65
   None the more did Jehane weep,
   She would only stand and keep
Saying, 'He will be here soon.'

Many times in the long day
   Miles and Giles and Gervaise past,   70
   Holding each some white hand fast,
Every time they heard her say:

'Summer cometh to an end,
   Undern cometh after noon;
   Golden wings will be here soon,   75
What if I some token send?'

Wherefore that night within the hall,
   With open mouth and open eyes,
   Like some one listening with surprise,
She sat before the sight of all.   80

Stoop'd down a little she sat there,
   With neck stretch'd out and chin thrown up,
   One hand around a golden cup;
And strangely with her fingers fair

She beat some tune upon the gold;   85
   The minstrels in the gallery
   Sung: 'Arthur, who will never die,
In Avallon he groweth old.'

And when the song was ended, she
90   Rose and caught up her gown and ran;
     None stopp'd her eager face and wan
Of all that pleasant company.

Right so within her own chamber
     Upon her bed she sat; and drew
95   Her breath in quick gasps; till she knew
That no man follow'd after her:

She took the garland from her head,
     Loosed all her hair, and let it lie
     Upon the coverlit; thereby
100 She laid the gown of white and red;

And she took off her scarlet shoon,
     And bared her feet; still more and more
     Her sweet face redden'd; evermore
She murmured: 'He will be here soon;

105 'Truly he cannot fail to know
     My tender body waits him here;
     And if he knows, I have no fear
For poor Jehane du Castel beau.'

She took a sword within her hand,
110   Whose hilts were silver, and she sung,
     Somehow like this, wild words that rung
A long way over the moonlit land: –

     Gold wings across the sea!
     Grey light from tree to tree,
115   Gold hair beside my knee,
     I pray thee come to me,
     Gold wings!

                                The water slips,
                The red-bill'd moorhen dips.
                Sweet kisses on red lips;
                Alas! the red rust grips,   120
                And the blood-red dagger rips,
                Yet, O knight, come to me!

                Are not my blue eyes sweet?
                The west wind from the wheat
                Blows cold across my feet;   125
                Is it not time to meet
                Gold wings across the sea?

                White swans on the green moat,
                Small feathers left afloat
                By the blue-painted boat;   130
                Swift running of the stoat;
                Sweet gurgling note by note
                Of sweet music.

                                O gold wings,
                Listen how gold hair sings,
                And the Ladies Castle rings,   135
                Gold wings across the sea.

                I sit on a purple bed,
                Outside, the wall is red,
                Thereby the apple hangs,
                And the wasp, caught by the fangs,   140

                Dies in the autumn night.
                And the bat flits till light,
                And the love-crazed knight

                Kisses the long wet grass:
                The weary days pass, –   145
                Gold wings across the sea!

       Gold wings across the sea!
       Moonlight from tree to tree,
       Sweet hair laid on my knee,
150   O, sweet knight, come to me!

       Gold wings, the short night slips,
       The white swan's long neck drips,
       I pray thee, kiss my lips,
       Gold wings across the sea.

155 No answer through the moonlit night;
      No answer in the cold grey dawn;
      No answer when the shaven lawn
Grew green, and all the roses bright.

Her tired feet look'd cold and thin,
160   Her lips were twitch'd, and wretched tears,
      Some, as she lay, roll'd past her ears,
Some fell from off her quivering chin.

Her long throat, stretch'd to its full length,
      Rose up and fell right brokenly;
165   As though the unhappy heart was nigh
Striving to break with all its strength.

And when she slipp'd from off the bed,
      Her cramp'd feet would not hold her; she
      Sank down and crept on hand and knee,
170 On the window-sill she laid her head.

There, with crooked arm upon the sill,
      She look'd out, muttering dismally:
      'There is no sail upon the sea,
No pennon on the empty hill.

'I cannot stay here all alone,   175
  Or meet their happy faces here,
  And wretchedly I have no fear;
A little while, and I am gone.'

Therewith she rose upon her feet,
  And totter'd; cold and misery   180
  Still made the deep sobs come, till she
At last stretch'd out her fingers sweet,

And caught the great sword in her hand;
  And, stealing down the silent stair,
  Barefooted in the morning air,   185
And only in her smock, did stand

Upright upon the green lawn grass;
  And hope grew in her as she said:
  'I have thrown off the white and red,
And pray God it may come to pass   190

'I meet him; if ten years go by
  Before I meet him; if, indeed,
  Meanwhile both soul and body bleed,
Yet there is end of misery,

'And I have hope. He could not come,   195
  But I can go to him and show
  These new things I have got to know,
And make him speak, who has been dumb.'

O Jehane! the red morning sun
  Changed her white feet to glowing gold,   200
  Upon her smock, on crease and fold,
Changed that to gold which had been dun.

O Miles, and Giles, and Isabeau,
  Fair Ellayne le Violet,
  Mary, Constance fille de fay!
Where is Jehane du Castel beau?

O big Gervaise ride apace!
  Down to the hard yellow sand,
  Where the water meets the land.
This is Jehane by her face;

Why has she a broken sword?
  Mary! she is slain outright;
  Verily a piteous sight;
Take her up without a word!

Giles and Miles and Gervaise there,
  Ladies' Gard must meet the war;
  Whatsoever knights these are,
Man the walls withouten fear!

Axes to the apple-trees,
  Axes to the aspens tall!
  Barriers without the wall
May be lightly made of these.

O poor shivering Isabeau;
  Poor Ellayne le Violet,
  Bent with fear! we miss to-day
Brave Jehane du Castel beau.

O poor Mary, weeping so!
  Wretched Constance fille de fay!
  Verily we miss to-day
Fair Jehane du Castel beau.

The apples now grow green and sour
  Upon the mouldering castle-wall,
  Before they ripen there they fall:
There are no banners on the tower.

The draggled swans most eagerly eat   235
  The green weeds trailing in the moat;
  Inside the rotting leaky boat
You see a slain man's stiffen'd feet.

The Haystack in the Floods

Had she come all the way for this,
To part at last without a kiss?
Yea, had she borne the dirt and rain
That her own eyes might see him slain
Beside the haystack in the floods?   5

Along the dripping leafless woods,
The stirrup touching either shoe,
She rode astride as troopers do;
With kirtle kilted to her knee,
To which the mud splash'd wretchedly;   10
And the wet dripp'd from every tree
Upon her head and heavy hair,
And on her eyelids broad and fair;
The tears and rain ran down her face.
By fits and starts they rode apace,   15
And very often was his place
Far off from her; he had to ride
Ahead, to see what might betide
When the roads cross'd; and sometimes, when
There rose a murmuring from his men,   20
Had to turn back with promises;
Ah me! she had but little ease;
And often for pure doubt and dread
She sobb'd, made giddy in the head

25   By the swift riding; while, for cold,
      Her slender fingers scarce could hold
      The wet reins; yea, and scarcely, too,
      She felt the foot within her shoe
      Against the stirrup: all for this,
30   To part at last without a kiss
      Beside the haystack in the floods.

      For when they near'd that old soak'd hay,
      They saw across the only way
      That Judas, Godmar, and the three
35   Red running lions dismally
      Grinn'd from his pennon, under which,
      In one straight line along the ditch,
      They counted thirty heads.

                              So then,
      While Robert turn'd round to his men,
40   She saw at once the wretched end,
      And, stooping down, tried hard to rend
      Her coif the wrong way from her head,
      And hid her eyes; while Robert said:
      'Nay, love, 'tis scarcely two to one,
45   At Poictiers where we made them run
      So fast – why, sweet my love, good cheer,
      The Gascon frontier is so near,
      Nought after this.'

                              But, 'O,' she said,
      'My God! my God! I have to tread
50   The long way back without you; then
      The court at Paris; those six men;
      The gratings of the Chatelet;
      The swift Seine on some rainy day
      Like this, and people standing by,
55   And laughing, while my weak hands try
      To recollect how strong men swim.
      All this, or else a life with him,

For which I should be damned at last,
Would God that this next hour were past!'

He answer'd not, but cried his cry,   60
'St George for Marny!' cheerily;
And laid his hand upon her rein.
Alas! no man of all his train
Gave back that cheery cry again;
And, while for rage his thumb beat fast   65
Upon his sword-hilts, some one cast
About his neck a kerchief long,
And bound him.

        Then they went along
To Godmar; who said: 'Now, Jehane,
Your lover's life is on the wane   70
So fast, that, if this very hour
You yield not as my paramour,
He will not see the rain leave off –
Nay, keep your tongue from gibe and scoff,
Sir Robert, or I slay you now.'   75

She laid her hand upon her brow,
Then gazed upon the palm, as though
She thought her forehead bled, and – 'No.'
She said, and turn'd her head away,
As there were nothing else to say,   80
And everything were settled: red
Grew Godmar's face from chin to head:
'Jehane, on yonder hill there stands
My castle, guarding well my lands:
What hinders me from taking you,   85
And doing that I list to do
To your fair wilful body, while
Your knight lies dead?'

                                 A wicked smile
Wrinkled her face, her lips grew thin,
A long way out she thrust her chin:
'You know that I should strangle you
While you were sleeping; or bite through
Your throat, by God's help – ah!' she said,
'Lord Jesus, pity your poor maid!
For in such wise they hem me in,
I cannot choose but sin and sin,
Whatever happens: yet I think
They could not make me eat or drink,
And so should I just reach my rest.'
'Nay, if you do not my behest,
O Jehane! though I love you well,'
Said Godmar, 'would I fail to tell
All that I know,' 'Foul lies,' she said.
'Eh? lies my Jehane? by God's head,
At Paris folks would deem them true!
Do you know, Jehane, they cry for you,
"Jehane the brown! Jehane the brown!
Give us Jehane to burn or drown!" –
Eh – gag me, Robert! – sweet my friend,
This were indeed a piteous end
For those long fingers, and long feet,
And long neck, and smooth shoulders sweet;
An end that few men would forget
That saw it – So, an hour yet:
Consider, Jehane, which to take
Of life or death!'

                            So, scarce awake,
Dismounting, did she leave that place,
And totter some yards: with her face
Turn'd upward to the sky she lay,
Her head on a wet heap of hay,
And fell asleep: and while she slept,
And did not dream, the minutes crept

Round to the twelve again; but she,
Being waked at last, sigh'd quietly,
And strangely childlike came, and said: 125
'I will not.' Straightway Godmar's head,
As though it hung on strong wires, turn'd
Most sharply round, and his' face burn'd.

For Robert – both his eyes were dry,
He could not weep, but gloomily   130
He seem'd to watch the rain; yea, too,
His lips were firm; he tried once more
To touch her lips; she reach'd out, sore
And vain desire so tortured them,
The poor grey lips, and now the hem   135
Of his sleeve brush'd them.

                                    With a start
Up Godmar rose, thrust them apart;
From Robert's throat he loosed the bands
Of silk and mail; with empty hands
Held out, she stood and gazed, and saw,   140
The long bright blade without a flaw
Glide out from Godmar's sheath, his hand
In Robert's hair; she saw him bend
Back Robert's head; she saw him send
The thin steel down; the blow told well,   145
Right backward the knight Robert fell,
And moan'd as dogs do, being half dead,
Unwitting, as I deem: so then
Godmar turn'd grinning to his men,
Who ran, some five or six, and beat   150
His head to pieces at their feet.

Then Godmar turn'd again and said:
'So, Jehane, the first fitte is read!
Take note, my lady, that your way
Lies backward to the Chatelet!'   155
She shook her head and gazed awhile

At her cold hands with a rueful smile,
As though this thing had made her mad.

This was the parting that they had
160   Beside the haystack in the floods.

Two Red Roses Across the Moon

There was a lady lived in a hall,
Large in the eyes, and slim and tall;
And ever she sung from noon to noon,
Two red roses across the moon.

5   There was a knight came riding by
In early spring, when the roads were dry;
And he heard that lady sing at the noon,
Two red roses across the moon.

Yet none the more he stopp'd at all,
10   But he rode a-gallop past the hall;
And left that lady singing at noon,
Two red roses across the moon.

Because, forsooth, the battle was set,
And the scarlet and blue had got to be met,
15   He rode on the spur till the next warm noon; –
Two red roses across the moon.

But the battle was scatter'd from hill to hill,
From the windmill to the watermill;
And he said to himself, as it near'd the noon,
20   *Two red roses across the moon.*

You scarce could see for the scarlet and blue,
A golden helm or a golden shoe:
So he cried, as the fight grew thick at the noon,
Two red roses across the moon!

Verily then the gold bore through   25
The huddled spears of the scarlet and blue;
And they cried, as they cut them down at the noon,
Two red roses across the moon!

I trow he stopp'd when he rode again
By the hall, though draggled sore with the rain: 30
And his lips were pinch'd to kiss at the noon,
Two red roses across the moon.

Under the may she stoop'd to the crown,
All was gold, there was nothing of brown;
And the horns blew up in the hall at noon,   35
Two red roses across the moon.

Near Avalon

A ship with shields before the sun,
Six maidens round the mast,
A red-gold crown on every one,
A green gown on the last.

The fluttering green banners there   5
Are wrought with ladies' heads most fair,
And a portraiture of Guenevere
The middle of each sail doth bear.

A ship with sails before the wind,
And round the helm six knights,   10
Their heaumes are on, whereby, half blind,
They pass by many sights,

The tatter'd scarlet banners there,
Right soon will leave the spear-heads bare.
Those six knights sorrowfully bear,   15
In all their heaumes some yellow hair.

Praise of My Lady

My lady seems of ivory
Forehead, straight nose, and cheeks that be
Hollow'd a little mournfully.
     Beata mea Domina!

5   Her forehead, overshadow'd much
By bows of hair, has a wave such
As God was good to make for me.
     Beata mea Domina!

Not greatly long my lady's hair,
10 Not yet with yellow colour fair,
But thick and crisped wonderfully:
     Beata mea Domina!

Heavy to make the pale face sad,
And dark, but dead as though it had
15 Been forged by God most wonderfully
     – Beata mea Domina! –

Of some strange metal, thread by thread,
To stand out from my lady's head,
Not moving much to tangle me.
20   *Beata mea Domina!*

Beneath her brows the lids fall slow,
The lashes a clear shadow throw
Where I would wish my lips to be.
     Beata mea Domina!

25 Her great eyes, standing far apart,
Draw up some memory from her heart,
And gaze out very mournfully;
     – Beata mea Domina! –

So beautiful and kind they are,
But most times looking out afar,   30
Waiting for something, not for me.
       Beata mea Domina!

I wonder if the lashes long
Are those that do her bright eyes wrong,
For always half tears seem to be   35
      – *Beata mea Domina!* –

Lurking below the underlid,
Darkening the place where they lie hid –
If they should rise and flow for me!
      Beata mea Domina!   40

Her full lips being made to kiss,
Curl'd up and pensive each one is;
This makes me faint to stand and see.
      Beata mea Domina!

Her lips are not contented now,   45
Because the hours pass so slow
Towards a sweet time: (pray for me),
      – *Beata mea Domina!* –

Nay, hold thy peace! for who can tell;
But this at least I know full well,   50
Her lips are parted longingly,
      – *Beata mea Domina!* –

So passionate and swift to move,
To pluck at any flying love,
That I grow faint to stand and see.   55
      Beata mea Domina!

Yea! there beneath them is her chin,
So fine and round, it were a sin
To feel no weaker when I see
60   – *Beata mea Domina!* –

God's dealings; for with so much care
And troublous, faint lines wrought in there,
He finishes her face for me.
                    Beata mea Domina!

65   Of her long neck what shall I say?
What things about her body's sway,
Like a knight's pennon or slim tree
                    – *Beata mea Domina!* –

Set gently waving in the wind;
70   Or her long hands that I may find
On some day sweet to move o'er me?
                    Beata mea Domina!

God pity me though, if I miss'd
The telling, how along her wrist
75   The veins creep, dying languidly
                    – *Beata mea Domina!* –

Inside her tender palm and thin.
Now give me pardon, dear, wherein
My voice is weak and vexes thee.
80   *Beata mea Domina!*

All men that see her any time,
I charge you straightly in this rhyme,
What, and wherever you may be,
                    – *Beata mea Domina!* –

To kneel before her; as for me,   85
I choke and grow quite faint to see
My lady moving graciously.
                    Beata mea Domina!

Summer Dawn

Pray but one prayer for me 'twixt thy closed lips,
    Think but one thought of me up in the stars.
The summer night waneth, the morning light slips,
    Faint and grey 'twixt the leaves of the aspen,
        betwixt the cloud-bars,
That are patiently waiting there for the dawn: 5
    Patient and colourless, though Heaven's gold
Waits to float through them along with the sun.
Far out in the meadows, above the young corn,
    The heavy elms wait, and restless and cold
The uneasy wind rises; the roses are dun;   10
Through the long twilight they pray for the dawn,
Round the lone house in the midst of the corn.
    Speak but one word to me over the corn,
    Over the tender, bow'd locks of the corn.

FROM *THE EARTHLY PARADISE*

An Apology

Of Heaven or Hell I have no power to sing,
I cannot ease the burden of your fears,
Or make quick-coming death a little thing,
Or bring again the pleasure of past years,
Nor for my words shall ye forget your tears,
Or hope again for aught that I can say,
The idle singer of an empty day.

But rather, when aweary of your mirth,
From full hearts still unsatisfied ye sigh,
And, feeling kindly unto all the earth,
Grudge every minute as it passes by,
Made the more mindful that the sweet days die –
– Remember me a little then I pray,
The idle singer of an empty day.

The heavy trouble, the bewildering care
That weighs us down who live and earn our bread,
These idle verses have no power to bear;
So let me sing of names remembered,
Because they, living not, can ne'er be dead,
Or long time take their memory quite away
From us poor singers of an empty day.

Dreamer of dreams, born out of my due time,
Why should I strive to set the crooked straight?
Let it suffice me that my murmuring rhyme
Beats with light wing against the ivory gate,
Telling a tale not too importunate
To those who in the sleepy region stay,
Lulled by the singer of an empty day.

Folk say, a wizard to a northern king
At Christmas-tide such wondrous things did show,   30
That through one window men beheld the spring,
And through another saw the summer glow,
And through a third the fruited vines a-row,
While still, unheard, but in its wonted way,
Piped the drear wind of that December day.   35

So with this Earthly Paradise it is,
If ye will read aright, and pardon me,
Who strive to build a shadowy isle of bliss
Midmost the beating of the steely sea,
Where tossed about all hearts of men must be;   40
Whose ravening monsters mighty men shall slay,
Not the poor singer of an empty day.

The Wanderers

Forget six counties overhung with smoke,
Forget the snorting steam and piston stroke,
Forget the spreading of the hideous town;
Think rather of the pack-horse on the down,
And dream of London, small, and white, and clean,   5
The clear Thames bordered by its gardens green;
Think, that below bridge the green lapping waves
Smite some few keels that bear Levantine staves,
Cut from the yew wood on the burnt-up hill,
And pointed jars that Greek hands toiled to fill,   10
And treasured scanty spice from some far sea,
Florence gold cloth, and Ypres napery,
And cloth of Bruges, and hogsheads of Guienne;
While nigh the thronged wharf Geoffrey Chaucer's
    pen
Moves over bills of lading – mid such times   15
Shall dwell the hollow puppets of my rhymes.

May

O Love, this morn when the sweet nightingale
Had so long finished all he had to say,
That thou hadst slept, and sleep had told his tale;
And midst a peaceful dream had stolen away
In fragrant dawning of the first of May,
Didst thou see aught? didst thou hear voices sing
Ere to the risen sun the bells 'gan ring?

For then methought the Lord of Love went by
To take possession of his flowery throne,
Ringed round with maids, and youths, and minstrelsy;
A little while I sighed to find him gone,
A little while the dawning was alone,
And the light gathered; then I held my breath,
And shuddered at the sight of Eld and Death.

Alas! Love passed me in the twilight dun,
His music hushed the wakening ousel's song;
But on these twain shone out the golden sun,
And o'er their heads the brown bird's tune was
        strong,
As shivering, twixt the trees they stole along;
None noted aught their noiseless passing by,
The world had quite forgotten it must die.

ALGERNON CHARLES SWINBURNE

A Ballad of Life

I found in dreams a place of wind and flowers,
  Full of sweet trees and colour of glad grass,
  In midst whereof there was
A lady clothed like summer with sweet hours.
Her beauty, fervent as a fiery moon,
  Made my blood burn and swoon
    Like a flame rained upon.
Sorrow had filled her shaken eyelids' blue,
And her mouth's sad red heavy rose all through
    Seemed sad with glad things gone.

She held a little cithern by the strings,
  Shaped heartwise, strung with subtle-coloured hair
  Of some dead lute-player
That in dead years had done delicious things.
The seven strings were named accordingly;
  The first string charity,
    The second tenderness,
The rest were pleasure, sorrow, sleep, and sin,
And loving-kindness, that is pity's kin
      And is most pitiless.

There were three men with her, each garmented
  With gold and shod with gold upon the feet;
  And with plucked ears of wheat
The first man's hair was wound upon his head:
His face was red, and his mouth curled and sad;
  All his gold garment had
    Pale stains of dust and rust.
A riven hood was pulled across his eyes;
The token of him being upon this wise
      Made for a sign of Lust.

The next was Shame, with hollow heavy face
   Coloured like green wood when flame kindles it.
   He hath such feeble feet
They may not well endure in any place.
His face was full of grey old miseries,   35
   And all his blood's increase
      Was even increase of pain.
The last was Fear, that is akin to Death;
He is Shame's friend, and always as Shame saith
      Fear answers him again.   40

My soul said in me; This is marvellous,
   Seeing the air's face is not so delicate
   Nor the sun's grace so great,
If sin and she be kin or amorous.
And seeing where maidens served her on their   45
     knees,
   I bade one crave of these
      To know the cause thereof.
Then Fear said: I am Pity that was dead.
And Shame said: I am Sorrow comforted.
      And Lust said: I am Love.   50

Thereat her hands began a lute-playing
   And her sweet mouth a song in a strange tongue;
   And all the while she sung
There was no sound but long tears following
Long tears upon men's faces, waxen white   55
   With extreme sad delight.
      But those three following men
Became as men raised up among the dead;
Great glad mouths open and fair cheeks made red
      With child's blood come again.   60

Then I said: Now assuredly I see
   My lady is perfect, and transfigureth
   All sin and sorrow and death,
Making them fair as her own eyelids be,

65 Or lips wherein my whole soul's life abides;
        Or as her sweet white sides
            And bosom carved to kiss.
    Now therefore, if her pity further me,
    Doubtless for her sake all my days shall be
70   As righteous as she is.

    Forth, ballad, and take roses in both arms,
        Even till the top rose touch thee in the throat
    Where the least thornprick harms;
        And girdled in thy golden singing-coat,
75 Come thou before my lady and say this;
        Borgia, thy gold hair's colour burns in me,
            Thy mouth makes beat my blood in feverish rhymes;
        Therefore so many as these roses be,
            Kiss me so many times.
80 Then it may be, seeing how sweet she is,
        That she will stoop herself none otherwise
            Than a blown vine-branch doth,
        And kiss thee with soft laughter on thine eyes,
            Ballad, and on thy mouth.

Laus Veneris

    Asleep or waking is it? for her neck,
    Kissed over close, wears yet a purple speck
        Wherein the pained blood falters and goes out;
    Soft, and stung softly – fairer for a fleck.

5   But though my lips shut sucking on the place,
    There is no vein at work upon her face;
        Her eyelids are so peaceable, no doubt
    Deep sleep has warmed her blood through all its ways.

Lo, this is she that was the world's delight;
The old grey years were parcels of her might;   10
   The strewings of the ways wherein she trod
Were the twain seasons of the day and night.

Lo, she was thus when her clear limbs enticed
All lips that now grow sad with kissing Christ,
   Stained with blood fallen from the feet of God,   15
The feet and hands whereat our souls were priced.

Alas, Lord, surely thou art great and fair.
But lo her wonderfully woven hair!
   And thou didst heal us with thy piteous kiss;
But see now, Lord; her mouth is lovelier.   20

She is right fair; what hath she done to thee?
Nay, fair Lord Christ, lift up thine eyes and see;
   Had now thy mother such a lip – like this?
Thou knowest how sweet a thing it is to me.

Inside the Horsel here the air is hot;   25
Right little peace one hath for it, God wot;
   The scented dusty daylight burns the air,
And my heart chokes me till I hear it not.

Behold, my Venus, my soul's body, lies
With my love laid upon her garment-wise,   30
   Feeling my love in all her limbs and hair
And shed between her eyelids through her eyes.

She holds my heart in her sweet open hands
Hanging asleep; hard by her head there stands,
   Crowned with gilt thorns and clothed with flesh   35
      like fire,
Love, wan as foam blown up the salt burnt sands –

Hot as the brackish waifs of yellow spume
That shift and steam – loose clots of arid fume
    From the sea's panting mouth of dry desire;
There stands he, like one labouring at a loom.

The warp holds fast across; and every thread
That makes the woof up has dry specks of red;
    Always the shuttle cleaves clean through, and he
Weaves with the hair of many a ruined head.

Love is not glad nor sorry, as I deem;
Labouring he dreams, and labours in the dream,
    Till when the spool is finished, lo I see
His web, reeled off, curls and goes out like steam.

Night falls like fire; the heavy lights run low,
And as they drop, my blood and body so
    Shake as the flame shakes, full of days and hours
That sleep not neither weep they as they go.

Ah yet would God this flesh of mine might be
Where air might wash and long leaves cover me,
    Where tides of grass break into foam of flowers,
Or where the wind's feet shine along the sea.

Ah yet would God that stems and roots were bred
Out of my weary body and my head,
    That sleep were sealed upon me with a seal,
And I were as the least of all his dead.

Would God my blood were dew to feed the grass,
Mine ears made deaf and mine eyes blind as glass,
    My body broken as a turnip wheel,
And my mouth stricken ere it saith Alas!

Ah God, that love were as a flower or flame,   65
That life were as the naming of a name,
   That death were not more pitiful than desire,
That these things were not one thing and the same!

Behold now, surely somewhere there is death:
For each man hath some space of years, he saith,   70
   A little space of time ere time expire,
A little day, a little way of breath.

And lo, between the sundawn and the sun,
His day's work and his night's work are undone;
   And lo, between the nightfall and the light,   75
He is not, and none knoweth of such an one.

Ah God, that I were as all souls that be,
As any herb or leaf of any tree,
   As men that toil through hours of labouring night,
As bones of men under the deep sharp sea.   80

Outside it must be winter among men;
For at the gold bars of the gates again
   I heard all night and all the hours of it
The wind's wet wings and fingers drip with rain.

Knights gather, riding sharp for cold; I know   85
The ways and woods are strangled with the snow;
   And with short song the maidens spin and sit
Until Christ's birthnight, lily-like, arow.

The scent and shadow shed about me make
The very soul in all my senses ache;   90
   The hot hard night is fed upon my breath,
And sleep beholds me from afar awake.

Alas, but surely where the hills grow deep,
Or where the wild ways of the sea are steep,
   Or in strange places somewhere there is death,
And on death's face the scattered hair of sleep.

There lover-like with lips and limbs that meet
They lie, they pluck sweet fruit of life and eat;
   But me the hot and hungry days devour,
And in my mouth no fruit of theirs is sweet.

No fruit of theirs, but fruit of my desire,
For her love's sake whose lips through mine respire;
   Her eyelids on her eyes like flower on flower,
Mine eyelids on mine eyes like fire on fire.

So lie we, not as sleep that lies by death,
With heavy kisses and with happy breath;
   Not as man lies by woman, when the bride
Laughs low for love's sake and the words he saith.

For she lies, laughing low with love; she lies
And turns his kisses on her lips to sighs,
   To sighing sound of lips unsatisfied,
And the sweet tears are tender with her eyes.

Ah, not as they, but as the souls that were
Slain in the old time, having found her fair;
   Who, sleeping with her lips upon their eyes,
Heard sudden serpents hiss across her hair.

Their blood runs round the roots of time like rain:
She casts them forth and gathers them again;
   With nerve and bone she weaves and multiplies
Exceeding pleasure out of extreme pain.

Her little chambers drip with flower-like red,
Her girdles, and the chaplets of her head,
    Her armlets and her anklets; with her feet
She tramples all that winepress of the dead.

Her gateways smoke with fume of flowers and   125
        fires,
With loves burnt out and unassuaged desires;
    Between her lips the steam of them is sweet,
The languor in her ears of many lyres.

Her beds are full of perfume and sad sound,
Her doors are made with music, and barred round   130
    With sighing and with laughter and with tears,
With tears whereby strong souls of men are bound.

There is the knight Adonis that was slain;
With flesh and blood she chains him for a chain;
    The body and the spirit in her ears   135
Cry, for her lips divide him vein by vein.

Yea, all she slayeth; yea, every man save me;
Me, love, thy lover that must cleave to thee
    Till the ending of the days and ways of earth,
The shaking of the sources of the sea.   140

Me, most forsaken of all souls that fell;
Me, satiated with things insatiable;
    Me, for whose sake the extreme hell makes mirth,
Yea, laughter kindles at the heart of hell.

Alas thy beauty! for thy mouth's sweet sake   145
My soul is bitter to me, my limbs quake
    As water, as the flesh of men that weep,
As their heart's vein whose heart goes nigh to break.

Ah God, that sleep with flower-sweet finger-tips
150 Would crush the fruit of death upon my lips;
Ah God, that death would tread the grapes of sleep
And wring their juice upon me as it drips.

There is no change of cheer for many days,
But change of chimes high up in the air, that sways
155   Rung by the running fingers of the wind;
And singing sorrows heard on hidden ways.

Day smiteth day in twain, night sundereth night,
And on mine eyes the dark sits as the light;
      Yea, Lord, thou knowest I know not, having sinned,
160 If heaven be clean or unclean in thy sight.

Yea, as if earth were sprinkled over me,
Such chafed harsh earth as chokes a sandy sea,
      Each pore doth yearn, and the dried blood thereof
Gasps by sick fits, my heart swims heavily,

165 There is a feverish famine in my veins;
Below her bosom, where a crushed grape stains
      The white and blue, there my lips caught and clove
An hour since, and what mark of me remains?

I dare not always touch her, lest the kiss
170 Leave my lips charred. Yea, Lord, a little bliss,
      Brief bitter bliss, one hath for a great sin;
Nathless thou knowest how sweet a thing it is.

Sin, is it sin whereby men's souls are thrust
Into the pit? yet had I a good trust
175   To save my soul before it slipped therein,
Trod under by the fire-shod feet of lust.

For if mine eyes fail and my soul takes breath,
I look between the iron sides of death
   Into sad hell where all sweet love hath end,
All but the pain that never finisheth.   180

There are the naked faces of great kings,
The singing folk with all their lute-playings;
   There when one cometh he shall have to friend
The grave that covets and the worm that clings.

There sit the knights that were so great of hand,   185
The ladies that were queens of fair green land,
   Grown grey and black now, brought unto the dust,
Soiled, without raiment, clad about with sand.

There is one end for all of them; they sit
Naked and sad, they drink the dregs of it,   190
   Trodden as grapes in the wine-press of lust,
Trampled and trodden by the fiery feet.

I see the marvellous mouth whereby there fell
Cities and people whom the gods loved well,
   Yet for her sake on them the fire gat hold,   195
And for their sakes on her the fire of hell.

And softer than the Egyptian lote-leaf is,
The queen whose face was worth the world to kiss,
   Wearing at breast a suckling snake of gold;
And large pale lips of strong Semiramis,   200

Curled like a tiger's that curl back to feed;
Red only where the last kiss made them bleed;
   Her hair most thick with many a carven gem,
Deep in the mane, great-chested, like a steed.

205   Yea, with red sin the faces of them shine;
But in all these there was no sin like mine;
   No, not in all the strange great sins of them
That made the wine-press froth and foam with wine.

For I was of Christ's choosing, I God's knight,
210   No blinkard heathen stumbling for scant light;
   I can well see, for all the dusty days
Gone past, the clean great time of goodly fight.

I smell the breathing battle sharp with blows,
With shriek of shafts and snapping short of bows;
215   The fair pure sword smites out in subtle ways,
Sounds and long lights are shed between the rows

Of beautiful mailed men; the edged light slips,
Most like a snake that takes short breath and dips
   Sharp from the beautifully bending head,
220   With all its gracious body lithe as lips

That curl in touching you; right in this wise
My sword doth, seeming fire in mine own eyes,
   Leaving all colours in them brown and red
And flecked with death; then the keen breaths like
     sighs,

225   The caught-up choked dry laughters following them,
When all the fighting face is grown a flame
   For pleasure, and the pulse that stuns the ears,
And the heart's gladness of the goodly game.

Let me think yet a little; I do know
230   These things were sweet, but sweet such years ago,
   Their savour is all turned now into tears;
Yea, ten years since, where the blue ripples blow,

The blue curled eddies of the blowing Rhine,
I felt the sharp wind shaking grass and vine
   Touch my blood too, and sting me with delight   235
Through all this waste and weary body of mine

That never feels clear air; right gladly then
I rode alone, a great way off my men,
   And heard the chiming bridle smite and smite,
And gave each rhyme thereof some rhyme again,   240

Till my song shifted to that iron one;
Seeing there rode up between me and the sun
   Some certain of my foe's men, for his three
White wolves across their painted coats did run.

The first red-bearded, with square checks – alack,   245
I made my knave's blood turn his beard to black;
   The slaying of him was a joy to see:
Perchance too, when at night he came not back,

Some woman fell a-weeping, whom this thief
Would beat when he had drunken; yet small grief   250
   Hath any for the ridding of such knaves;
Yea, if one wept, I doubt her teen was brief.

This bitter love is sorrow in all lands,
Draining of eyelids, wringing of drenched hands,
   Sighing of hearts and filling up of graves;   255
A sign across the head of the world he stands,

An one that hath a plague-mark on his brows;
Dust and spilt blood do track him to his house
   Down under earth; sweet smells of lip and cheek,
Like a sweet snake's breath made more poisonous   260

With chewing of some perfumed deadly grass,
Are shed all round his passage if he pass,
     And their quenched savour leaves the whole soul weak,
Sick with keen guessing whence the perfume was.

265   As one who hidden in deep sedge and reeds
Smells the rare scent made where a panther feeds,
     And tracking ever slotwise the warm smell
Is snapped upon by the sweet mouth and bleeds,

His head far down the hot sweet throat of her –
270   So one tracks love, whose breath is deadlier,
     And lo, one springe and you are fast in hell,
Fast as the gin's grip of a wayfarer.

I think now, as the heavy hours decease
One after one, and bitter thoughts increase
275   One upon one, of all sweet finished things;
The breaking of the battle; the long peace

Wherein we sat clothed softly, each man's hair
Crowned with green leaves beneath white hoods of vair;
     The sounds of sharp spears at great tourneyings,
280   And noise of singing in the late sweet air.

I sang of love too, knowing nought thereof;
'Sweeter,' I said, 'the little laugh of love
     Than tears out of the eyes of Magdalen,
Or any fallen feather of the Dove.

285   'The broken little laugh that spoils a kiss,
The ache of purple pulses, and the bliss
     Of blinded eyelids that expand again –
Love draws them open with those lips of his,

'Lips that cling hard till the kissed face has grown
Of one same fire and colour with their own;   290
   Then ere one sleep, appeased with sacrifice,
Where his lips wounded, there his lips atone.'

I sang these things long since and knew them not;
'Lo, here is love, or there is love, God wot,
   This man and that finds favour in his eyes,'   295
I said, 'but I, what guerdon have I got?

'The dust of praise that is blown everywhere
In all men's faces with the common air;
   The bay-leaf that wants chafing to be sweet
Before they wind it in a singer's hair.'   300

So that one dawn I rode forth sorrowing;
I had no hope but of some evil thing,
   And so rode slowly past the windy wheat
And past the vineyard and the water-spring,

Up to the Horsel. A great elder-tree   305
Held back its heaps of flowers to let me see
   The ripe tall grass, and one that walked therein,
Naked, with hair shed over to the knee.

She walked between the blossom and the grass;
I knew the beauty of her, what she was,   310
   The beauty of her body and her sin,
And in my flesh the sin of hers, alas!

Alas! for sorrow is all the end of this.
O sad kissed mouth, how sorrowful it is!
   O breast whereat some suckling sorrow clings,   315
Red with the bitter blossom of a kiss!

Ah, with blind lips I felt for you, and found
About my neck your hands and hair enwound,
   The hands that stifle and the hair that stings,
320   I felt them fasten sharply without sound.

Yea, for my sin I had great store of bliss:
Rise up, make answer for me, let thy kiss
   Seal my lips hard from speaking of my sin,
Lest one go mad to hear how sweet it is.

325   Yet I waxed faint with fume of barren bowers,
And murmuring of the heavy-headed hours;
   And let the dove's beak fret and peck within
My lips in vain, and Love shed fruitless flowers.

So that God looked upon me when your hands
330   Were hot about me; yea, God brake my bands
   To save my soul alive, and I came forth
Like a man blind and naked in strange lands

That hears men laugh and weep, and knows not whence
Nor wherefore, but is broken in his sense;
335   Howbeit I met folk riding from the north
Towards Rome, to purge them of their souls' offence,

And rode with them, and spake to none; the day
Stunned me like lights upon some wizard way,
   And ate like fire mine eyes and mine eyesight;
340   So rode I, hearing all these chant and pray,

And marvelled; till before us rose and fell
White cursed hills, like outer skirts of hell
   Seen where men's eyes look through the day to night,
Like a jagged shell's lips, harsh, untunable,

Blown in between by devils' wrangling breath;   345
Nathless we won well past that hell and death,
  Down to the sweet land where all airs are good,
Even unto Rome where God's grace tarrieth.

Then came each man and worshipped at his knees
Who in the Lord God's likeness bears the keys   350
  To bind or loose, and called on Christ's shed
      blood,
And so the sweet-souled father gave him ease.

But when I came I fell down at his feet,
Saying, 'Father, though the Lord's blood be right
      sweet,
  The spot it takes not off the panther's skin,   355
Nor shall an Ethiop's stain be bleached with it.

'Lo, I have sinned and have spat out at God,
Wherefore his hand is heavier and his rod
  More sharp because of mine exceeding sin,
And all his raiment redder than bright blood   360

'Before mine eyes; yea, for my sake I wot
The heat of hell is waxen seven times hot
  Through my great sin.' Then spake he some sweet
      word,
Giving me cheer; which thing availed me not;

Yea, scarce I wist if such indeed were said;   365
For when I ceased – lo, as one newly dead
  Who hears a great cry out of hell, I heard
The crying of his voice across my head.

'Until this dry shred staff, that hath no whit
Of leaf nor bark, bear blossom and smell sweet,   370
  Seek thou not any mercy in God's sight,
For so long shalt thou be cast out from it.'

Yea, what if dried-up stems wax red and green,
Shall that thing be which is not nor has been?
375   Yea, what if sapless bark wax green and white,
Shall any good fruit grow upon my sin?

Nay, though sweet fruit were plucked of a dry tree,
And though men drew sweet waters of the sea,
      There should not grow sweet leaves on this dead stem,
380   This waste wan body and shaken soul of me.

Yea, though God search it warily enough,
There is not one sound thing in all thereof;
      Though he search all my veins through, searching
          them
He shall find nothing whole therein but love.

385   For I came home right heavy, with small cheer,
And lo my love, mine own soul's heart, more dear
      Than mine own soul, more beautiful than God,
Who hath my being between the hands of her –

Fair still, but fair for no man saving me,
390   As when she came out of the naked sea
      Making the foam as fire whereon she trod,
And as the inner flower of fire was she.

Yea, she laid hold upon me, and her mouth
Clove unto mine as soul to body doth,
395   And, laughing, made her lips luxurious;
Her hair had smells of all the sunburnt south,

Strange spice and flower, strange savour of crushed fruit,
And perfume the swart kings tread underfoot
      For pleasure when their minds wax amorous,
400   Charred frankincense and grated sandal-root.

And I forgot fear and all weary things,
All ended prayers and perished thanksgivings,
  Feeling her face with all her eager hair
Cleave to me, clinging as a fire that clings

To the body and to the raiment, burning them;   405
As after death I know that such-like flame
  Shall cleave to me for ever; yea, what care,
Albeit I burn then, having felt the same?

Ah love, there is no better life than this;
To have known love, how bitter a thing it is,   410
  And afterward be cast out of God's sight;
Yea, these that know not, shall they have such bliss

High up in barren heaven before his face
As we twain in the heavy-hearted place,
  Remembering love and all the dead delight,   415
And all that time was sweet with for a space?

For till the thunder in the trumpet be,
Soul may divide from body, but not we
  One from another; I hold thee with my hand,
I let mine eyes have all their will of thee,   420

I seal myself upon thee with my might,
Abiding alway out of all men's sight
  Until God loosen over sea and land
The thunder of the trumpets of the night.

A Match

If love were what the rose is,
    And I were like the leaf,
Our lives would grow together
In sad or singing weather,
Blown fields or flowerful closes,
    Green pleasure or grey grief;
If love were what the rose is,
    And I were like the leaf.

If I were what the words are,
    And love were like the tune,
With double sound and single
Delight our lips would mingle,
With kisses glad as birds are
    That get sweet rain at noon;
If I were what the words are,
    And love were like the tune.

If you were life, my darling,
    And I your love were death,
We'd shine and snow together
Ere March made sweet the weather
With daffodil and starling
    And hours of fruitful breath;
If you were life, my darling,
    And I your love were death.

If you were thrall to sorrow,
    And I were page to joy,
We'd play for lives and seasons
With loving looks and treasons
And tears of night and morrow
    And laughs of maid and boy;
If you were thrall to sorrow,
    And I were page to joy.

    If you were April's lady,
      And I were lord in May,
    We'd throw with leaves for hours   35
    And draw for days with flowers,
    Till day like night were shady
      And night were bright like day;
    If you were April's lady,
      And I were lord in May.   40

    If you were queen of pleasure,
      And I were king of pain,
    We'd hunt down love together,
    Pluck out his flying-feather,
    And teach his feet a measure,   45
      And find his mouth a rein;
    If you were queen of pleasure,
      And I were king of pain.

A Cameo

There was a graven image of Desire
    Painted with red blood on a ground of gold
    Passing between the young men and the old,
And by him Pain, whose body shone like fire,
And Pleasure with gaunt hands that grasped their hire.   5
    Of his left wrist, with fingers clenched and cold,
    The insatiable Satiety kept hold,
Walking with feet unshod that pashed the mire.
The senses and the sorrows and the sins,
    And the strange loves that suck the breasts of   10
      Hate
Till lips and teeth bite in their sharp indenture,
Followed like beasts with flap of wings and fins.
    Death stood aloof behind a gaping grate,
Upon whose lock was written *Peradventure*.

The Leper

Nothing is better, I well think,
   Than love; the hidden well-water
Is not so delicate to drink:
   This was well seen of me and her.

5   I served her in a royal house;
   I served her wine and curious meat.
For will to kiss between her brows,
   I had no heart to sleep or eat.

Mere scorn God knows she had of me,
10   A poor scribe, nowise great or fair,
Who plucked his clerk's hood back to see
   Her curled-up lips and amorous hair.

I vex my head with thinking this.
   Yea, though God always hated me,
15   And hates me now that I can kiss
   Her eyes, plait up her hair to see

How she then wore it on the brows,
   Yet am I glad to have her dead
Here in this wretched wattled house
20   Where I can kiss her eyes and head.

Nothing is better, I well know,
   Than love; no amber in cold sea
Or gathered berries under snow:
   That is well seen of her and me.

25   Three thoughts I make my pleasure of:
   First I take heart and think of this:
That knight's gold hair she chose to love,
   His mouth she had such will to kiss.

Then I remember that sundawn
   I brought him by a privy way   30
Out at her lattice, and thereon
   What gracious words she found to say.

(Cold rushes for such little feet –
   Both feet could lie into my hand.
A marvel was it of my sweet   35
   Her upright body could so stand.)

'Sweet friend, God give you thank and grace;
   Now am I clean and whole of shame,
Nor shall men burn me in the face
   For my sweet fault that scandals them.'   40

I tell you over word by word.
   She, sitting edgewise on her bed,
Holding her feet, said thus. The third,
   A sweeter thing than these, I said.

God, that makes time and ruins it   45
   And alters not, abiding God,
Changed with disease her body sweet,
   The body of love wherein she abode.

Love is more sweet and comelier
   Than a dove's throat strained out to sing.   50
All they spat out and cursed at her
   And cast her forth for a base thing.

They cursed her, seeing how God had wrought
   This curse to plague her, a curse of his.
Fools were they surely, seeing not   55
   How sweeter than all sweet she is.

He that had held her by the hair,
　　With kissing lips blinding her eyes,
Felt her bright bosom, strained and bare,
60　　　Sigh under him, with short mad cries

Out of her throat and sobbing mouth
　　And body broken up with love,
With sweet hot tears his lips were loth
　　Her own should taste the savour of,

65　Yea, he inside whose grasp all night
　　Her fervent body leapt or lay,
Stained with sharp kisses red and white,
　　Found her a plague to spurn away.

I hid her in this wattled house,
70　　I served her water and poor bread.
For joy to kiss between her brows
　　Time upon time I was nigh dead.

Bread failed; we got but well-water
　　And gathered grass with dropping seed.
75　I had such joy of kissing her,
　　I had small care to sleep or feed.

Sometimes when service made me glad
　　The sharp tears leapt between my lids,
Falling on her, such joy I had
80　　To do the service God forbids.

'I pray you let me be at peace,
　　Get hence, make room for me to die.'
She said that: her poor lip would cease,
　　Put up to mine, and turn to cry.

I said, 'Bethink yourself how love   85
    Fared in us twain, what either did;
Shall I unclothe my soul thereof?
    That I should do this, God forbid.'

Yea, though God hateth us, he knows
    That hardly in a little thing   90
Love faileth of the work it does
    Till it grow ripe for gathering.

Six months, and now my sweet is dead
    A trouble takes me; I know not
If all were done well, all well said,   95
    No word or tender deed forgot.

Too sweet, for the least part in her,
    To have shed life out by fragments; yet,
Could the close mouth catch breath and stir,
    I might see something I forget.   100

Six months, and I sit still and hold
    In two cold palms her cold two feet.
Her hair, half grey half ruined gold,
    Thrills me and burns me in kissing it.

Love bites and stings me through, to see   105
    Her keen face made of sunken bones.
Her worn-off eyelids madden me,
    That were shot through with purple once.

She said, 'Be good with me; I grow
    So tired for shame's sake, I shall die   110
If you say nothing:' even so.
    And she is dead now, and shame put by.

Yea, and the scorn she had of me
  In the old time, doubtless vexed her then.
115 I never should have kissed her. See
    What fools God's anger makes of men!

She might have loved me a little too,
  Had I been humbler for her sake.
But that new shame could make love new
120   She saw not – yet her shame did make.

I took too much upon my love,
  Having for such mean service done
Her beauty and all the ways thereof,
  Her face and all the sweet thereon.

125 Yea, all this while I tended her,
    I know the old love held fast his part:
I know the old scorn waxed heavier,
    Mixed with sad wonder, in her heart.

It may be all my love went wrong –
130   A scribe's work writ awry and blurred,
Scrawled after the blind evensong –
    Spoilt music with no perfect word.

But surely I would fain have done
  All things the best I could. Perchance
135 Because I failed, came short of one,
    She kept at heart that other man's.

I am grown blind with all these things:
  It may be now she hath in sight
Some better knowledge; still there clings
140   The old question. Will not God do right?

A Ballad of Burdens

The burden of fair women. Vain delight,
   And love self-slain in some sweet shameful way,
And sorrowful old age that comes by night
   As a thief comes that has no heart by day,
   And change that finds fair cheeks and leaves them 5
     grey,
And weariness that keeps awake for hire,
   And grief that says what pleasure used to say;
This is the end of every man's desire.

The burden of bought kisses. This is sore,
   A burden without fruit in childbearing;   10
Between the nightfall and the dawn threescore,
   Threescore between the dawn and evening.
   The shuddering in thy lips, the shuddering
In thy sad eyelids tremulous like fire,
   Makes love seem shameful and a wretched thing.   15
This is the end of every man's desire.

The burden of sweet speeches. Nay, kneel down,
   Cover thy head, and weep; for verily
These market-men that buy thy white and brown
   In the last days shall take no thought for thee.   20
   In the last days like earth thy face shall be,
Yea, like sea-marsh made thick with brine and mire,
   Sad with sick leavings of the sterile sea.
This is the end of every man's desire.

The burden of long living. Thou shalt fear   25
   Waking, and sleeping mourn upon thy bed;
And say at night 'Would God the day were here,'
   And say at dawn 'Would God the day were dead.'
   With weary days thou shalt be clothed and fed,
And wear remorse of heart for thine attire,   30
   Pain for thy girdle and sorrow upon thine head;
This is the end of every man's desire.

The burden of bright colours. Thou shalt see
   Gold tarnished, and the grey above the green;
35 And as the thing thou seest thy face shall be,
   And no more as the thing beforetime seen.
   And thou shalt say of mercy 'It hath been,'
And living, watch the old lips and loves expire,
   And talking, tears shall take thy breath between;
40 This is the end of every man's desire.

The burden of sad sayings. In that day
   Thou shalt tell all thy days and hours, and tell
Thy times and ways and words of love, and say
   How one was dear and one desirable,
45 And sweet was life to hear and sweet to smell,
But now with lights reverse the old hours retire
   And the last hour is shod with fire from hell.
This is the end of every man's desire.

The burden of four seasons. Rain in spring,
50 White rain and wind among the tender trees;
A summer of green sorrows gathering,
   Rank autumn in a mist of miseries,
   With sad face set towards the year, that sees
The charred ash drop out of the dropping pyre,
55 And winter wan with many maladies;
This is the end of every man's desire.

The burden of dead faces. Out of sight
   And out of love, beyond the reach of hands,
Changed in the changing of the dark and light,
60 They walk and weep about the barren lands
   Where no seed is nor any garner stands,
Where in short breaths the doubtful days respire,
   And time's turned glass lets through the sighing sands;
This is the end of every man's desire.

The burden of much gladness. Life and lust   65
   Forsake thee, and the face of thy delight;
And underfoot the heavy hour strews dust,
   And overhead strange weathers burn and bite;
   And where the red was, lo the bloodless white,
And where truth was, the likeness of a liar,   70
   And where day was, the likeness of the night;
This is the end of every man's desire.

L'ENVOY

Princes, and ye whom pleasure quickeneth,
   Heed well this rhyme before your pleasure tire;
For life is sweet, but after life is death.   75
   This is the end of every man's desire.

The Garden of Proserpine

Here, where the world is quiet;
   Here, where all trouble seems
Dead winds' and spent waves' riot
   In doubtful dreams of dreams;
I watch the green field growing   5
For reaping folk and sowing,
For harvest-time and mowing,
   A sleepy world of streams.

I am tired of tears and laughter,
   And men that laugh and weep;   10
Of what may come hereafter
   For men that sow to reap:
I am weary of days and hours,
Blown buds of barren flowers,
Desires and dreams and powers   15
   And everything but sleep.

Here life has death for neighbour,
        And far from eye or ear
Wan waves and wet winds labour,
        Weak ships and spirits steer;
They drive adrift, and whither
They wot not who make thither;
But no such winds blow hither,
        And no such things grow here.

No growth of moor or coppice,
        No heather-flower or vine,
But bloomless buds of poppies,
        Green grapes of Proserpine,
Pale beds of blowing rushes
Where no leaf blooms or blushes
Save this whereout she crushes
        For dead men deadly wine.

Pale, without name or number,
        In fruitless fields of corn,
They bow themselves and slumber
        All night till light is born;
And like a soul belated,
In hell and heaven unmated,
By cloud and mist abated
        Comes out of darkness morn.

Though one were strong as seven,
        He too with death shall dwell,
Nor wake with wings in heaven,
        Nor weep for pains in hell;
Though one were fair as roses,
His beauty clouds and closes;
And well though love reposes,
        In the end it is not well.

Pale, beyond porch and portal,
   Crowned with calm leaves, she stands   50
Who gathers all things mortal
   With cold immortal hands;
Her languid lips are sweeter
Than love's who fears to greet her
To men that mix and meet her   55
   From many times and lands.

She waits for each and other,
   She waits for all men born;
Forgets the earth her mother,
   The life of fruits and corn;   60
And spring and seed and swallow
Take wing for her and follow
Where summer song rings hollow
   And flowers are put to scorn.

There go the loves that wither,   65
   The old loves with wearier wings;
And all dead years draw thither,
   And all disastrous things;
Dead dreams of days forsaken,
Blind buds that snows have shaken,   70
Wild leaves that winds have taken,
   Red strays of ruined springs.

We are not sure of sorrow,
   And joy was never sure;
To-day will die to-morrow;   75
   Time stoops to no man's lure;
And love, grown faint and fretful,
With lips but half regretful
Sighs, and with eyes forgetful
   Weeps that no loves endure.   80

From too much love of living,
   From hope and fear set free,
We thank with brief thanksgiving
   Whatever gods may be
85   That no life lives for ever;
That dead men rise up never;
That even the weariest river
   Winds somewhere safe to sea.

Then star nor sun shall waken,
90   Nor any change of light:
Nor sound of waters shaken,
   Nor any sound or sight:
Nor wintry leaves nor vernal,
Nor days nor things diurnal;
95   Only the sleep eternal
   In an eternal night.

Before Parting

A month or twain to live on honeycomb
Is pleasant; but one tires of scented time,
Cold sweet recurrence of accepted rhyme,
And that strong purple under juice and foam
5   Where the wine's heart has burst;
Nor feel the latter kisses like the first.

Once yet, this poor one time; I will not pray
Even to change the bitterness of it,
The bitter taste ensuing on the sweet,
10   To make your tears fall where your soft hair lay
All blurred and heavy in some perfumed wise
Over my face and eyes.

And yet who knows what end the scythèd wheat
Makes of its foolish poppies' mouths of red?
15   These were not sown, these are not harvested,

They grow a month and are cast under feet
   And none has care thereof,
   As none has care of a divided love.

I know each shadow of your lips by rote,
   Each change of love in eyelids and eyebrows;   20
The fashion of fair temples tremulous
With tender blood, and colour of your throat;
   I know not how love is gone out of this,
   Seeing that all was his.

Love's likeness there endures upon all these: 25
   But out of these one shall not gather love.
Day hath not strength nor the night shade enough
To make love whole and fill his lips with ease,
   As some bee-builded cell
   Feels at filled lips the heavy honey swell.   30

I know not how this last month leaves your hair
   Less full of purple colour and hid spice,
   And that luxurious trouble of closed eyes
Is mixed with meaner shadow and waste care;
   And love, kissed out by pleasure, seems not yet   35
   Worth patience to regret.

Love and Sleep

Lying asleep between the strokes of night
   I saw my love lean over my sad bed,
   Pale as the duskiest lily's leaf or head,
Smooth-skinned and dark, with bare throat made to bite,
Too wan for blushing and too warm for white,   5
   But perfect-coloured without white or red,
   And her lips opened amorously, and said –
I wist not what, saving one word – Delight.
And all her face was honey to my mouth,
   And all her body pasture to mine eyes;   10

The long lithe arms and hotter hands than fire,
The quivering flanks, hair smelling of the south,
The bright light feet, the splendid supple thighs
And glittering eyelids of my soul's desire.

The King's Daughter

We were ten maidens in the green corn,
    Small red leaves in the mill-water:
Fairer maidens never were born,
    Apples of gold for the king's daughter.

We were ten maidens by a well-head,
    Small white birds in the mill-water:
Sweeter maidens never were wed,
    Rings of red for the king's daughter.

The first to spin, the second to sing,
    Seeds of wheat in the mill-water;
The third may was a goodly thing,
    White bread and brown for the king's daughter.

The fourth to sew and the fifth to play,
    Fair green weed in the mill-water;
The sixth may was a goodly may,
    White wine and red for the king's daughter.

The seventh to woo, the eighth to wed,
    Fair thin reeds in the mill-water;
The ninth had gold work on her head,
    Honey in the comb for the king's daughter.

The ninth had gold work round her hair,
    Fallen flowers in the mill-water;
The tenth may was goodly and fair,
    Golden gloves for the king's daughter.

We were ten maidens in a field green,   25
   Fallen fruit in the mill-water;
Fairer maidens never have been,
   Golden sleeves for the king's daughter.

By there comes the king's young son,
   A little wind in the mill-water;   30
'Out of ten maidens ye'll grant me one,'
   A crown of red for the king's daughter.

'Out of ten mays ye'll give me the best,'
   A little rain in the mill-water;
A bed of yellow straw for all the rest,   35
   A bed of gold for the king's daughter.

He's ta'en out the goodliest,
   Rain that rains in the mill-water;
A comb of yellow shell for all the rest,
   A comb of gold for the king's daughter.   40

He's made her bed to the goodliest,
   Wind and hail in the mill-water;
A grass girdle for all the rest,
   A girdle of arms for the king's daughter.

He's set his heart to the goodliest,   45
   Snow that snows in the mill-water;
Nine little kisses for all the rest,
   An hundredfold for the king's daughter.

He's ta'en his leave at the goodliest,
   Broken boats in the mill-water;   50
Golden gifts for all the rest,
   Sorrow of heart for the king's daughter.

'Ye'll make a grave for my fair body,'
   Running rain in the mill-water;
55 'And ye'll streek my brother at the side of me,'
   The pains of hell for the king's daughter.

A Ballad of Dreamland

I hid my heart in a nest of roses,
   Out of the sun's way, hidden apart;
In a softer bed than the soft white snow's is,
   Under the roses I hid my heart.
5   Why would it sleep not? why should it start,
When never a leaf of the rose-tree stirred?
   What made sleep flutter his wings and part?
Only the song of a secret bird.

Lie still, I said, for the wind's wing closes,
10   And mild leaves muffle the keen sun's dart;
Lie still, for the wind on the warm sea dozes,
   And the wind is unquieter yet than thou art.
   Does a thought in thee still as a thorn's wound smart?
Does the fang still fret thee of hope deferred?
15   What bids the lids of thy sleep dispart?
Only the song of a secret bird.

The green land's name that a charm encloses,
   It never was writ in the traveller's chart,
And sweet on its trees as the fruit that grows is,
20   It never was sold in the merchant's mart.
   The swallows of dreams through its dim fields dart,
And sleep's are the tunes in its tree-tops heard;
   No hound's note wakens the wildwood hart,
Only the song of a secret bird.

ENVOI

In the world of dreams I have chosen my part,   25
   To sleep for a season and hear no word
Of true love's truth or of light love's art,
Only the song of a secret bird.

Sonnet for a Picture

That nose is out of drawing. With a gasp,
   She pants upon the passionate lips that ache
   With the red drain of her own mouth, and make
A monochord of colour. Like an asp,
One lithe lock wriggles in his rutilant grasp.   5
   Her bosom is an oven of myrrh, to bake
   Love's white warm shewbread to a browner cake.
The lock his fingers clench has burst its hasp.
The legs are absolutely abominable.
   Ah! what keen overgust of wild-eyed woes   10
   Flags in that bosom, flushes in that nose?
Nay! Death sets riddles for desire to spell,
   Responsive. What red hem earth's passion sews,
But may be ravenously unripped in hell?

From *Tristram of Lyonesse*

I

THE SAILING OF THE SWALLOW

About the middle music of the spring
Came from the castled shore of Ireland's king
A fair ship stoutly sailing, eastward bound
And south by Wales and all its wonders round
To the loud rocks and ringing reaches home   5
That take the wild wrath of the Cornish foam,

Past Lyonesse unswallowed of the tides
And high Carlion that now the steep sea hides
To the wind-hollowed heights and gusty bays
10   Of sheer Tintagel, fair with famous days.
Above the stem a gilded swallow shone,
Wrought with straight wings and eyes of glittering stone
As flying sunward oversea, to bear
Green summer with it through the singing air.
15   And on the deck between the rowers at dawn,
As the bright sail with brightening wind was drawn,
Sat with full face against the strengthening light
Iseult, more fair than foam or dawn was white.
Her gaze was glad past love's own singing of,
20   And her face lovely past desire of love.
Past thought and speech her maiden motions were,
And a more golden sunrise was her hair.
The very veil of her bright flesh was made
As of light woven and moonbeam-coloured shade
25   More fine than moonbeams; white her eyelids shone
As snow sun-stricken that endures the sun,
And through their curled and coloured clouds of deep
Luminous lashes thick as dreams in sleep
Shone as the sea's depth swallowing up the sky's
30   The springs of unimaginable eyes.
As the wave's subtler emerald is pierced through
With the utmost heaven's inextricable blue,
And both are woven and molten in one sleight
Of amorous colour and implicated light
35   Under the golden guard and gaze of noon,
So glowed their awless amorous plenilune,
Azure and gold and ardent grey, made strange
With fiery difference and deep interchange
Inexplicable of glories multiform;
40   Now as the sullen sapphire swells toward storm
Foamless, their bitter beauty grew acold,
And now afire with ardour of fine gold.
Her flower-soft lips were meek and passionate,
For love upon them like a shadow sate

Patient, a foreseen vision of sweet things,   45
A dream with eyes fast shut and plumeless wings
That knew not what man's love or life should be,
Nor had it sight nor heart to hope or see
What thing should come, but childlike satisfied
Watched out its virgin vigil in soft pride   50
And unkissed expectation; and the glad
Clear cheeks and throat and tender temples had
Such maiden heat as if a rose's blood
Beat in the live heart of a lily-bud.
Between the small round breasts a white way led   55
Heavenward, and from slight foot to slender head
The whole fair body flower-like swayed and shone
Moving, and what her light hand leant upon
Grew blossom-scented: her warm arms began
To round and ripen for delight of man   60
That they should clasp and circle: her fresh hands,
Like regent lilies of reflowering lands
Whose vassal firstlings, crown and star and plume,
Bow down to the empire of that sovereign bloom,
Shone sceptreless, and from her face there went   65
A silent light as of a God content;
Save when, more swift and keen than love or shame,
Some flash of blood, light as the laugh of flame,
Broke it with sudden beam and shining speech,
As dream by dream shot through her eyes, and   70
   each
Outshone the last that lightened, and not one
Showed her such things as should be borne and done.
Though hard against her shone the sunlike face
That in all change and wreck of time and place
Should be the star of her sweet living soul.   75

A Death on Easter Day

The strong spring sun rejoicingly may rise,
   Rise and make revel, as of old men said,
   Like dancing hearts of lovers newly wed:
A light more bright than ever bathed the skies
5 Departs for all time out of all men's eyes.
   The crowns that girt last night a living head
   Shine only now, though deathless, on the dead:
Art that mocks death, and Song that never dies.
Albeit the bright sweet mothlike wings be furled,
10   Hope sees, past all division and defection,
    And higher than swims the mist of human breath,
The soul most radiant once in all the world
   Requickened to regenerate resurrection
    Out of the likeness of the shadow of death.

A Ballad of Appeal
To Christina G. Rossetti

Song wakes with every wakening year
   From hearts of birds that only feel
Brief spring's deciduous flower-time near:
   And song more strong to help or heal
5   Shall silence worse than winter seal?
From love-lit thought's remurmuring cave
The notes that rippled, wave on wave,
   Were clear as love, as faith were strong;
And all souls blessed the soul that gave
10   Sweet water from the well of song.

All hearts bore fruit of joy to hear,
   All eyes felt mist upon them steal
For joy's sake, trembling toward a tear,
   When, loud as marriage-bells that peal,
15   Or flutelike soft, or keen like steel,

Sprang the sheer music; sharp or grave,
We heard the drift of winds that drave,
   And saw, swept round by ghosts in throng,
Dark rocks, that yielded, where they clave,
   Sweet water from the well of song.   20

Blithe verse made all the dim sense clear
   That smiles of babbling babes conceal:
Prayer's perfect heart spake here: and here
   Rose notes of blameless woe and weal,
   More soft than this poor song's appeal.   25
Where orchards bask, where cornfields wave,
They dropped like rains that cleanse and lave,
   And scattered all the year along,
Like dewfall on an April grave,
   Sweet water from the well of song.   30

Ballad, go bear our prayer, and crave
Pardon, because thy lowlier stave
   Can do this plea no right, but wrong.
Ask nought beside thy pardon, save
   Sweet water from the well of song.   35

JOHN PAYNE

This is the House of Dreams. Whoso is fain
   To enter in this shadow-land of mine,
   He must forget the utter Summer's shine
And all the daylight ways of hand and brain:
Here is the white moon ever on the wane,
   And here the air is sad with many a sign
   Of haunting mysteries, – the golden wine
Of June falls never, nor the silver rain
   Of hawthorns pallid with the joy of Spring;
But many a mirage of pale memories
Veils up the sunless aisles: upon the breeze
   A music of waste sighs doth float and sing;
And in the shadow of the sad-flower'd trees,
   The ghosts of men's desire walk wandering.

From *Sir Floris*

I

THE FIRST COMING OF THE DOVE

Hard by the confluence of Rhone
A castle of old times alone
   Upon a high grey hill did stand,
   And look'd across the pleasant land;
And of the castle castellain
And lord of all the wide domain
   Of golden field and purple wood
   And vineyards where the vine-rows stood
In many a trellis, Floris was;
A good knight and a valorous,
   And in all courtesies approved,
   That unto valiantise behoved.
Full young he was and fair of face,
And among ladies had much grace,
   And favour of all men likewise:
   For in such stout and valiant guise

His years of manhood had he spent
In knightly quest and tournament,
   There was no knight in all the land
   Whose name in more renown did stand,   20
And the foe quaked to look upon
The white plume of his morion,
   When through the grinding shock of spears
   Sir Floris' war-cry pierced their ears
And over all the din was blown   25
The silver of his clarion.

   So was much ease prepared for him,
   And safety from the need and grim
Hard battle against gibe and sneer
That must full oft be foughten here –   30
   For evil fortune and the lack
   Of strength to thrust the envious back –
By many a noble soul and true;
And had he chosen to ensue
   The well-worn path that many tread   35
   For worship, all his life were spread
Before him, level with delight.
But if in shock of arms and fight
   Of squadrons he disdainèd not
   To win renown, the silken lot   40
Of those that pass their days in ease
And dalliance on the flower'd leas
   Of life was hateful to his soul;
   And so – when once the battle's roll
And thunder was from off the lands   45
Turn'd back and from the war-worn hands
   The weapons fell – he could not bring
   His heart to brook the wearying
Of peace and indolent disport
Of ease. Wherefore he left the court –   50
   So secretly that no one knew
   Awhile his absence – and withdrew

A season to his own demesne,
And there in solitude was fain
    To yearn for some fair chance to hap
    And win his living from the lap
Of drowsy idlesse with some quest,
That should from that unlovely rest
    Redeem him to the old delight
    Of plucking – in the bold despite
Of danger – from the brows of Fate
Some laurel. Nor had he to wait
    The cooling of his knightly fire;
    There was vouchsafed to his desire,
Ere long, a very parlous quest,
That should unto the utterest
Assay his knightly worth and test
    The temper of his soul full well
    And sore. And in this wise it fell.

It chanced one night, – most nigh the time
When through the mist-wreaths and the rime
    The hours begin to draw toward
    The enchanted birthnight of the Lord, –
That in the midnight, on his bed,
He heard in dreams a voice that said
    'Arise, Sir Floris, get thee forth,
    'An thou wouldst prove thee knight of worth!'

A Birthday Song

I

The rose-time and the roses
    Call to me, dove of mine;
I hear the birdsong-closes
    Ring out in the sunshine;
In all the wood-reposes

There runs a magic wine
Of music all divine.

All things have scent and singing;
The happy earth is ringing
  With praise of love and June: 10
  Have I alone no tune,
No sound of music-making
To greet my love's awaking
  This golden summer noon?

II

Ah, love! my roses linger   15
  For sunshine of thine eyes;
For Love the music-bringer,
  My linnets wait to rise;
All dumb are birds and singer:
  The song in kisses dies   20
  And sound of happy sighs.

What need of songs and singing,
When love for us is ringing
  Bells of enchanted gold?
  Dear, whilst my arms enfold   25
My love, our kisses fashion
Tunes of more perfect passion
  Than verses new or old.

Dream-Life

It seems to me sometimes that I am dead
  And watch the live world in its ceaseless stream
  Pass by me through the pauses of a dream.
The dawn breaks blue on them, the sunset's red
Burns on their smiles and on the tears they shed;   5

The moonlight floods them with its silver gleam:
To me they are as ghosts, that do but seem;
Their grief is strange to me, their gladness dread.

Life lapses, like a vision dim and grey,
Before my sight, a cloud-wrack in the sky:
Since I am dead I can no longer die:
Ah, can it be this doom is laid on me,
To see the tired world slowly pass away,
Nor die, but live on everlastingly?

Love's Amulet

Song, be strong and true to hold
Love within thy locks of gold:
Bind my lady's thought with rhyme;
Kiss her if her lips grow cold;
Bring her thoughts of Summer-prime,
Lest her heart catch winter-time.
Song, be quick and bold.

Take her flowers of love and light,
Blossoms of her soul's delight,
Roses of her heart's desire;
Bind her brow with lilies white;
Lilies' snow and roses' fire
Hold love's summer ever by her,
In the world's despite.

Strew the Springtime in her way,
Lest she weary of the day,
Lest the lonely hours be long;
Be her season ever May,
May, when Love is safe from wrong
And with larks' and linnets' song
All the world is gay.

Sweet, I wind thee with a chain,
Verses linked in one refrain,
'Love me, love, who love but thee,'
Piping ever and again;   25
Bind thy thought and heart to be
Constant aye to Love and me
    Thorow joy and pain.

Faded Love

Farewell, sweetheart! Farewell, our golden days!
  So runs the cadence, ringing out the tune
  Of sighs and kisses: for the tale of June
Is told, and all the length of flowered ways
Fades in the distance, as the new life lays   5
  Its hand upon the strings, and all too soon
  Breaks the brief song of birds and flowers and moon
That held the Maytime – what is this that stays?
– A white-robed figure, with sad eyes that hold
  A far-off dream of never-travelled ways, –   10
Wan with white lips and hands as pale and cold
  As woven garlands of long-vanished Mays,
And the sun's memory halo-like above
Its head? – It is the thought of faded Love.

Rondeau

Life lapses by for you and me,
Our sweet days pass us by and flee,
And evermore Death draws us nigh:
The blue fades fast out of our sky,
The ripple ceases from our sea.   5
What would we not give, you and I,
The early sweet of life to buy!
Alas! sweetheart, that cannot we;
    Life lapses by.

10   But though our young years buried lie,
      Shall love with Spring and Summer die?
      What if the roses faded be!
      We in each other's eyes will see
      New Springs, nor question how or why
15   Life lapses by.

Sad Summer

Ah Summer, lady of the flowered lands,
    When shall thy lovely looks bring back to me
    – To me who strain into the grey sad sea
Of dreams unsatisfied, and with stretched hands
5   Implore the stern sky and the changeless sands
    For some faint sign of that which was to be
    So perfect and so fair a life to see –
The time of songs and season of flower-bands?

At least, for guerdon of full many a lay
10   In praise of thee and of thy youngling Spring,
    What time my lips were yet attuned to sing,
Let not thy roses redden in my way
Too flauntingly, nor all thy golden day
    Insult my silence with too glad a ring.

ARTHUR O'SHAUGHNESSY

Ode

We are the music makers,
   And we are the dreamers of dreams,
Wandering by lone sea-breakers,
   And sitting by desolate streams; –
World-losers and world-forsakers,
   On whom the pale moon gleams:
Yet we are the movers and shakers
   Of the world for ever, it seems.

With wonderful deathless ditties
We build up the world's great cities,
   And out of a fabulous story
   We fashion an empire's glory:
One man with a dream, at pleasure,
   Shall go forth and conquer a crown;
And three with a new song's measure
   Can trample a kingdom down.

We, in the ages lying
   In the buried past of the earth,
Built Nineveh with our sighing,
   And Babel itself in our mirth;
And o'erthrew them with prophesying
   To the old of the new world's worth;
For each age is a dream that is dying,
   Or one that is coming to birth.

A breath of our inspiration
Is the life of each generation;
   A wondrous thing of our dreaming
   Unearthly, impossible seeming –
The soldier, the king, and the peasant
   Are working together in one,
Till our dream shall become their present,
   And their work in the world be done.

They had no vision amazing
Of the goodly house they are raising;
   They had no divine foreshowing   35
   Of the land to which they are going:
But on one man's soul it hath broken,
   A light that doth not depart;
And his look, or a word he hath spoken,
   Wrought flame in another man's heart.   40

And therefore to-day is thrilling
With a past day's late fulfilling;
   And the multitudes are enlisted
   In the faith that their fathers resisted,
And, scorning the dream of to-morrow,   45
   Are bringing to pass, as they may,
In the world, for its joy or its sorrow,
   The dream that was scorned yesterday.

But we, with our dreaming and singing,
   Ceaseless and sorrowless we!   50
The glory about us clinging
   Of the glorious futures we see,
Our souls with high music ringing:
   O men! it must ever be
That we dwell, in our dreaming and singing,   55
   A little apart from ye.

For we are afar with the dawning
   And the suns that are not yet high,
And out of the infinite morning
   Intrepid you hear us cry –   60
How, spite of your human scorning,
   Once more God's future draws nigh,
And already goes forth the warning
   That ye of the past must die.

65 Great hail! we cry to the comers
        From the dazzling unknown shore;
    Bring us hither your sun and your summers,
        And renew our world as of yore;
    You shall teach us your song's new numbers,
70   And things that we dreamed not before:
    Yea, in spite of a dreamer who slumbers,
        And a singer who sings no more.

Song

    I made another garden, yea,
        For my new love;
    I left the dead rose where it lay,
        And set the new above.
5   Why did the summer not begin?
        Why did my heart not haste?
    My old love came and walked therein,
        And laid the garden waste.

    She entered with her weary smile,
10   Just as of old;
    She looked around a little while,
        And shivered at the cold.
    Her passing touch was death to all,
        Her passing look a blight:
15 She made the white rose-petals fall,
        And turned the red rose white.

    Her pale robe, clinging to the grass,
        Seemed like a snake
    That bit the grass and ground, alas!
20   And a sad trail did make.
    She went up slowly to the gate;
        And there, just as of yore,
    She turned back at the last to wait,
        And say farewell once more.

Song

I went to her who loveth me no more,
  And prayed her bear with me, if so she might;
For I had found day after day too sore,
  And tears that would not cease night after night.
And so I prayed her, weeping, that she bore   5
To let me be with her a little; yea,
  To soothe myself a little with her sight,
Who loved me once, ah! many a night and day.

Then she who loveth me no more, maybe
  She pitied somewhat: and I took a chain   10
To bind myself to her, and her to me;
  Yea, so that I might call her mine again.
Lo! she forbade me not; but I and she
Fettered her fair limbs, and her neck more fair,
  Chained the fair wasted white of love's domain,   15
And put gold fetters on her golden hair.

Oh! the vain joy it is to see her lie
  Beside me once again; beyond release,
Her hair, her hand, her body, till she die,
  All mine, for me to do with as I please!   20
For, after all, I find no chain whereby
To chain her heart to love me as before,
  Nor fetter for her lips, to make them cease
From saying still she loveth me no more.

The Great Encounter

Such as I am become, I walked one day
Along a sombre and descending way,
Not boldly, but with dull and desperate thought:
Then one who seemed an angel – for 'twas He,
My old aspiring self, no longer *Me* –   5

Came up against me terrible, and sought
To slay me with the dread I had to see
His sinless and exalted brow. We fought;
And, full of hate, he smote me, saying, 'Thee
10   I curse this hour: go downward to thine hell.'
And in that hour I felt his curse and fell.

Living Marble

When her large, fair, reluctant eyelids fell,
    And dreams o'erthrew her blond head mutinous,
That lollingly surrendered to the spell
    Of sleep's warm death, whose tomb is odorous
5   And made of recent roses; then unchid
I gazed more rapturously than I may tell
On that vain-hearted queen with whom I dwell,
    The wayward Venus who for days hath hid
    Her peerless, priceless beauty, and forbid,
10   With impious shames and child-like airs perverse,
        My great, fond soul from worshipping the sight
        That gives religion to my day and night –
Her shape sublime that should be none of hers.

The wonder of her nakedness, unspoiled
15   By fear or feigning, showed each passionate limb
In reckless grace that failed not nor recoiled;
    And all the sweet, rebellious body, slim,
    Exuberant, lay abandoned to the whim
And miracle of unabashed repose.
20   I joyed to see her glorious side left bare,
        Each snow-born flow'ret of her breast displayed,
One white hand vaguely touching one red rose,
    One white arm gleaming through thick golden hair.
    I gazed; then broke the marble I had made,
25   And yearned, restraining heart and holding breath,
That sleep indeed were endless, even as death.

The Line of Beauty

When mountains crumble and rivers all run dry,
  When every flower has fallen and summer fails
  To come again, when the sun's splendour pales,
And earth with lagging footsteps seems well-nigh
Spent in her annual circuit through the sky;   5
  When love is a quenched flame, and nought avails
  To save decrepit man, who feebly wails
And lies down lost in the great grave to die;
What is eternal? What escapes decay?
  A certain faultless, matchless, deathless line,   10
    Curving consummate. Death, Eternity,
Add nought to it, from it take nought away;
  'Twas all God's gift and all man's mastery,
    God become human and man grown divine.

Pentelicos

In dark days bitter between dream and dream,
  I go bowed down with many a load of pain,
  Increasing memory gathers to remain
From paths where now, all snakelike, lurk and gleam
Love's last deceits that loveliest did seem,   5
  Or hurrying on with hope and thought astrain,
  To reunite love's worn just broken chain,
Whose links fall through my fingers in a stream;
When, sometimes, mid these semblances of love,
  Pursued with feverish joy or mad despair,   10
    There flashes suddenly on my unrest
Some marble shape of Venus, high above
  All pain or changing, fair above all fair,
    Still more and more desired, still unpossest.

Paros

When I took clay – with eager passionate hand
   Inspired by love – to mould the yielding curves
   Of all her shape consummate that deserves,
Immortal in the sight of heaven, to stand;
5 Then, undismayed, as at a god's command,
   Laborious, with the obedient tool that serves
   The sculptor's mighty art and never swerves,
Beside the crumbling form I carved the grand
Imperishable marble. Henceforth – seeing
10 The glory of her nakedness divine –
    My heart is raised, I bend the knee and deem her
   Not simply woman and not merely mine,
    But goddess, as the future age shall deem her,
Ideal love of man's eternal being.

Carrara

I am the body purified by fire;
A man shall look on me without desire,
But rather think what miracles of faith
Made me to trample without fear or scathe
5 The burning shares; the thick-set bristling paths
Of martyrdom; to lie on painful laths
Under the torturer's malice; to be torn
And racked and broken, all-victorious scorn
Strengthening the inward spirit to reject
10 The frame of flesh, with sins and lusts infect,
Whose punishment, like to the sin, was gross,
And man the executioner. I arose
Changed from those beds of pain, and shriven at last
From the whole shameful history of the past –
15 Of earth-bound pride and revelry; yea, shriven
From Love, at first the one sin, and forgiven:

Beauty that other, with the vanity
That set me crowned before humanity;
So I was led, a priestess or a saint,
Robed solemnly, leaving the latest taint   20
Of earthliness in some far desert cell
Ascetic; and the hand late used to tell
Rough rosaries, the hand for ever chilled
With fingering the death-symbol, feels unthrilled
With any passionate luxury forbidden   25
The world's new wedlock. Man and woman chidden
For all their life on earth wed timorously,
And full of shames, fearing lest each should see
The other's greater sin; so they unite,
Two penitential spirits, to take flight,   30
In one ethereal vision sanctified,
Two bodies for the grave. I am the bride
Who clings with terror, suppliant and pale,
And fears the lifting of her virgin veil,
Because the shrinking form, spite of her prayers,   35
Has grown to know its earthliness, and bears
The names of sins that gave up shameful ghosts
On antique crosses. Raised now amid the hosts
Of living men, my effigy is grown
Passionless, speechless through the postured stone   40
That holds one changeless meaning in its pose;
The murmuring myriads pass, and each man knows
And sees me with a cold thought at his heart;
For I am that from which the soul must part.

PHILIP BOURKE MARSTON

Love's Shrines

All places that have known my love at all
  Have grown as sympathetic friends to me,
  And each for song has some dear memory,
Some perfume of her presence clings to all;
How then, to me, O love, shall it befall,
  When I no longer in my life shall see
  The places that through love have grown to be
Of buried dreams the mute memorial?
  Then surely shall I seem as one who stands
  Exiled from home in unfamiliar lands,
And strains across the weary sea and long
  His desolate sad eyes, and wrings his hands,
While round him press an undiscerning throng
Of strange men talking in an alien tongue.

Love Past Utterance

I am a painter, and I love you so
  I cannot paint your face for very love;
  My heart is like a sea the tempests move
Wherein no ship a certain path may know;
I can but gaze upon you till you grow
  Lovely and distant as the skies above:
  How then to man shall I my worship prove,
And unto coming worlds your beauty show?
  I am a poet, and my love is such
    I cannot tell the marvel of your voice,
Or show the laugh that thrills me like a kiss;
  The very recollection of your touch
    O'ercomes me like a sudden tide of joys,
And my heart gasps for breath 'twixt waves of bliss.

Shake Hands and Go

Come now, behold, how small a thing is love;
 How long ago is it since, side by side,
 We stood together, in that summer-tide,
 And heard the June sea, blue, and deep, and wide,
Murmuring as one that in her dreams doth move   5
 To thoughts of love's first kiss and beauty's pride?

How long is it? But one brief year ago;
 One autumn, and one winter, and one spring;
 Now, as last year, the birds awake and sing,
 Once more unto the hills the hill-flowers cling;   10
How is it with you? What heart you have, I know,
 Changes with every comer and fresh thing.

And yet, I think, you loved me for a space;
 At all events you loved my love of you:
 Whether to me or that, your love was due   15
 I know not; while it lived perchance 'twas true;
But you forget each season and each face,
 And love the new as long as it is new.

Scan o'er that time, as at the close of day
 One thinks what he has done or left undone;   20
 Know you those days when noontide heats of sun
 Smote full upon us, and we strove to shun
Their flaming force, and took the sheltered way
 Of shading trees with green leaves softly spun?

There in an island of dim green and shade   25
 We stretched, while round, like a great silent sea,
 Lay the blue, blinding, burning day; but we
 Knew nothing save our own life's melody,
And there, until the day was done, delayed;
 Then homeward wended o'er the dewy lea.   30

Know you those moonlit nights spent on the sand –
    The golden sand beside the lucid deep –
    Where soft waves rippled as they sang in sleep;
    How there we sowed what I alone shall reap?
35   Nay, feign not thus to draw away your hand,
    Nor droop your lids; I know you cannot weep.

O pliant crimson lips and bright cold eyes,
    Lips that my lips have pressed, and fingers sweet
    That lay about my neck, or soft, would meet
40   Around my eyes to screen them from the heat,
Where are your words, where is our paradise?
    Your love was warm as summer – and as fleet.

And yet, behold, with some how strong is love;
    How helpless is the dupe that boasts a heart!
45   I know you now – and yet regret to part:
    Fairer than ever, in the marriage mart
You'll fetch your price; time's dealings that are rough
    With nature, leave untouched the works of art.

Well, kiss once more as in the gone-by time,
50   Let your hair mix with mine, take hands again;
    Your kiss is sweet – and do you only feign?
    There, look once more on jutting cliff and main;
And now go hence, while I in some sad rhyme
    Weave our love's tale – its brief joy, lasting pain.

55   Go, go thy way; return not to the gates
    Of the fair past, forsake the dear dead days;
    I know thou wilt. I to some distant place
    May wander and forget your voice and face:
No anger, say 'Good-bye!' I know one waits:
60   He paid his price and for his purchase stays.

Love's Warfare

'And are these cold, light words your last?' he said,
And rose, his face made pale with outraged love.
She answered gaily, 'Are they not enough?'
And lightly laughed until his spirit bled,
While snake-like on his grief her beauty fed.   5
He looked upon her face once more for proof,
Then through and through his lips the sharp teeth drove,
Till with the bitter dew of blood made red.
At length he said, 'And so 'twas but a jest,
A well-conceived, well-executed plan;   10
Yet now may God forgive you, if God can!'
And, passing, left her calm and self-possessed.
She watched him cross the lawn with eyes bent low,
Where she had kissed his face one hour ago.

Stronger Than Sleep

Weary, my limbs upon my couch I laid,
And dreamt; and in my dream I seemed to see
My lady, who was soon my bride to be,
Silently standing, gazing on my bed,
A crown of bright red roses on her head.   5
I said, 'O love! this hour is sweet to me;
Stretch out your throat and let us kiss.' Then she
Bowed down her body and brows garlanded.
'Stretch out your hand and feel,' her deep eyes said:
I touched, and through soft raiment felt her form   10
Panting and glowing with the want of love.
Then all the waves of pleasure, deep and warm,
Burst through my veins. My eyes love's hot tears bled,
And I awoke, too weak to speak or move.

The New Religion

They shall not be forgotten, these my lays;
   I know that they shall live when I am dead.
   A thousand things I might have sung and said,
And no man hearkened to my blame or praise;
5 I might have moved the veil from off the face
   Of awful Destiny; I might have spread
   Rebellion through a land misused, and made
My song the weapon of an injured race,
   And men forgotten all the same; but now
10 I come among ye, and to each I cry,
   'He that hath ears to hearken, let him hear,'
I sing of love, made manifest in her.
   I preach the Gospel of her life, and so
I feel these words, though mine, not born to die!

OLIVER MADOX BROWN

Sonnet
Written at the Age of Thirteen for a Picture by
Mrs Stillman

Leaning against the window, rapt in thought,
   Of what sweet past do thy soft brown eyes dream
   That so expressionlessly sweet they seem?
Or what great image hath thy fancy wrought
5 To wonder round and gaze at? or doth aught
   Of legend move thee, o'er which eyes oft stream,
   Telling of some sweet saint who rose supreme
From martyrdom to God, with glory fraught?
Or art thou listening to the gondolier,
10   Whose song is dying o'er the waters wide,
Trying the faintly-sounding tune to hear
   Before it mixes with the rippling tide?
Or dost thou think of one that comes not near,
   And whose false heart, in thine, thine own doth chide?

Song

Lady, we are growing tired!
   Lo! our faltering breath,
Once with new-born love inspired,
Holds the love we once desired, as weary unto death.

5 Lady, Love is very fleet,
   All too fleet for sorrow:
But if we part in time, my sweet,
We'll overtake Love's flying feet, –
If we part to-day, my love, we'll find new love to-morrow.

Abbreviations

Frequently Mentioned Names

ACS	Algernon Charles Swinburne
DGR	Dante Gabriel Rossetti
CGR	Christina Georgina Rossetti
EBJ	Edward Burne-Jones
FMB	Ford Madox Brown
JEM	John Everett Millais
OMB	Oliver Madox Brown
PRB	Pre-Raphaelite Brotherhood
RA	Royal Academy
WBS	William Bell Scott
WHD	Walter Howell Deverell
WHH	William Holman Hunt
WM	William Morris
WMR	William Michael Rossetti

Frequently Mentioned Works

DGR, Works	*The Works of Dante Gabriel Rossetti*, ed. with a preface and notes by WMR (Ellis and Elvey, 1911)
FLM	*Dante Gabriel Rossetti: His Family Letters with a Memoir*, ed. WMR, 2 vols. (Ellis and Elvey, 1895)
FS	'The Fleshly School of Poetry: Mr D. G. Rossetti' by Robert Buchanan (as Thomas Maitland), *Contemporary Review* 18 (October 1871), pp. 334–50
Malory	*Le Morte d'Arthur* (William Caxton, 1485) by Sir Thomas Malory (a useful modern edition is *Caxton's Malory: A New Edition of Sir Thomas Malory's 'Le Morte d'Arthur'*, ed. James W. Spisak, University of California Press, 1983)
PP	*The Painter-Poets*, ed. Kineton Parkes (Walter Scott, 1890)
RRP	*Ruskin: Rossetti: Preraphaelitism: Papers 1854–1862*, ed. WMR (George Allen, 1899)
SR	*Some Reminiscences of William Michael Rossetti*, 2 vols. (Brown, Langham & Co., 1906)

Biographical Notes

These notes follow the sequence of the poems as they occur in the book. All members of the PRB are included here, even those who did not write poetry, namely Frederic George Stephens, William Holman Hunt and John Everett Millais. Edward Burne-Jones is also included, as he was a formative influence in Pre-Raphaelitism's second wave, and PRB associate Simeon Solomon. Biographical information has been taken from the *Dictionary of National Biography* as well as more specialized works such as William E. Fredeman's *Pre-Raphaelitism: A Bibliocritical Study* (Harvard University Press, 1965) and Lionel Stevenson's *The Pre-Raphaelite Poets* (University of North Carolina Press, 1972).

A selected list of publications is given for each author, which includes works from which the poems have been taken, in some cases selected volumes from multi-volume works. The focus is necessarily on poetic works, as a complete list of novels, stories and essays could fill a volume in itself. A list of significant paintings and illustrations follows separately.

The exhaustive research of William E. Fredeman in *Pre-Raphaelitism: A Bibliocritical Study* (Harvard University Press, 1965) has been of particular help, along with Derek Stanford's *Pre-Raphaelite Writing* (Dent, 1973) and Inga Bryden's *The Pre-Raphaelites: Writings and Sources*, 4 vols. (Routledge, 1998). I strongly recommend their work to readers interested in Pre-Raphaelitism.

William Bell Scott (1811–90)

Poet and painter; born in Edinburgh; studied fine art at Trustees' Academy, Edinburgh; moved to London, 1837; married Letitia Margery Norquoy, 1839; exhibited at the RA, 1842; met the Rossettis in 1847; contributed to the *Germ*, 1850; taught at the Government School of Design in Newcastle, 1843–64; between 1855 and 1861, painted the Northumbrian History Cycle murals at Wallington, home of Pauline Trevelyan; close friend of ACS, who dedicated *Poems and Ballads III*

(1889) to him; *Autobiographical Notes* (published 1892), in which his critical remarks about Rossetti and the PRB were viewed as a betrayal by the Pre-Raphaelites and associates.

Works: *Poems by a Painter* (1854); *Poems: Ballads, Studies from Nature, Sonnets, Etc.* (1875); *A Poet's Harvest Home*, dedicated to WMR (1882); *Autobiographical Notes* (1892).

John Ruskin (1819–1900)

Art critic and collector, social critic; born in London to a wealthy family; educated at Oxford, where he won the Newdigate Prize for poetry, 1839; patron and mentor to the PRB, DGR in particular; also supported Elizabeth Siddal; married Euphemia ('Effie') Chalmers Gray, 1848; poems privately printed by his father, 1850; defended the PRB painters in letters to *The Times*, 1851 and 1854; portrait painted by JEM, 1854; marriage annulled on ground of non-consummation, 1854, after which Effie married JEM, 1855; member of the Hogarth Club; became a patron of EBJ in 1859, and godfather to his son, 1861; elected first Slade Professor of Fine Art at Oxford, 1869.

Works: *Modern Painters* (1843–60); *Pre-Raphaelitism*, a pamphlet (1851); *The Stones of Venice* (1851–3); *Sesame and Lilies* (1864–5); *Poems* (1882); *The Poems of John Ruskin*, vol. 2 (1891); *The Works of John Ruskin*, vol. 2 (1903).

Ford Madox Brown (1821–93)

Painter, designer; born in Calais; married Elisabeth Bromley, 1841; she died in 1846; took a studio in London, 1844; tutored DGR in painting; declined formal PRB membership because he 'had no faith in coteries' (*FLM* 1, 130), but remained its closest associate; best known as the painter of *Work* (1852–65) and *The Last of England* (1855); married Emma Hill, 1853; organized a Pre-Raphaelite exhibition, 1857; designed furniture and stained glass as a partner of Morris, Marshall, Faulkner & Co., 1861–74; father of OMB, grandfather of novelist Ford Madox Ford; daughter Lucy, also a painter, married WMR, 1874; poems appeared in the *Germ* 1 (January 1850), and in the 1865 exhibition catalogues accompanying his paintings.

Coventry Kersey Dighton Patmore (1823–96)

Poet and literary essayist; born in Essex; worked in the Printed Books Department at the British Museum, 1846; married Emily Andrews,

1847, the inspiration for *The Angel in the House* series; she died in 1862; on the Cyclographic Society's 'List of Immortals'; contributed two poems and an article on *Macbeth* to the *Germ*, 1850; suggested to Ruskin that he come to the defence of the PRB, 1851; connections to major literary figures of the day, such as Alfred Tennyson and Robert Browning, proved helpful to the Pre-Raphaelites; association with them lasted throughout the 1850s; became a Roman Catholic, 1864, and married Marianne Caroline Byles, whose income allowed him to quit the British Museum in 1865; Byles died in 1880 and Patmore married Harriet Robson, 1881.

Works: *Poems* (1844); *The Angel in the House* (complete version, 1863), comprising *The Betrothal* (1854), *The Espousals* (1856), *Faithful For Ever* (1860) and *The Victories of Love* (1862); *The Unknown Eros* (1877).

William Allingham (1824–89)

Poet; born in Ballyshannon, County Donegal; became a bank manager and got a Customs Service job, 1846; met Coventry Patmore in 1849, through whom he was introduced to Thomas Carlyle, the Rossettis and the PRB; DGR, JEM and Arthur Hughes illustrated *The Music Master* (1855); befriended WM, EBJ, Alfred Tennyson and the Brownings; became editor of the influential *Fraser's Magazine*,1874; dedicated *Flower Pieces* (1888) to DGR.

Works: *Day and Night Songs* (1854); *The Music Master, a Love Story, and Two Series of Day and Night Songs* (1855); *Songs, Ballads and Stories* (1877); *The Fairies* (1883); *Flower Pieces and Other Poems*, illustrated by DGR (1888); *Life and Phantasy*, illustrated by JEM and Arthur Hughes (1889).

James Collinson (1825–81)

Painter, PRB member; born in Mansfield; met DGR and WHH at the RA Schools; raised in the Anglican Church, he converted to Roman Catholicism; became engaged to CGR, 1848; re-converted to Anglicanism; exhibited with PRB members at the RA, 1849; exhibited *Answering the Emigrant's Letter* (1850) at the RA; contributed a poem to the *Germ* 2 (February 1850); reverted to Roman Catholicism, 1850, and gave up PRB membership for religious reasons; CGR subsequently broke off the engagement; entered Jesuit community at Stonyhurst College in Lancashire, 1852–3; left before completing novitiate, 1854; married Eliza Wheeler, 1858.

Thomas Woolner (1825–92)

Sculptor and poet; PRB member; born in Suffolk; entered the RA Schools, 1842; met DGR and joined the Cyclographic Society, 1847; verse appeared in the *Germ*, 1850; prospected for gold in Australia, 1852; returned to England, 1854, to become a successful maker of busts (Alfred Tennyson, 1857 and 1874; Charles Darwin, 1870; Charles Dickens, 1872) and portrait medallions (Tennyson, 1848; Coventry Patmore, 1849; William Wordsworth, 1851; Robert Browning, 1856); married Alice Gertrude Waugh, 1864; sculpture *Mother and Child* installed at Wallington, 1866; made Associate of the RA, 1871, and Royal Academician, 1874.

Works: *My Beautiful Lady* (1863); *Pygmalion* (1881); *Silenus* (1884).

John Lucas Tupper (1826?–79)

Drawing-master, sculptor and poet; born in London; studied at the RA Schools, where he met the PRB; worked as an anatomical artist at Guy's Hospital, 1849–69; wrote 'The Subject in Art', an essay in two parts, for the *Germ* 1 and 3 (January and March 1850) and contributed poems to the magazine; exhibited at the RA, but not with great success; became a drawing-master at Rugby, 1865; the Tupper Firm, run by his brothers George and Alexander, printed the *Germ*; married Annie Amelia French, 1871.

Works: *Poems by the Late John Lucas Tupper*, ed. WMR (1897).

William Holman Hunt (1827–1910)

Painter, PRB member; born in London; studied at the RA Schools, 1844; exhibited *The Eve of St Agnes* at the RA in 1848; DGR, WMR and JEM sat for *Rienzi* (1849), shown at the RA; *A Converted British Family* (1850) shown at the RA; WHH depicted both contemporary subjects (*The Awakening Conscience*, 1853) and biblical allegories (*The Scape-goat*, 1854); travelled to the Middle East, 1854–6; illustrated the Moxon edition of Tennyson's *Poems* (1857); married Fanny Waugh in 1865, who died shortly after; associate member of the Old Watercolour Society, 1869; travelled to Florence, 1868–9; worked on religious subjects (including *The Shadow of Death*, 1870–73, and *The Triumph of the Innocents*, 1883–4); married late wife's younger sister, 1875; published his memoirs, *Pre-Raphaelitism and the Pre-Raphaelite Brotherhood* (1905), which argued for his and JEM's importance to the PRB and disassociated himself from Pre-Raphaelitism's second wave.

Walter Howell Deverell (1827–54)

Painter; born to an English family in Virginia, USA; studied at Sass's Academy with DGR; exhibited at the RA, 1847–53; nominated for PRB membership when James Collinson resigned, 1850, but not selected; poems appeared in the *Germ*, 1850; shared a studio with DGR in 1851; died of a kidney disease.

Frederic George Stephens (1827–1907)

Art critic, art historian and PRB member; born in London; studied as a painter at the RA; began working as an artist, then abandoned painting in the 1850s; wrote seminal essay for the *Germ* 2 (February 1850), 'The Purpose and Tendency of Early Italian Art'; art critic at the *Athenaeum* for forty years; promoted PRB painters, but became increasingly critical of them from the 1880s onwards; wrote hundreds of articles, produced monographs and catalogues on artists such as Lawrence Alma-Tadema, Joshua Reynolds, Edwin Landseer and William Mulready.

George Meredith (1828–1909)

Novelist and poet; born in Portsmouth; married writer Mary Ellen Nicholls, daughter of Thomas Love Peacock, 1849; Mary left Meredith, 1857, to join her lover, the painter Henry Wells; shared lodgings with DGR and ACS, 1862–3; Mary died, 1862; first marriage is said to have inspired the *Modern Love* sonnets and the novel *The Ordeal of Richard Feverel* (1859); *Modern Love* attacked by many, but defended by ACS; became a reader at the publisher Chapman and Hall; married Marie Vulliamy, 1864; Tracey Runningbrook in *Emilia in England* (1864) is based on ACS; success of *Beauchamp's Career* (1876) established him as a novelist; President of Society of Authors, 1892; received the Order of Merit, 1905.

    Works: *Poems* (1851); *Modern Love and Poems of the English Roadside, with poems and ballads* (1862); *Poems and Lyrics of the Joy of Earth* (1883); *Ballads and Poems of Tragic Life* (1887); *A Reading of Life* (1901).

Dante Gabriel Rossetti (1828–82)

Painter, poet and translator; PRB member; born in London to Gabriele Rossetti, an exiled Italian poet, and Frances Polidori; elder brother of

WMR and CGR; maternal uncle John Polidori was Byron's physician; studied at the RA Schools, where he met WHH and JEM; contributed poems to the *Germ*, 1850, and the *Oxford and Cambridge Magazine*, 1856, among other journals, but did not publish his own volume of poetry until 1870; met EBJ and WM in 1856; worked on Oxford Union murals, 1857; illustrated Moxon edition of Tennyson's *Poems* (1857); member of Hogarth Club, 1858; married model Elizabeth Siddal, 1860, who died of a possibly intentional laudanum overdose, 1862; published *The Early Italian Poets* and became founder member of Morris, Marshall, Faulkner & Co., 1861; ACS and George Meredith were tenants at his Cheyne Walk home, 1862–3; helped prepare Alexander Gilchrist's 1863 biography of William Blake; during 1860s and 1870s, produced commercially successful paintings of beautiful women such as *Venus Verticordia* (1864–8) and *Astarte Syriaca* (1877); poems criticized by Robert Buchanan in 'The Fleshly School of Poetry' (1871); replied with 'The Stealthy School of Criticism' (1872); became addicted to chloral and alcohol, dying of organ failure.

Works: *Poems*, including first part of *The House of Life* sonnet sequence (1870); *Ballads and Sonnets*, including completed *House of Life* (1881); *Poems: A New Edition* (1881); *The Works of Dante Gabriel Rossetti*, ed. WMR (1911).

John Everett Millais (1829–96)

Painter; PRB member; born in Southampton; met WHH at the RA Schools; PRB inaugurated at his Gower Street house, 1848; PRB painting *Christ in the House of His Parents* (1850) was the subject of fierce criticism; Elizabeth Siddal modelled for *Ophelia* (1852); found success with *A Huguenot* (1852) and *The Rescue* (1855); elected Associate of the RA, 1853; painted John Ruskin's portrait, 1854; married Ruskin's ex-wife, Effie, 1855; atmospheric paintings such as *Autumn Leaves* (1856) and *The Vale of Rest* (1858–9) presaged the rise of Aestheticism; illustrated Moxon edition of Tennyson's *Poems* (1857), Anthony Trollope's serialized novels and *The Parables of Our Lord* (1864); after the 1860s, became known for portraiture and paintings of children; most successful PRB painter; became a baronet, 1885; elected RA President, 1896.

Elizabeth Eleanor Siddal (1829–62)

Artist's model, poet and artist; born in London; worked as a dressmaker and milliner, reputedly 'discovered' by Walter Deverell, 1850; best known as the model for JEM's *Ophelia* (1852); sat for many DGR works, among them *A Christmas Carol* (1857–8) and *Beata Beatrix* (1860); inspired CGR's sonnet 'In an Artist's Studio'; John Ruskin offered an annuity for her drawings and watercolours, some of which appeared in the Pre-Raphaelite exhibition of 1857; married DGR, 1860; gave birth to a stillborn baby, 1861, and died of a laudanum overdose, 1862; DGR buried his poetic works in her coffin, but had her body exhumed in 1869 to retrieve them for publication in *Poems* (1870); own poems not published in her lifetime but appeared posthumously in *RRP* and *SR*.

William Michael Rossetti (1829–1910)

Art and literary critic, editor, secretary to the PRB and unofficial archivist of Pre-Raphaelite and Rossetti family activities; born in London; for family, see entry on DGR; contributed poems to the *Germ*, 1850; the most politically radical of the Rossetti siblings, he supported revolutions in Europe and female suffrage; wrote political sonnets which he withheld until his retirement; worked as a civil servant at the Inland Revenue, 1845–94; art critic for the *Critic*, *Spectator* and *Crayon*, among others; wrote the long poem 'Mrs Holmes Gray', 1849 (not published until 1868); married FMB's daughter Lucy, 1874; edited and introduced many volumes for the Moxon Popular Poets series; produced editions of Percy Bysshe Shelley, William Blake and Walt Whitman (among the first English critics to champion Whitman); wrote a biography of John Keats, 1887; published multiple works on DGR, CGR and the Pre-Raphaelites, including *Ruskin: Rossetti: Preraphaelitism: Papers 1854–1862* (1899), *Rossetti Papers, 1862–1870* (1903) and *Some Reminiscences of William Michael Rossetti* (1906).

Works: 'Mrs Holmes Gray', *Broadway Annual* (1868); *Democratic Sonnets* (1907).

Christina Georgina Rossetti (1830–94)

Poet, short-story and devotional prose writer; born in London; for family, see entry on DGR; raised as a devout High Anglican; modelled for DGR's early paintings; her gender precluded PRB membership, but her early work is associated with Pre-Raphaelitism; only woman to publish poems in the *Germ*; engaged to James Collinson, 1848, but broke engagement on his re-conversion to Roman Catholicism, 1850; *Goblin Market* (1862) is the first book of Pre-Raphaelite associated poetry to win critical acclaim; ACS a fervent admirer of her poems;

work was illustrated by DGR and Arthur Hughes; wrote short stories and poems for children; later work almost exclusively devotional; diagnosed with Graves' disease in 1872; died of breast cancer; EBJ designed decorations for her memorial in Christ Church, Woburn Square.

Works: *Goblin Market and Other Poems*, illustrated by DGR (1862); *The Prince's Progress and Other Poems*, illustrated by DGR (1866); *Commonplace and Other Short Stories* (1870); *Sing-Song: A Nursery Rhyme Book*, illustrated by Arthur Hughes (1872); *Speaking Likenesses*, illustrated by Arthur Hughes (1874); *A Pageant and Other Poems* (1881); *Verses* (1893); *New Poems*, dedicated to ACS by WMR (1896); *The Poetical Works of Christina Rossetti*, ed. WMR (1904).

Arthur Hughes (1832–1915)

Painter and illustrator; born in London; attended the RA Schools, 1847; met FMB and DGR, 1851, and JEM in 1852; married Tryphena Foord in 1855; one of the illustrators of William Allingham's *The Music Master* (1855); WMR writes that 'he was one of those who most sympathized with the ideas which guided the Praeraphaelite Brotherhood, and his style conformed pretty faithfully (not servilely) to theirs; if the organization had been kept up a little longer, and if new members had ever been admitted ... Mr Hughes would doubtless have been invited to join' (*SR* 1, 147); participated in the Pre-Raphaelite exhibition and helped paint the Oxford Union murals, 1857; founder member of the Hogarth Club, 1858; illustrated Alfred Tennyson's *Enoch Arden* (1865), the frontispiece of Thomas Woolner's *My Beautiful Lady*, third edition (1866), CGR's *Sing-Song: A Nursery Rhyme Book* (1872) and *Speaking Likenesses* (1874).

Edward Coley Burne-Jones (1833–98)

Painter, designer; born in Birmingham; studied at Oxford, where he met WM, 1853; read Ruskin and saw Pre-Raphaelite pictures; admired Pre-Raphaelite illustrations for William Allingham's *The Music Master* (1855); read Thomas Malory's *Le Morte d'Arthur*; published short stories in the *Oxford and Cambridge Magazine*, 1856; met DGR and ACS, moved to London and shared rooms with WM; helped paint Oxford Union murals, 1857; became a member of the Hogarth Club, 1858; married Georgiana Macdonald, 1860; founder member of Morris, Marshall, Faulkner & Co., 1861; designed stained glass, textiles and ceramics; elected to the Old Watercolour Society, 1864; resigned,

1870; produced illustrations (never published) for WM's *The Earthly Paradise* (1868–70); exhibited at Grosvenor Gallery, 1877; elected Associate of the RA, 1885; baronetcy in 1894.

William Morris (1834–96)

Poet, translator, designer, painter; born in London, educated at Exeter College, Oxford, where he met EBJ and DGR; contributed poetry to the *Oxford and Cambridge Magazine*, 1856; helped paint the Oxford Union murals, 1857; member of Hogarth Club; stimulated Pre-Raphaelite interest in Arthurian legend; married Pre-Raphaelite model Jane Burden, 1859, who later became DGR's muse and lover; moved into Red House, Upton, 1860; active in the Arts and Crafts Movement; founder member of Morris, Marshall, Faulkner & Co., 1861, along with DGR, FMB and EBJ, among others, which became William Morris & Co., 1875; other interests were Icelandic literature and folklore, also socialist politics; contributed to and edited Socialist League journal the *Commonweal*, 1885–90; befriended W. B. Yeats in the late 1880s; set up Kelmscott Press, 1891.

Works: *The Defence of Guenevere and Other Poems* (1858); *The Life and Death of Jason: A Poem* (1867); *The Earthly Paradise: A Poem* (1868–70); *Love is Enough, or the Freeing of the Pharamond: A Morality* (1873); *Sigurd the Volsung and the Fall of the Niblungs* (1877); *Poems by the Way* (1891).

Algernon Charles Swinburne (1837–1909)

Poet, literary critic; born in London to an admiral in the Royal Navy and a daughter of the 3rd Earl of Ashburnham; raised Anglican but later rejected Christianity; educated at Eton and Oxford, where he met DGR, WM and EBJ; lifelong friend of WBS; published pieces in *Undergraduate Papers*, 1856–8; sent away for a term, then left Oxford for London without a degree, 1860; famous for unconventional behaviour, interest in flagellation, shared by his friend homosexual painter and Pre-Raphaelite associate Simeon Solomon; defended George Meredith's *Modern Love* (1862); in 1866 caused a literary scandal with the explicit *Poems and Ballads* and defended his own work in *Notes on Poems and Reviews*, as did WMR in *Swinburne's Poems and Ballads*; sympathy with the struggle for Italian independence inspired *A Song of Italy* (1867); a remarkably prolific writer, he produced critical essays and verse plays, along with many volumes of poetry, including influential pieces on Blake and Baudelaire; rescued from alcoholism by Rossetti friend Theodore Watts-Dunton, with whose family he lived until his death.

Works: *Poems and Ballads* (1866); *Songs Before Sunrise* (1871); *Songs of Two Nations* (1875); *Poems and Ballads II* (1878); *Studies in Song* (1880); *The Heptalogia* (1880);*Tristram of Lyonesse and Other Poems* (1882); *A Century of Roundels* (1883); *A Midsummer Holiday and Other Poems* (1884); *Poems and Ballads III* (1889); *Astrophel and Other Poems*, 1894; *A Channel Passage* (1904); *The Poems of Algernon Charles Swinburne*, 6 vols. (1904).

Simeon Solomon (1840–1905)

Painter, born in London to a Jewish merchant family; attended RA Schools, 1856; first RA painting exhibited, 1857; received critical acclaim and commissions; interest in painting Jewish subjects and themes such as *Carrying the Scrolls of the Law* (1867); friend of DGR and EBJ, but especially close to ACS; painting strongly influenced by DGR, as in *Dante's First Meeting with Beatrice* (1859–63); became member of the Savile Club, 1868; produced stained-glass designs for Morris, Marshall, Faulkner & Co.; in the 1860s and 1870s his work began to emphasize the erotic and the mystical, such as *The Sleepers and the One Who Watcheth* (1870), increasingly featuring androgynous figures; wrote prose tale, *A Vision of Love Revealed in Sleep* (1871); arrested for homosexual offences, 1873; subsequently abandoned by Pre-Raphaelite friends and patrons; spent time in the workhouse; his reputation revived in 1880s, but he died destitute and alcoholic.

John Payne (1842–1916)

Poet and translator; born in Devon; met Arthur O'Shaughnessy and the Pre-Raphaelite circle in the 1860s; dedicated *The Masque of Shadows* (1870) to O'Shaughnessy; skilled in languages, he translated François Villon, Boccaccio, *One Thousand and One Nights* and *The Quatrains of Omar Kheyyam of Nishapour*, among other works; own poems heavily influenced by DGR; Robert Buchanan's essay mentions his 'queer allegories' (*FS*, 347).

Works: *The Masque of Shadows and Other Poems* (1870); *Intaglios: Sonnets* (1871); *Songs of Life and Death* (1872); *New Poems* (1880).

Arthur William Edgar O'Shaughnessy (1844–81)

Poet; born in London, of Irish descent; protégé of his mother's friend Lord Lytton; junior assistant at the British Museum, 1861; became senior assistant in the Natural History Department, 1863 until his death; first volume of poems, *An Epic of Women* (1870), dedicated to fellow poet John Payne, who dedicated *The Masque of Shadows* to O'Shaughnessy in the same year; frequent guest at FMB's home where he met the Rossetti siblings, WM, WBS, ACS and OMB; married Eleanor Kyme Marston, sister of Philip Bourke Marston, 1873; poems heavily influenced by ACS and Baudelaire; Buchanan calls him 'a second-hand Mr Swinburne' (*FS*, 347).

Works: *An Epic of Women* (1870); *Lays of France* (1872); *Music and Moonlight* (1874); *Songs of a Worker* (1881).

Philip Bourke Marston (1850–87)

Poet; born in London; blind from age three; DGR and ACS were family friends; known for melancholy poetry and his tragic life story, which involves the deaths of his mother in 1870, his fiancée Mary Nesbit in 1871, his closest friend OMB in 1874, his two sisters in 1878 and 1879 respectively; close friend of Arthur O'Shaughnessy, who married his sister Eleanor; began a literary club, 'The Vagabonds', 1883; heavily influenced by DGR and ACS; Robert Buchanan writes that 'every poem of Mr Marston's reminds us of Mr Rossetti' (*FS*, 347).

Works: *Song-Tide and Other Poems* (1871); *All in All: Poems and Sonnets* (1875); *Wind-Voices* (1883).

Oliver Madox Brown (1855–74)

Poet, painter and author; born at Finchley, Middlesex; son of FMB; close friend of Philip Bourke Marston and Arthur O'Shaughnessy; first-exhibited painting, *The Infant Jason Delivered to the Centaur* (1869), based on events in WM's *The Life and Death of Jason* (1867); showed promise when he turned from painting to writing in 1871; his gothic novel, *Gabriel Denver* (1873), and its earlier version, *The Black Swan*, were admired by DGR and friends; died of peritonitis; WMR and Francis Hueffer brought out an edition of his unpublished works, *The Dwale Bluth* (1876).

Works: *Gabriel Denver* (1873); *The Dwale Bluth, Hebditch's Legacy, and Other Literary Remains*, ed. WMR and Francis Hueffer, vol. 2 (1876).

Selected List of Paintings and Illustrations

This list is intended as a starting point for those interested in Pre-Raphaelite visual culture, and is by no means comprehensive. It includes paintings and illustrations cited in the biographical and textual notes.

PAINTINGS AND DRAWINGS

Ford Madox Brown: *Lear and Cordelia* (1849–54); *The Pretty Baa-Lambs* (1851–9); *Jesus Washing Peter's Feet* (1852–6); *Work* (1852–65); *The Last of England* (1855); *The Death of Sir Tristram* (1864).

Oliver Madox Brown: *The Infant Jason Delivered to the Centaur* (1869); *Exercize, Obstinacy* (1870); *Mazeppa, Prospero and the Infant Miranda* (1871); *Silas Marner* (1872).

Edward Coley Burne-Jones: *Sidonia von Bork* (1860); *The Madness of Sir Tristram* (1862); *The Wine of Circe* (1863–9); *The Beguiling of Merlin* (1870–74); *Laus Veneris* (1873–5); *The Hours* (1882); *The Last Sleep of Arthur in Avalon* (1881–98).

James Collinson: *The Charity Boy's Debut* (1847); *Italian Image Makers at a Roadside Alehouse* (1849); *Answering the Emigrant's Letter, The Renunciation of St Elizabeth of Hungary* (1850); *To Let, For Sale* (1857).

Walter Howell Deverell: *Twelfth Night* (1850); *The Grey Parrot* (1852–3); *The Mock Marriage of Orlando and Rosalind, A Pet* (1853).

Arthur Hughes: *Ophelia* (1852); *April Love* (1855–6); *The Eve of St Agnes* (1856); *The Annunciation* (1858); *Aurora Leigh's Dismissal of Romney* (1860); *La Belle Dame Sans Merci* (1861–3); *The Lady of Shalott* (1873).

William Holman Hunt: *The Eve of St Agnes* (1848); *Rienzi* (1849); *Claudio and Isabella, A Converted British Family* (1850); *The Hireling Shepherd* (1851); *The Light of the World* (1851–3); *Our*

English Coasts (1852); *The Awakening Conscience* (1853); *The Great Pyramid* (1854); *The Scapegoat* (1854); *Isabella and the Pot of Basil* (1867); *The Shadow of Death* (1870–73); *The Triumph of the Innocents* (1883–4); *The Lady of Shalott* (1886–1905).

John Everett Millais: *Isabella* (1849); *Christ in the House of His Parents* (1850); *Mariana, The Woodman's Daughter* (1851); *A Huguenot, Ophelia* (1852); *The Rescue* (1855); *The Blind Girl* (1856); *Autumn Leaves* (1856); *The Vale of Rest* (1858–9); *Esther* (1863–5); *The Sound of Many Waters* (1876).

William Morris: *La Belle Iseult* (or *Queen Guenevere*) (1858).

Dante Gabriel Rossetti: *The Girlhood of Mary Virgin* (1849); *The Annunciation* (or *Ecce Ancilla Domini!*) (1849–50); *Arthur's Tomb* (1855); *The Blue Closet, The Tune of the Seven Towers* (1857); *A Christmas Carol* (1857–8); *Bocca Baciata* (1859); *Beata Beatrix* (1860); *Venus Verticordia* (1864–8); *Monna Vanna* (1866); *Proserpine* (1874); *The Blessed Damozel* (1875–8); *Astarte Syriaca* (1877).

William Bell Scott: *King Arthur Carried from the Battlefield to the Land of Enchantment* (1847); *Iron and Coal* (*c.*1855–60); *The Gloaming* (1862); *The Eve of the Deluge* (1865).

Elizabeth Eleanor Siddal: *The Lady of Shalott* (1853); *Lovers Listening to Egyptian Girls Playing Music, Pippa Passes* (1854); *The Quest of the Holy Grail* (1855), a collaboration with DGR; *The Eve of St Agnes, Lady Affixing Pennant to a Knight's Spear, Sir Patrick Spens* (*c.*1856); *Clerk Saunders, Lady Clare, The Ladies' Lament* (1857).

Simeon Solomon: *Dante's First Meeting with Beatrice* (1859–63); *The Mother of Moses* (1860); *Love in Autumn, Damon and Aglae* (1866); *Carrying the Scrolls of the Law* (1867); *The Sleepers and the One Who Watcheth, Dawn* (1870).

ILLUSTRATIONS

Ford Madox Brown: 'Cordelia' in the *Germ* 3 (March 1850); 'Ehud and Eglon', 'The Coat of Many Colours', 'Elijah and the Widow's Son' in *Dalziels' Bible Gallery*, a collection of wood engravings of the Old Testament by a number of Pre-Raphaelite artists (1881).

Oliver Madox Brown: 'Mazeppa' and 'The Deformed Transformed' in *The Poetical Works of Byron* (1870), ed. WMR.

Edward Coley Burne-Jones: 'Ezekiel and the Boiling Pot' in *Dalziels' Bible Gallery* (1881); frontispiece, 'The Frankleynes Tale', 'The Tale of the Wife of Bath', 'Troilus and Criseyde' in the Kelmscott edition of *The Works of Geoffrey Chaucer* (1896).

James Collinson: 'The Child Jesus' in the *Germ* 2 (February 1850).

Walter Howell Deverell: 'Viola and Olivia' in the *Germ* 4 (April 1850).

Arthur Hughes: eight illustrations for William Allingham's *The Music Master* (1855), including 'The Fairies', 'Crossing the Stile' and 'Lady Alice'; over twenty illustrations in Alfred Tennyson's *Enoch Arden* (1865); frontispiece for Thomas Woolner's *My Beautiful Lady*, third edition (1866); illustrations for CGR's *Sing-Song: A Nursery Rhyme Book* (1872) and *Speaking Likenesses* (1874) and for Allingham's *Life and Phantasy* (1889).

William Holman Hunt: 'My Beautiful Lady' in the *Germ* 1 (January 1850); 'The Beggar Maid', 'The Lady of Shalott', 'Godiva' in the Moxon edition of Tennyson's *Poems* (1857); 'The Lent Jewels' in Robert Willmott's *English Sacred Poetry* (1862); 'Eliezer and Rebekah at the Well' in *Dalziels' Bible Gallery* (1881).

John Everett Millais: 'The Fireside Story' in Allingham's *The Music Master* (1855); 'Mariana', 'St Agnes' Eve', 'The Day-Dream', 'A Dream of Fair Women' in the Moxon edition of Tennyson's *Poems* (1857); 'The Lost Piece of Silver', 'The Lost Sheep', 'The Prodigal Son' in *The Parables of Our Lord* (1864); frontispiece for Allingham's *Life and Phantasy* (1889).

Dante Gabriel Rossetti: 'The Maids of Elfen-Mere' in Allingham's *The Music Master* (1855); 'The Lady of Shalott', 'The Palace of Art', 'St Cecilia', 'Sir Galahad' in the Moxon edition of Tennyson's *Poems* (1857); 'Golden head by golden head' and 'Buy from us with a golden curl' in CGR's *Goblin Market* (1862); 'The long hours go and come and go', 'You should have wept her yesterday' in CGR's *The Prince's Progress* (1866); 'The Queen's Page' in Allingham's *Flower Pieces and Other Poems* (1888).

Simeon Solomon: 'Abraham and Isaac', 'Hagar and Ishmael', 'Hosannah', 'The Infant Moses' and 'Melchizedek Blesses Abram' in *Dalziels' Bible Gallery* (1881).

Notes

The notes to each poem provide the date of its first publication. This is the first date given in each case, unless preceded by a composition date (not available for every poem). The phrase 'First poetry volume', together with a date, is used only if the poem first appeared in a particularly significant Pre-Raphaelite journal, magazine or other collection. (Some poems originally appeared in other contemporary journals, but I have noted only those publications of particular relevance to the Pre-Raphaelites.) The first volume of poetry cited is the source for the copy-text for each poem unless the poem wasn't subsequently published in book form. Any exceptions to this are mentioned in the notes. Where a group of poems is drawn from the same source, this is stated at the top of the relevant section of notes. Note numbers refer to line numbers (marked in the margin of the poems themselves).

While some of the Pre-Raphaelite poets were in thrall to medieval legend and lore, all were very much engaged with the poetry of their own age. In order to emphasize the extent to which Pre-Raphaelitism was reshaping contemporary poetry, the notes themselves focus on the influence of Romantic and Victorian poetry. They also highlight the influence of the Pre-Raphaelite poets on one another. These ambitious writers responded to and promoted each other's work, self-consciously creating their own poetic lexicons and traditions.

Notes also take account of other important works such as Thomas Malory's *Le Morte d'Arthur*, Dante Alighieri's *Divine Comedy* and the Bible. I have translated all foreign words that appear in the poems and provided limited summaries of some medieval stories to which the poems frequently allude. More scholarly work in general is needed on the influence of French, German and Italian literature on Pre-Raphaelite poetry, which often references Jean Froissart, Tannhäuser, Petrarch and Dante. Commenting on the vexed question of English translation in the nineteenth century, or on which poets were able to read poems in original European languages and how they used that experience to shape their own poetry, was considered beyond this volume's scope.

WILLIAM BELL SCOTT

From *Rosabell*

Monthly Repository (February–March 1838). A heavily revised version entitled 'Maryanne' appeared in *Poems* (Smith, Elder & Co., 1854). The original version, from which stanza 12 is reproduced here, appeared in WBS's *Autobiographical Notes* (Harper, 1892). DGR wrote of his admiration for this poem in his first letter to WBS in 1847. WBS claimed this 'fallen woman' poem inspired DGR's unfinished painting *Found* and his poem 'Jenny'.

25. *She cannot wash Christ's feet with them* alludes to an unidentified female sinner in Luke 7:37–50, who washes Christ's feet with her tears and dries them with her hair. The woman is associated with Mary Magdalene, a figure frequently represented as a reformed prostitute.

27. *without the pale* outside an area with defined boundaries.

Morning Sleep

Germ 2 (February 1850). First poetry volume *Poems* (Smith, Elder & Co., 1854).

36. *unzoned* unconstrained by a corset.

43. *Haroun* Harun al-Rashid (763–809), Caliph of Baghdad, appears in *One Thousand and One Nights*.

44. *Bagdat* Baghdad.

46. *Giafar* (767–803), vizier of Caliph Harun al-Rashid, appears in *One Thousand and One Nights*.

47. *Assad* one of the principal characters in the *One Thousand and One Nights* story of the princes Amgiad and Assad.

48–9. *long wearying / For his lost brother's step* WBS has confused the brothers here. In the story, it is Amgiad who waits for Assad.

60. *bourne* destination.

65. *tedious* moving very slowly.

68. *sward* grass.

82. *Merlin* magician and adviser to King Arthur.

115. *Chaucer* Geoffrey Chaucer (1342–1400), author of *The Canterbury Tales*.

117. *Spenser* Edmund Spenser (1552–99), author of *The Faerie Queene* (1590–96).

132. *Comus* Greek god of festivity and excess; *nectar* drink of the gods.

Sonnet: Early Aspirations

Germ 3 (March 1850).

To the Artists Called P.R.B.

Composed 1851. *Poems* (Longmans, Green & Co., 1875). See also John Tupper's 'A Quiet Evening', DGR's 'To the P.R.B.' and 'St Wagnes' Eve' and CGR's 'The P.R.B.'.

3.   *humbly stands apart* WBS was not an official member of the PRB.

5.   *old marionettes* presumably artists who conformed to Royal Academy tradition.

8.   *Uniting life with 'nature'* truth to nature was part of the Pre-Raphaelite creed.

'I Go to be Cured at Avilion'

Poems (Longmans, Green & Co., 1875).

Title. Avilion Avalon, the mythical island to which King Arthur is brought after his final battle, and from which it is hoped he will return one day. Composed for WBS's painting *King Arthur Carried from the Battlefield to the Land of Enchantment* (1847). See WM's 'Near Avalon'.

3.   *pall* a cloth spread over a coffin or bier; also a robe or cloak; *marge* margin, edge.

9.   *cresset* torch.

Art for Art's Sake

A Poet's Harvest Home (Elkin Matthews and John Lane, 1882).

7.   *stalls and boxes* of a theatre.

13.   *Fletcher* John Fletcher (1579–1625), Jacobean playwright.

JOHN RUSKIN

All poems are taken from *The Works of John Ruskin*, ed. E. T. Cook and Alexander Wedderburn, vol. 2 (George Allen, 1903).

The Last Smile

Composed 1836. *Friendship's Offering* (1837). First poetry volume *Poems* (John Wiley, 1882).

Christ Church, Oxford

Composed 1837. *Friendship's Offering* (1838). First poetry volume *Poems* (John Wiley, 1882). '... no miscellany for the boudoir was considered complete without a copy of ... "Christ Church, Oxford"' (*The Works of John Ruskin*, p. xix).

17. *oriel* bay window which projects from a wall without extending to the ground.

The Mirror

Composed 1837. *London Monthly Miscellany* (1839). First poetry volume *The Poems of John Ruskin*, vol. 2 (George Allen, 1891).

IV

4.   *Elysian* relating to the Elysian Fields, where the heroes of Greek mythology went after death.

The Old Water-Wheel

Composed 1840. *Friendship's Offering* (1841). First poetry volume *Poems* (John Wiley, 1882).

The Hills of Carrara

Composed 1841. *Friendship's Offering* (1842). First poetry volume *Poems* (John Wiley, 1882). See Arthur O'Shaughnessy's 'Carrara'.

Title. City in Tuscany, Italy, famous for its white marble.

I

3.   *cumbrous* heavily.

V

3.   *couchant* latent, deriving from the heraldic term for an animal lying down with its head raised.

FORD MADOX BROWN

All three poems are taken from *PP*, where 'Angela Damnifera' was first published. The other two poems were first published in an exhibition catalogue, *The Exhibition of 'Work' and Other Paintings by Ford Madox Brown*, at the Gallery, 191 Piccadilly, London, 1865.

Angela Damnifera

Composed 1858.

3.   *Nemesis* goddess of divine punishment for wrongdoing or hubris (excessive pride or arrogance in the face of the gods).
10. *basilisk* mythical reptile whose gaze or breath is lethal.
12. *Beatrice* Beatrice Portinari (1266–90), muse of the the poet Dante Alighieri (1265–1321).
13. *surcease* cessation.

For the Picture 'The Last of England'

Title. Refers to a major FMB painting (1855), the subject of which is immigration. FMB used himself and his family as models for this painting, now in Birmingham Museum and Art Gallery.

5.   *sots* drunkards.

For the Picture Called 'Work'

Title. Refers to a major FMB painting depicting workers digging up a road (1852–65), now in Manchester Art Gallery.

COVENTRY PATMORE

The Seasons

Germ 1 (January 1850).

Stars and Moon

Germ 2 (February 1850).

13. *boon* blessing, favour.

FROM *THE ANGEL IN THE HOUSE:*
THE BETROTHAL

Both poems were first published in (and are taken from) Book 1 of *The Angel in the House: The Betrothal* (J. W. Parker, 1854), which Patmore had begun writing around 1850, during his association with the early Pre-Raphaelites. He revised this work and continued the verse sequence of *The Angel in the House* over three additional books: *The Espousals* (J. W. Parker, 1856), *Faithful For Ever* (Macmillan, 1860) and *The Victories of Love* (Macmillan, 1862). All parts were published together in one volume in 1863. 'The Gracious Chivalry' and 'Love Liberal' constitute numbers 1 and 2 from 'The Accompaniments' in 'Canto 10: Going to Church'.

The Gracious Chivalry

18.   *gust* a passionate outburst.

WILLIAM ALLINGHAM

The Fairies

Day and Night Songs (Routledge, 1854). Illustrated by Arthur Hughes in *The Music Master* (Routledge, 1855). See CGR's 'Goblin Market'.

22.   *Columbkill* a parish in County Longford in the Irish Midlands.
24.   *Slieveleague* cliffs off the coast of County Donegal; *Rosses* region in the west of County Donegal.

Lady Alice

Day and Night Songs (Routledge, 1854). Illustrated by Arthur Hughes in *The Music Master* (Routledge, 1855), from which this text is taken. See WM's 'Golden Wings'.

II

4.   *bier* a frame to carry a coffin or a corpse to burial.

The Maids of Elfen-Mere

The Music Master, a Love Story, and Two Series of Day and Night Songs (Routledge, 1855). Illustrated by DGR. See also WM's 'The Blue Closet'.

11.   *Lilies* emblems of innocence.
17.   *sued* appealed.

Three Sisters of Haworth

Life and Phantasy (Reeves and Turner, 1889).

Title. Refers to the Brontë sisters.

3.   *sacristan* person in charge of the room where a priest prepares for a service.

Express

Life and Phantasy (Reeves and Turner, 1889).

6.   *fleet* swift.
13. *kine* cattle.

Vivant!

Life and Phantasy (Reeves and Turner, 1889).

Title. Living, alive (French).

18. *Oberon and Titania* king and queen of the fairies in William Shakespeare's *A Midsummer Night's Dream*.

JAMES COLLINSON

From *The Child Jesus*

Germ 2 (February 1850). Illustrated by Collinson.

Subtitle. Five Sorrowful Mysteries refers to five episodes leading up to Christ's crucifixion, commonly meditated upon during rosary prayer. Collinson divides his long poem into these five 'mysteries', the first of which is given here.

I
THE AGONY IN THE GARDEN

Title. After the Last Supper, Christ prays in the Garden of Gethsemane before he is betrayed by Judas. See Matthew 26:36–46 and Luke 22:40–48.

47. *oriel* bay window which projects from a wall without extending to the ground.

THOMAS WOOLNER

My Beautiful Lady

Germ 1 (January 1850). Illustrated in two panels by WHH. First poetry volume *My Beautiful Lady* (Macmillan, 1863). Because of Woolner's extensive revisions for the 1863 volume, the text is taken from the *Germ*.

26. *august* respected, impressive.
61. *ounce* snow leopard.
120. *blent* blended.

Of My Lady in Death

Germ 1 (January 1850). Although WHH is credited with being the illustrator of 'My Beautiful Lady' only, the second panel of his illustration corresponds more closely with the subject matter of 'Of My Lady in Death'. First poetry volume *My Beautiful Lady* (Macmillan, 1863). Because of Woolner's extensive revisions for the 1863 volume, the text is taken from the *Germ*.

46.   *blent* blended.

O When and Where

Germ 2 (February 1850).

Emblems

Germ 3 (March 1850). See DGR's 'The Woodspurge'.

39.   *main* ocean.
56.   *chidden* chided, scolded.

JOHN TUPPER

A Sketch from Nature

Composed 1849 – 'in Sydenham Wood', according to a note in the original text. *Germ* 1 (January 1850).

8.   *corbies* ravens or crows.
26.   *merle* blackbird.

Viola and Olivia

Germ 4 (April 1850). Illustrated by WHD.

Title. Characters from William Shakespeare's comedy *Twelfth Night*. Viola, disguised as the male page Cesario, works for the Duke, Orsino. She presents his suit to Olivia, a mourning widow. Olivia falls in love with the disguised Viola, while Viola falls in love with Orsino and Orsino with 'Cesario'. Mayhem ensues.

A Quiet Evening

Composed 1850. *Poems by the Late John Lucas Tupper* (Longmans, Green & Co., 1897). See WBS's 'To the Artists Called P.R.B.', DGR's 'To the P.R.B.' and 'St Wagnes' Eve' and CGR's 'The P.R.B.'.

1.   *ennui* boredom (French).

3.   *Gabriel* Dante Gabriel Rossetti – see Biographical Notes.
4.   *Stephens* Frederick George Stephens – see Biographical Notes.
6.   *William* William Michael Rossetti – see Biographical Notes.
9.   *John* John Lucas Tupper – see Biographical Notes.
13.   *Aleck* Alexander Tupper, John Tupper's brother, whose firm printed the *Germ*.
18.   *mundungus* smelly tobacco.
53.   *George* George Tupper, brother of John and Alexander.
77.   *Thomas* Thomas Woolner – see Biographical Notes.
78.   *like Burns 'among the three'* see ll. 19–20 of Robert Burns's drinking song 'Willie Brew'd a Peck o'Maut' (1789): 'Wha first beside his chair shall fa' / He is the King amang us three.'

WALTER HOWELL DEVERELL

The Sight Beyond

Germ 2 (February 1850).

I

2.   *Noah's dove* after the flood, Noah releases a dove three times from the ark to seek land (Genesis 8:8–12).
8.   *egress* exit, way out.

II

8.   *welkin* sky.

III

1.   *Vanity . . . quoting him of old* 'Vanity of vanities, saith the Preacher, vanity of vanities; all is vanity' (Ecclesiastes 1:2).
6.   *demesne* domain.
10.   *Jacob's ladder* in his dream, Jacob sees a ladder reaching from earth to heaven, on which angels ascend and descend. See Genesis 28:11–19.
11.   *terrene* earthly.
12.   *ken* range of knowledge or sight.
14.   *bow* rainbow, symbol of the covenant between God and mankind.

A Modern Idyl

Germ 4 (April 1850).

13.   *lilies* emblems of innocence.

GEORGE MEREDITH

From *Modern Love*

All poems were first published in (and are taken from) Meredith's sonnet sequence *Modern Love* in *Modern Love and Poems of the English Roadside, with poems and ballads* (Chapman & Hall, 1862). There are fifty sonnets in total in this sequence and, unusually, each sonnet is sixteen rather than fourteen lines long. Compare with Coventry Patmore's *Angel in the House* and DGR's sonnet sequence *The House of Life*.

VII

See DGR's 'Body's Beauty' (Sonnet LXXVIII of *The House of Life*).

5. *Cupid* Roman god of love and beauty.
7. *serpent dwelling in rich hair* recalls Medusa, a mythological monster with snakes for hair whose gaze turns men to stone. See l. 4 of CGR's 'The World': 'And subtle serpents gliding in her hair.'

IX

2. *rude* rough, ungentle, violent.

XVI

14. *Her cheek was salt* tear-streaked.

XVII

5. *ply* practise, work at diligently.
12. *ephemerioe* something short-lived, transitory, ephemeral.

XXI

13–14. *Fainting points ... in wedlock* fainting could be a sign of pregnancy.

XXIX

13–16. *A kiss is but a kiss ... on the grave* compare to ACS's 'Before Parting'.

XXXVII

4. *chariot* in Greek mythology, the chariot of the sun driven by the sun god Helios.
11. *rosed* risen.

XXXIX

2.   *rose* emblem of love.
4.   *violet* symbol of innocence and modesty as well as faithfulness.

XLV

5.   *Hesper* Venus, the evening star.

DANTE GABRIEL ROSSETTI

Rossetti was a notoriously heavy reviser, and readers should be aware that there is wide textual variation among versions of his poems. No variorum edition of his complete works exists, but there is a variorum edition of his *House of Life* sonnet sequence, edited by Roger C. Lewis (Boydell & Brewer, 2007). Other useful modern collections of his poems are Jan Marsh's *Dante Gabriel Rossetti: Collected Writings* (Dent, 1999) and Jerome McGann's *Dante Gabriel Rossetti: Collected Poetry and Prose* (Yale University Press, 2003). See also Jerome J. McGann's online archive, *The Complete Writings and Pictures of Dante Gabriel Rossetti: A Hypermedia Archive* at www.rossettiarchive.org.

Unless otherwise noted, texts here are taken from *Poems: A New Edition* (Ellis and White, 1881). The last volume Rossetti released before his death in 1882, it was a companion volume to his *Ballads and Sonnets* (F. S. Ellis, 1881). Along with new poems, *Poems* (1881) contained many works which had appeared initially in *Poems* (F. S. Ellis, 1870). A notable exception is *The House of Life* sonnet sequence. Composed between 1847 and 1881, the sonnets were published in two parts, with the first fifty sonnets appearing in *Poems* (1870) and the complete sequence of 101 sonnets in *Ballads and Sonnets* (1881) – from which the texts here are taken. The shape of this sequence changed considerably from DGR's first publication of a sixteen-sonnet version in the *Fortnightly Review* (1869) through to the sequence's appearance in *The House of Life*. For more on the complicated publishing history of the sonnets, see the variorum edition of *The House of Life*. *House of Life* sonnets which also appeared in *Poems* (1870) are indicated in the notes to individual poems, as are texts taken from other sources such as magazines and posthumously published collections.

The Blessed Damozel

Composed 1846–7. *Germ* 2 (February 1850). First poetry volume *Poems* (1870). This poem exists in several different versions as it went through various revisions from 1850 to 1881. See Elizabeth Siddal's 'He and She and Angels Three'.

Title. DGR painted *The Blessed Damozel* in 1875–8. Now in the Fogg Museum, Harvard University. The first four stanzas appear on the frame, which was designed by DGR.

1. *damozel* sixteenth- or seventeenth-century term for a young, unmarried lady of noble birth.
5. *lilies* emblems of innocence.
7. *ungirt* undone.
9. *white rose of Mary's gift* the white rose is associated with the Virgin Mary.
10. *meetly* suitably.
24. *apace* swiftly.
32. *ether* the sky above the clouds.
54. *stars sang in their spheres* in ancient philosophy, the movements of celestial bodies (which were believed to revolve around the earth) were thought to produce a kind of music.
73. *aureole* circle of light, like a halo.
107–8. *Cecily* Cecilia, virgin martyr and patron saint of musicians; *Gertrude* patron saint of pilgrims, travellers and the recently dead; *Magdalen* Mary Magdalene, a woman to whom Christ appears after his resurrection; she is often depicted as a reformed prostitute (see also note for l. 25 of WBS's 'Rosabell'); *Margaret*: virgin martyr and one of the 'Fourteen Holy Helpers', a group of saints celebrated for their intercessory powers in human affairs; *Rosalys* this name may be suggestive of the rosary; possibly also Rosalie, patron saint of Palermo, who, though descended from royalty, chose to live a life of solitude and penance.
126. *citherns and citoles* stringed instruments similar to lutes.

The Card-Dealer

Composed 1848. *Athenaeum* (1852). First poetry volume *Poems* (1870). This poem was inspired by Theodore Von Holst's painting *The Wish* (1840). See CGR's 'The Queen of Hearts'.

Title. Originally 'The Card-Dealer; or, Vingt-et-un'.
19–24. *Her fingers . . . eyes of her rings* see ll. 218–21 of John Keats's 'The Eve of St Agnes' (1819) for a similar visual effect as the moonlight shines through a stained-glass window:

> And threw warm gules on Madeline's fair breast,
> As down she knelt for heaven's grace and boon;

Rose-bloom fell on her hands, together prest,
And on her silver cross soft amethyst . . .

The Burden of Nineveh

Composed 1850. *Oxford and Cambridge Magazine* (1856). First poetry volume *Poems* (1870). Influenced by Percy Bysshe Shelley's 'Ozymandias' (1817) and John Keats's 'Ode on a Grecian Urn' (1820). See also Robert Browning's 'Love Among the Ruins' (1855).

Title. Burden a load of labour, duty, responsibility; a refrain; the primary theme or leading argument of a song or literary work. DGR's poem makes use of all these meanings. See ACS's 'A Ballad of Burdens'. *Nineveh* oldest city and capital of the ancient Assyrian empire.

2–3. *To-day I lingered . . . to living eyes* the Elgin Marbles at the British Museum.

10. *wingèd beast from Nineveh* DGR's poem was inspired by the British Museum's colossal statue, probably that of a winged lion from the Northwest Palace of Ashurnasirpal II, 883–859 BC, in northern Iraq.

14. *mitred* wearing an Assyrian headdress; *Minotaur* monster from Greek mythology with the head of a bull and the body of a man.

17. *scathe* harm or injury.

19. *cerements* cloths for wrapping a corpse.

23–7. *What song . . . strange image heard?* see ll. 8–10 of Keats's 'Ode on a Grecian Urn':

> What men or gods are these? What maidens loath?
> What mad pursuit? What struggle to escape?
> What pipes and timbrels? What wild ecstasy?

53. *Sheltered His Jonah with a gourd* refers to an episode in Jonah when God displays his power by making a giant gourd grow in order to shelter Jonah, then infesting it with a worm so that it withers and dies. See Jonah 4; see also Jonah 3, where God, having vowed to destroy Nineveh, spares the city.

60. *Sardanapalus* the last King of Assyria.

62. *Sennacherib* Assyrian king who rebuilt Nineveh and made it his capital. Assassinated by his sons. He is described in Lord Byron's 'The Destruction of Sennacherib' (1815).

64. *Semiramis* the mythological daughter of an Assyrian king and a goddess. Wife of Nineveh's founder.

70. DGR's footnote refers to the works on Nineveh of contemporary explorer, excavator and archaeologist Austen Henry Layard

(1817–94): *Nineveh and Its Remains* (1840) and *A Popular Account of Discoveries at Nineveh* (1852).

109. *Isis* principal goddess of ancient Egypt, goddess of fertility – the cow (see l. 108) was sacred to her; *Ibis* a long-legged wading bird, sacred to Isis.

110. *Thebes* Greek name for the ancient Egyptian capital under the eighteenth dynasty. The site of the major temples of Luxor and Karnak, it is famous for its monuments and Egyptian treasures.

113. *teraphim* small objects used in ancient times as household gods or oracles.

125. *sardonyx* type of onyx (a semi-precious stone) containing bands of sard, a reddish mineral; *porphyry* semi-precious, reddish-purple stone with large crystals.

148. *taboring* drumming.

164. *gypsum* soft mineral found in sedimentary deposits from which plaster of Paris is made.

166. *erst* long ago, formerly.

171–5. *For as that Bull-god . . . with destiny* see ll. 2–4 and 12–14 of Shelley's 'Ozymandias': '. . . Two vast and trunkless legs of stone / Stand in the desert. Near them, on the sand, / Half sunk, a shattered visage lies . . .'; '. . . Round the decay / Of that colossal wreck, boundless and bare / The lone and level sands stretch far away.'

181–90. *Or it may chance . . . God of Nineveh* see ll. 46–8 of Keats's 'Ode on a Grecian Urn': 'When old age shall this generation waste, / Thou shalt remain, in midst of other woe, / Than ours . . .'

182. *hoary* having white or grey hair, aged.

Jenny

Composed 1847–8. *Poems* (1870). Singled out for criticism by Robert Buchanan in *FS*, in which he accuses DGR of plagiarizing it from his own poem 'Artist and Model'. WBS claimed his 'Rosabell', which DGR knew well, was also an inspiration.

Epigraph. William Shakespeare's *Merry Wives of Windsor* IV.i.63–4.

21. *lodestar* a star used to guide ships, in particular the pole star.

24. *serried* arranged in rows.

48–9. *Your silk ungirdled . . . to the waist* see l. 7 of 'The Blessed Damozel': 'Her robe, ungirt from clasp to hem'.

100–101. *Behold the lilies . . . do they spin* 'And why take ye thought for raiment? Consider the lilies of the field, how they grow; they toil not, neither do they spin: And yet I say unto you, That even

Solomon in all his glory was not arrayed like one of these'
(Matthew 6:28–9). See also Luke 12:27. Christ's parable of the
lilies is a recurring theme of DGR's poetry. Lilies also symbolize
innocence.

116. *roses* emblems of love and beauty.

133. *broil* commotion, quarrel; *bale* torment, sorrow.

166. *Lethe* a river in Hades whose waters cause the dead to forget their
lives on earth.

230. *aureole* circle of light, like a halo.

233. *descried* seen, espied.

237. *Raffael* Raphael Sanzio (1483–1520), Italian Renaissance artist;
Leonardo Leonardo da Vinci (1452–1519), Italian Renaissance
artist.

270. *sanguine* ruddy.

278. *cipher* a secret manner of writing, a code; also a person of no
importance or worth, a nonentity. The poem makes use of both
these meanings.

280–81. *A riddle ... scornful sphinx* to enter the city of Thebes,
according to Greek mythology, travellers had to answer a riddle
posed by the Sphinx (a monster with a woman's head and lion's
body) guarding the entrance. Incorrect guesses resulted in death.

282. *Like a toad within a stone* DGR inverts the image of the toadstone,
a stone believed to form within the body of a toad and to have
magical or healing properties. See also William Shakespeare's *As
You Like It*, II.i.12–17:

> Sweet are the uses of adversity,
> Which, like the toad, ugly and venemous,
> Wears yet a precious jewel in his head;
> And this our life, exempt from public haunt,
> Finds tongues in trees, books in the running brooks,
> Sermons in stones, and good in everything.

315–16. *Your lamp, my Jenny ... Like a wise virgin's* refers to the
biblical parable of the wise and foolish virgins. While awaiting
the arrival of the bridegroom, the wise virgins bring extra oil for
their lamps, while the foolish virgins run out of oil. The foolish
virgins go out to seek more oil, but return to find the bridegroom
has arrived and shut the door against them. See Matthew 25:1–13.

322. *pier-glass* long mirror placed on a wall between two windows and
frequently of the same shape.

345. *purse* slang for 'vagina', and 'scrotum'.
366. *Paphian* relating to Paphos, a city of Cyprus where Venus was worshipped – 'Cyprian' (inhabitant of Cyprus) is slang for 'prostitute'; *Venus* Roman goddess of beauty and sensual love.
370. *Priapus* mythological Greek god of fertility.
380. *Danaë* in Greek mythology, the daughter of Acrisius, King of Argos. She is imprisoned to prevent her from conceiving the son who it is prophesied will murder the king. Zeus appears to her, disguised in the form of a shower of gold, and her son Perseus is conceived. Years later, Perseus kills Acrisius accidentally with a discus during games.

The Portrait

Composed 1847. *Poems* (1870).

1–9. *This is her picture . . . earth is over her* see the opening lines of Robert Browning's 'My Last Duchess' (1842): 'That's my last Duchess painted on the wall, / Looking as if she were alive . . .' See also 'The Portrait' and 'Willowwood' (Sonnets X and XLIX, L, LI, LII of *The House of Life*) and CGR's 'In an Artist's Studio'.
3. *glass* mirror, looking-glass.
11. *rude* rough, basic.
41–5. *And with her . . . another echo there* see 'Willowwood', Sonnet IV, ll. 9–11: '. . . I leaned low and drank / A long draught from the water where she sank, / Her breath and all her tears and all her soul'.
97. *music of the suns* see note for l. 54 of 'The Blessed Damozel'.

Nuptial Sleep

Composed 1869. *Poems* (1870), from which the text is taken and where it is Sonnet V in *The House of Life* sequence; DGR removed it from *Poems: A New Edition* (1881). It was singled out for attack by Robert Buchanan's 1871 review (*FS*, 338):

> Here is a full-grown man, presumably intelligent and cultivated, putting on record, for other full-grown men to read, the most secret mysteries of sexual connection, and that with so sickening a desire to reproduce the sensual mood, so careful a choice of epithet to convey mere animal sensations, that we merely shudder at the shameless nakedness . . . It is simply nasty.

The Woodspurge

Composed 1856. *Poems* (1870). See Thomas Woolner's 'Emblems'.

The Honeysuckle

Composed 1853. *Poems* (1870). See ACS's 'Before Parting'.

Title. Wild honeysuckle is an emblem of inconstancy in love.

4.   *quag-water* marshy or boggy water.
12.   *virgin lamps* see note for ll. 315–16 of 'Jenny'.

The Sea-Limits

Composed 1849. An early version of this poem appears in the *Germ* (March 1850) as a two-stanza poem, 'From the Cliffs: Noon'. First poetry volume *Poems* (1870).

15–20. *Listen alone . . . surge again* see ll. 9–14 of Matthew Arnold's 'Dover Beach' (1867).

> Listen! You hear the grating roar
> Of pebbles which the waves draw back, and fling,
> At their return, up the high strand,
> Begin, and cease, and then again begin,
> With tremulous cadence slow, and bring
> The eternal note of sadness in.

For 'The Wine of Circe' by Edward Burne-Jones

Composed 1870. *Poems* (1870).

Title. Refers to an episode in *The Odyssey* where Odysseus' men turn into pigs after drinking the witch Circe's wine. The EBJ painting (1863–9) is now in a private collection.

5.   *Helios* in Greek mythology, the sun god; *Hecatè* in Greek mythology, goddess of dark places; associated with sorcery.
6.   *votaress* a devoted follower or advocate.
8.   *countersign* password given in reply to a soldier on guard.

Mary's Girlhood

Composed 1848–9. *Poems* (1870). The sonnet's close attention to detail, explicit iconography and heavy symbolism are typical of the early Pre-Raphaelite period. This sonnet has a second part which WMR included in his brother's posthumous *Works* (1911).

Title. Refers to DGR's first completed oil painting, *The Girlhood of Mary Virgin*, a significant early work (1849), now in Tate Britain. The sonnet was inscribed on the picture frame. CGR posed for Mary.

7.   *Faithful . . . in charity* 'And now abideth faith, hope, charity, these three; but the greatest of these is charity' (1 Corinthians 13:13).
10.   *lily* emblem of innocence; associated with the Virgin Mary.
12.   *She woke in her white bed* WMR notes that this line has 'a more direct connection' with DGR's second painting – *The Annunciation* (or *Ecce Ancilla Domini!*) (1849–50), now in Tate Britain – which depicts Mary in white on a white bed.
14.   *fulness of the time* 'But when the fulness of the time was come, God sent forth his Son, made of a woman, made under the law' (Galatians 4:4).

On the 'Vita Nuova' of Dante

Composed 1852. *Poems* (1870).

Title. *Vita Nuova*, or 'New Life' (Italian), the autobiography of Florentine poet Dante Alighieri (1265–1321), which details his love for his muse, Beatrice Portinari (1266–90). DGR wrote this sonnet for his own translation of the *Vita Nuova*.

5.   *threefold* refers to the *terza rima* form of Dante's most famous work, *The Divine Comedy*.

Beauty and the Bird

Composed c.1854. *Poems* (1870). May have been inspired by WHD's *The Pet (or Lady Feeding a Bird)* (1850–52), now in Tate Britain.

9–11.   *the child in Chaucer . . . name in song* 'The Prioress's Tale' from Geoffrey Chaucer's *The Canterbury Tales*. In the story, Satan incites Jews to murder a boy who sings a hymn about the Virgin Mary. After his death, the boy goes on singing until an abbot removes a grain that Mary has placed on the boy's tongue.

A Match with the Moon

Composed 1854. *Poems* (1870).

4–5.   *doubled on my sight / in ponds* was reflected.
8.   *welkin's* sky's.

John Keats

Composed 1880. *Ballads and Sonnets* (1881), from which the text is taken. Sonnet IV of the sequence 'Five English Poets'. Other poets are

Thomas Chatterton, William Blake, Samuel Taylor Coleridge and Percy Bysshe Shelley.

Title. John Keats (1795–1821), poet whose early death from tuberculosis was popularly attributed to his poems' harsh treatment at the hands of reviewers. Prompted by the publication of Monkton Milnes's *Life and Letters of John Keats* (1848) and Alfred Tennyson's appreciation of Keats's work, the Pre-Raphaelites did much to revive his reputation in the nineteenth century, portraying Keatsian figures and themes in both painting and poetry. DGR identified powerfully with Keats, and a similar mythology grew around DGR's early death. Buchanan's 'Fleshly School' review (see the Introduction) has been credited with beginning Rossetti's demise. See also Shelley's poem on Keats's death, 'Adonias' (1821) and CGR's sonnet 'On Keats'. WMR notes that 'in his last few years, the poetry of Keats was more constantly present to my brother's thoughts than that of any one else' (DGR, *Works*, 671).

4.   *Castalian* Castalia was a spring on Mount Parnassus sacred to Apollo and the Muses; *Latmos* mountain where the Greek goddess Selene falls in love with Endymion and swears to protect him for ever, a reference to Keats's 'Endymion' (1818).
6.   *Lethe* see note for l. 166 of 'Jenny'. See also l. 1 of Keats's 'Ode on Melancholy' (1820): 'No, no! go not to Lethe . . .'
7.   *labour spurned* refers to poor notices from reviewers.
8.   *Rome's sheltering shadow* Keats died and was buried in Rome.
12–13. *not writ / But rumour'd in water* refers to Keats's epitaph, 'Here lies one whose name was writ in water'.

Words on the Window-Pane

Composed 1853. *Ballads and Sonnets* (1881), from which the text is taken.

4.   *tettered* afflicted with a 'tetter', a skin irritation characterized by itchy patches; *cark* troubled state of mind, distress, anxiety.
9.   *Howbeit* nevertheless, however.

Astarte Syriaca

Composed 1877. *Ballads and Sonnets* (1881), from which the text is taken.

Title. Phoenician goddess of love and fertility, identified with the Greek goddess Aphrodite and the Roman goddess Venus (see ll. 2–3). The title and subtitle '(For a Picture)' refer to a DGR painting of 1877, now in Manchester Art Gallery.

8. *spheres' dominant tune* see note for l. 54 of 'The Blessed Damozel'.

FROM *THE HOUSE OF LIFE*

For editions of *The House of Life* sequence, see the introduction to this section on DGR's poems. The sonnets from 'V. Heart's Hope' up to and including 'LIII. Without Her' are from 'Part I: Youth and Change', while the remaining sonnets are from 'Part II: Change and Fate'.

A Sonnet is a moment's monument

Composed 1880.

4. *lustral* relating to ceremonial purification.
8. *orient* lustrous, specifically in reference to a fine-quality pearl.
12. *dower* a dowry, a bride's assets offered to her husband's estate upon marriage.
14. *In Charon's palm . . . to Death* in Greek mythology, Charon is an old man who ferries the dead across the River Styx to Hades, the underworld. His passengers pay him to take them across.

V
Heart's Hope

Composed 1871.

4. *Even as that sea . . . dryshod* biblical episode in Exodus 14 in which Moses parts the waters of the Red Sea to lead the Israelites out of Egypt.
7–8. *Thy soul I know not . . . from myself* the separation and union of body and soul is a recurring theme of this sonnet sequence.

VI
The Kiss

Composed 1869. *Poems* (1870).

7. *Orpheus* in Greek mythology, a musician poet who fails to secure his wife Eurydice's release from the dead when he disobeys the command to resist looking back at her during their journey out of the underworld.
8. *lay* medieval narrative poem, often sung.

X
The Portrait

Composed 1869. *Poems* (1870). See CGR's sonnet 'In an Artist's Studio' for a very different treatment of the same subject. See also Robert Browning's 'My Last Duchess' (1842).

7.   *refluent* ebbing.

XI
The Love-Letter

Composed 1870. *Poems* (1870).

XVIII
Genius in Beauty

Composed 1871. *Ballads and Sonnets* (1881).

2.   *Homer* (eighth century BC) Greek epic poet and author of *The Odyssey* and *The Iliad*; *Dante* Dante Alighieri (1265–1321), Italian poet and author of *The Divine Comedy* and the *Vita Nuova*; see also the title note for 'On the "Vita Nuova" of Dante'.
3.   *Michael* the Italian Renaissance artist Michelangelo (1475–1564).
13.   *void of ruth* with no pity.

XIX
Silent Noon

Composed 1871. *Ballads and Sonnets* (1881).

12.   *dower* a dowry, a bride's assets offered to her husband's estate upon marriage.

XXV
Winged Hours

Composed 1869. *Poems* (1870).

3.   *covert* thicket, also feathers covering the bases of a bird's wing and tail feathers.
11.   *unleaved* with leaves removed.
12.   *brake* thicket.

XXVII
Heart's Compass

Composed 1871. *Ballads and Sonnets* (1881).

4. *halcyon* a time gone by that was peaceful and happy.
7. *oracular* of or relating to an oracle, a figure who acts as a medium for the advice and prophecy of the gods.
13. *gage* object, often a glove, thrown down by way of issuing a challenge for a duel or combat.

XXIX
The Moonstar

Composed 1871. *Ballads and Sonnets* (1881). See sonnet 218 of Petrarch's *Canzoniere* ('*Tra quantunque leggiadre donne et belle*' ('However many lovely, charming ladies')), whose language and themes Rossetti's English sonnet echoes.

8. *votaress* a devoted follower or acolyte.
11. *emulous* seeking to match, surpass or imitate.

XL
Severed Selves

Composed 1871. *Ballads and Sonnets* (1881).

XLIX, L, LI, LII
Willowwood

Composed 1868. *Fortnightly Review* (March 1869). First poetry volume *Poems* (1870). 'Willowwood' comprises four sonnets, numbers XLIX, L, LI and LII in the sequence.

I

11. *drouth* drought.

IV

2. *wellaway* lamentation.
14. *aureole* circle of light, like a halo.

LIII
Without Her

Composed 1871. *Ballads and Sonnets* (1881).

1. *glass* mirror, looking glass.

LXIII
Inclusiveness

Fortnightly Review (March 1869). *Poems* (1870). WMR comments: 'I question whether the word "Inclusiveness" quite indicates to the reader what the author meant to convey in this sonnet. The uncouth word, "many-sidedness," or "divergent identity," might be more apt' (DGR, *Works*, 655).

4.   *board* a table.

LXIX

Autumn Idleness

Composed November 1850. *Poems* (1870). See John Keats's 'To Autumn' (1820).

LXXVIII

Body's Beauty

Composed 1864–5. *Notes on the Royal Academy Exhibition* (1868) by ACS. First poetry volume *Poems* (1870). Inscribed on the frame of DGR's painting *Lady Lilith* (1866–8; altered 1872–3), now in the Delaware Art Museum. See Sonnet VII of George Meredith's *Modern Love*.

1.   *Lilith* the first wife of Adam before Eve's creation.
9.   *rose* emblem of love and beauty; *poppy* symbol of evanescent pleasure, also of sleep; here the opium poppy.
14. *And round his heart one strangling golden hair* from Goethe's *Faust*. WMR's note on the poem (DGR, *Works*, 656) provides Percy Bysshe Shelley's translation of Scene II from *Scenes from the Faust of Goethe* (1824):

> Lilith, the first wife of Adam.
> Beware of her fair hair, for she excels
> All women in the magic of her locks;
> And, when she winds them round a young man's neck,
> She will not ever set him free again.

LXXXIII

Barren Spring

Composed 1870. *Poems* (1870).
9.   *crocus* signifies youthful gladness.
10. *snowdrop* emblem of consolation, hope; *apple-blossom* symbolizes preference.
13. *lily* emblem of innocence.

LXXXV
Vain Virtues

Composed 1869. *Poems* (1870).

12.   *deigns no whit* does not condescend.

LXXXVI
Lost Days

A Welcome (1863). First poetry volume *Poems* (1870).

XCV
The Vase of Life

Composed 1869. *Fortnightly Review* (March 1869). First poetry volume *Poems* (1870).

4.   *girt* prepared and strengthened.

XCVII
A Superscription

Composed 1868–9. *Fortnightly Review* (March 1869). First poetry volume *Poems* (1870).

Title. Inscription written at the top of, above or over an existing line, letter or document.
5.   *glass* mirror, looking glass.

CI
The One Hope

Composed 1970. *Poems* (1870).

13.   *the one Hope's one name* according to WMR's notes, 'the name of the woman supremely beloved upon earth' (DGR, *Works*, 659).

To the P.R.B.

Composed 1849. *FLM* 2. See WBS's 'To the Artists Called P.R.B.', John Tupper's 'A Quiet Evening' and CGR's 'The P.R.B.'.

1.   *Woolner* Thomas Woolner; *Stephens* Frederic George Stephens; *Collinson* James Collinson; *Millais* John Everett Millais. See Biographical Notes.
12.   *Browning* the poet Robert Browning (1812–89).

14.   *Sordello* the title of a critically reviled Browning poem (1840)
       which DGR particularly admired.

St Wagnes' Eve

Composed 1851. *FLM* 2. See WBS's 'To the Artists Called P.R.B.', John
Tupper's 'A Quiet Evening' and CGR's 'The P.R.B.'.

Title. Alludes to John Keats's 'The Eve of St Agnes' (1819) and Alfred
Tennyson's 'St Agnes' Eve' (1837), works which inspired Pre-Raphaelite
paintings and poems. *Wagnes* based on 'wag', a joker.
1.   *hop-shop* dancing academy held in the house in which DGR was
       renting a studio.
2.   *Collinson* James Collinson – see Biographical Notes. He was
       known for falling asleep early and in company.
3.   *Deverell* Walter Deverell – see Biographical Notes.
5.   *Hancock* John Hancock (1825–69), sculptor and member of the
       Cyclographic Society.
7.   *Guardami ben . . . Beatrice* 'Observe me well. I am, in sooth, I
       am / Beatrice', Dante Alighieri, *Purgatorio* 30.72–3 (Henry Francis
       Cary translation, 1814); *Beatrice* see note for l. 12 of FMB's
       'Angela Damnifera'.
8.   *Bernhard Smith* (1820–85), sculptor and painter, close Pre-
       Raphaelite associate.
13.   *William North* (d. 1855), a writer, author of 'The Infinite Republic'
       (1851) and the posthumous novel *The Slave of the Lamp* (1855).

NONSENSE VERSES

Composed 1869–71. All limericks first published in *The Rossetti Papers
1862–1870*, ed. WMR (Sands & Co., 1903), except for 'There was a
young rascal called Nolly' and 'As a critic, the Poet Buchanan', which
appeared in DGR, *Works*. WMR grouped these limericks under the
heading 'Nonsense Verses', noting that they had been inspired by
Edward Lear's *Book of Nonsense* (1846).

There's an infantine Artist named Hughes

1.   *Hughes* Arthur Hughes – see Biographical Notes.
2.   *R.A.* Royal Academy.

There is a young Artist named Jones

1.   *Jones* Edward Burne-Jones – see Biographical Notes.

There is a young Painter called Jones

1.   *Jones* Edward Burne-Jones – see Biographical Notes.

There's a combative Artist named Whistler

1.   *Whistler* James McNeill Whistler (1834–1903), American painter.
2.   *hog-hairs* paint brushes (made of hog's hair).

A Historical Painter named Brown

1.   *Brown* Ford Madox Brown – see Biographical Notes.
3.   *epochs of victual* mealtimes.
4.   *pudden . . . kittle* mispronunciation of 'pudding' and 'kettle'.

There was a young rascal called Nolly

1.   *Nolly* Oliver Madox Brown – see Biographical Notes.

There's a Scotch correspondent named Scott

1.   *Scott* William Bell Scott – see Biographical Notes.

There once was a painter named Scott

1.   *Scott* William Bell Scott – see Biographical Notes.

There's the Irishman Arthur O'Shaughnessy

1.   *Arthur O'Shaughnessy* see Biographical Notes.

There is a poor sneak called Rossetti

1.   *Rossetti* Dante Gabriel Rossetti – see Biographical Notes.

As a critic, the Poet Buchanan

1.   *Buchanan* Robert Buchanan (1841–1901), author of *FS*.
3.   *Into Maitland he shrunk* Buchanan published his review under
       the pseudonym 'Thomas Maitland'.

ELIZABETH SIDDAL

'True Love', 'Dead Love', 'Shepherd Turned Sailor', 'Gone', 'Speechless',
'The Lust of the Eyes', 'Worn Out' and 'At Last' are taken from *RRP*.
Although he is uncertain, WMR puts their composition dates at roughly
1855–7. 'Early Death', 'He and She and Angels Three', 'A Silent Wood',
'Love and Hate', 'The Passing of Love', 'Lord, May I Come?' are taken
from *SR* 1. WMR supplied the titles for these. He writes that he cannot
provide composition dates, but guesses that 'Lord, May I Come?',

'written in a very shaky and straggling way . . . must have been done under the influence of laudanum, . . . and probably not long before her death' (*SR* 1, 196). 'A Year and A Day' is taken from *FLM* 1.

True Love

1 *Earl Richard* refers to a Scottish ballad, 'Earl Richard', adapted by Walter Scott in *Minstrelsy of the Scottish Border* (1833). This volume also contains 'Clerk Saunders', for which Siddal painted a watercolour of the same name in 1857. The ballad concerns the murder of Earl Richard by his jealous lover, and the discovery of her guilt through the chattering of a tell-tale bird.

Dead Love

3.   *blue . . . red* the colour blue is associated with chastity and loyalty, while red commonly symbolizes passion.

Shepherd Turned Sailor

See CGR's 'An End'.

Gone

11–12. *tender dove / That left the ark* after the flood, Noah releases a dove three times from the ark to seek land. After the third time, the dove does not return (Genesis 8:8–12).

Speechless

Liana Cheney in *Pre-Raphaelitism and Medievalism in the Arts* (E. Mellen Press, 1992) suggests that this poem is influenced by the poetry of Christine de Pisan (1363–*c*.1434).

The Lust of the Eyes

See DGR's 'The Portrait' (1870), CGR's 'In an Artist's Studio', ACS's 'Before Parting' and Arthur O'Shaughnessy's 'Paros'.

Worn Out

5–8. *For I am but . . . away from thee* see ll. 11–14 of DGR's 'Winged Hours':

> When, wandering round my life unleaved, I know
> The bloodied feathers scattered in the brake,
>   And think how she, far from me, with like eyes
> Sees through the untuneful bough the wingless skies?

At Last

See CGR's 'After Death'.

12. *winding-sheet* shroud.

He and She and Angels Three

See DGR's 'Blessed Damozel'.

A Silent Wood

First published by WMR in the *Burlington Magazine* (May 1903). See DGR's 'Willowwood' (Sonnets XLIX, L, LI, LII of *The House of Life*).

1–2. *O silent wood . . . full of misery* see the opening lines of Canto I of Dante Alighieri's *Inferno*, where the poet finds himself in crisis while wandering through '*una selva oscura*' ('a dark wood').

7. *boon* blessing, favour.

Love and Hate

19. *poisonous tree* refers to Eve's sampling of the forbidden fruit of the tree of knowledge in Genesis 3. See also note for l. 260 of CGR's 'Goblin Market' and Matthew 12:33: 'Either make the tree good, and his fruit good; or else make the tree corrupt, and his fruit corrupt: for the tree is known by his fruit.'

The Passing of Love

19–20. *That dragged my idol . . . all its shrine* see Exodus 32, where Moses destroys the golden calf and forbids the worship of idols.

Lord, May I Come?

16. *lilies* emblems of innocence.

A Year and a Day

7–10. *I lie among . . . in its bed* see ll. 7–10 of DGR's 'The Woodspurge':

> My hair was over in the grass,
> My naked ears heard the day pass.
>
> My eyes, wide open, had the run
> Of some ten weeds to fix upon . . .

WILLIAM MICHAEL ROSSETTI

Her First Season

Germ 1 (January 1850).

'Jesus Wept'

Germ 4 (April 1850).

Title. John 11:35.
9.   *Mary and Martha* sisters of Lazarus, whom Jesus raises from the dead.
10–11. *'Where / Have ye . . . come and see'* (John 11:34).

The Evil Under the Sun

Germ 4 (April 1850).

Title. A common phrase of Ecclesiastes, appearing in several chapters: 4:3, 5:13, 6:1, 9:3 and 10:5.
1.   *How long, oh Lord?* 'My soul is also sore vexed: but thou, O Lord, how long?' (Psalms 6:3).
3.   *John Evangelist* one of Christ's twelve apostles.
4.   *Patmos* Greek island in the Aegean Sea where St John was living when he had the visions of Revelation.
6.   *day of the great reckoning* Judgement Day.

Dedication

Democratic Sonnets (Alston Rivers, 1907).

11.   *mortal Easter-day* DGR died on Easter Sunday, 9 April 1882.

Mary Shelley

Composed 1851. *Democratic Sonnets* (Alston Rivers, 1907).

Title. Née Wollstonecraft Godwin (1797–1851). Author of *Frankenstein* (1818) and wife of the poet Percy Bysshe Shelley (1792–1822).
1–2. *her who . . . women's cause* Mary Wollestonecraft (1759–97), feminist and author of *A Vindication of the Rights of Woman* (1792).
3–4. *him who reasoned . . . balance weighed* William Godwin (1756–1836), radical and political philosopher.
9.   *for aye* for ever.
11–12. *thirtieth year of severance . . . drowned Shelley* Shelley famously drowned when his sailing boat sank in a storm off the coast of Italy in 1822, twenty-nine years before she died (i.e. the 'thirtieth year' of their time apart).

12. *Harriet* Harriet Westbrook (1795–1816), Shelley's first wife, who committed suicide by drowning.

CHRISTINA GEORGINA ROSSETTI

Dream Land

Composed April 1849. *Germ* 1 (January 1850). First poetry volume *Goblin Market* (Macmillan, 1862). See Samuel Taylor Coleridge, 'Kubla Khan, or, A Vision in a Dream, a Fragment' (1816). See also ACS's 'The Garden of Proserpine' and 'A Ballad of Dreamland'.

15–16. *And hears the nightingale . . . sadly sings* see John Keats's 'Ode to a Nightingale' (1819).

An End

Composed 5 March 1849. *Germ* 1 (January 1850). First poetry volume *Goblin Market* (Macmillan, 1862).

1. *Love, strong as Death* 'Set me as a seal upon thine heart, as a seal upon thine arm: for love is strong as death; jealousy is cruel as the grave . . .' (Song of Solomon, 8:6). See also Sonnet 7, ll. 13–14, of 'Monna Innominata': 'Though jealousy be cruel as the grave, / And death be strong, yet love is strong as death.'
4–5. *A green turf . . . at his feet* See Ophelia's 'Song' in William Shakespeare's *Hamlet* IV.v:

> He is dead and gone, lady,
> He is dead and gone;
> At his head a grass-green turf,
> At his heels a stone.

A Pause of Thought

Composed 14 February 1848. *Germ* 2 (February 1850). First poetry volume *Goblin Market* (Macmillan, 1862).

2. *hope deferred made my heart sick* 'Hope deferred maketh the heart sick: but when the desire cometh, it is a tree of life' (Proverbs 13:12).

Sweet Death

Composed 9 February 1849. *Germ* 2 (March 1850). First poetry volume *Goblin Market* (Macmillan, 1862).

16.   *grass* emblem of utility, submission; biblical symbol of mortality.
24.   *glean with Ruth* the widowed Ruth marries Boaz after he sees her
      gleaning (gathering what was left by the reapers) in his cornfield.
      Their union begins the earthly lineage of Christ (Ruth 2–3). See
      also ll. 65–7 of John Keats's 'Ode to a Nightingale' (1819):
      'Perhaps the self-same song that found a path / Through the sad
      heart of Ruth, when, sick for home, / She stood in tears amid the
      alien corn'.

Goblin Market

Composed 22 April 1859. *Goblin Market* (Macmillan, 1862), for which
DGR provided two illustrations. See William Allingham's 'The Fairies'.

3–4.   *'Come buy . . . come buy'* 'Ho, everyone that thirsteth, come ye
       to the waters and he that hath no money, come ye, buy, and eat;
       yea, come buy wine and milk without money and without price'
       (Isaiah 55:1).
10.   *Swart-headed* dark.
76.   *ratel* badger-like animal, also known as a 'honey badger'.
83.   *lily* emblem of innocence.
126.   *precious golden lock* in folklore, fairies prize golden hair,
       kidnapping or seducing golden-haired girls for fairy brides.
129.   *honey from the rock* 'He made him ride on the high places of the
       earth, that he might eat the increase of the fields; and he made
       him to suck honey out of the rock, and oil out of the flinty rock'
       (Deuteronomy 32:13).
160.   *daisies* emblems of innocence.
185.   *Like two pigeons* 'And if she be not able to bring a lamb, then she
       shall bring . . . two young pigeons; the one for the burnt offering,
       the other for a sin offering; and the priest shall make an atonement
       for her, and she shall be clean' (Leviticus 12:7).
220.   *flags* irises, symbolizing eloquence.
258.   *succous* containing juice or sap.
260.   *Her tree of life* the tree of life grew in the Garden of Eden: 'And
       out of the ground made the Lord God to grow every tree that is
       pleasant to the sight, and good for food: the tree of life also in the
       midst of the garden, and the tree of knowledge of good and evil'
       (Genesis 2:9). See also Revelation 22:2 and note for l. 2 of 'A Pause
       of Thought'.
290.   *drouth* drought.
395.   *Cross-grained* contrary, intractable, perverse.
410.   *Like a rock of blue-veined stone* 'He is like a man which built an
       house, and digged deep, and laid the foundation upon a rock, and

when the flood arose, the stream beat vehemently upon that house, and could not shake it; for it was founded upon a rock' (Luke 6:48).

415–16. *orange-tree / White with blossoms* orange blossom signifies chastity.

451. *dingle* hollow or dell.

471. *Eat me, drink me* 'And when he had given thanks, he brake it, and said, Take, eat: this is my body, which is broken for you: this do in remembrance of me' (1 Corinthians 11:24). See also Christ's words to his disciples during the sacrament of the Eucharist (Matthew 26:26–9, Mark 14:22–5 and Luke 22:17–20). See also Chapter 1 of Lewis Carroll's *Alice's Adventures in Wonderland* (1865), where Alice follows the instructions 'Eat me' and 'Drink Me'.

479. *fruit forbidden* see note for l. 19 of Elizabeth Siddal's 'Love and Hate'.

491. *aguish* feverish.

494. *wormwood* a bitter ingredient of vermouth and absinthe, used as a tonic.

A Birthday

Composed 18 November 1857. *Goblin Market* (Macmillan, 1862). See John Payne's 'A Birthday Song'.

6.   *halcyon* happy and peaceful.
9.   *dais* platform for a throne.
10.   *vair* fur used for trimming garments.

After Death

Composed 28 April 1849. *Goblin Market* (Macmillan, 1862).

My Dream

Composed 9 March 1855. *Goblin Market* (Macmillan, 1862).

15.   *waxed* grew in size.
48.   *appropriate tears* 'crocodile' tears.

The World

Composed 27 June 1854. *Goblin Market* (Macmillan, 1862). See John Keats's 'La Belle Dame Sans Merci' (1820).

4.   *subtle serpents gliding in her hair* allusion to the snake-haired gorgon Medusa whose looks turn men to stone. See Sonnet VII, l. 7, of George Meredith's *Modern Love*: 'serpent dwelling in rich hair'.

14. *Till my feet, cloven too, take hold on hell?* 'For the lips of a strange
   woman drop as an honeycomb, and her mouth is smoother than
   oil: But her end is bitter as wormwood, sharp as a two-edged
   sword. Her feet go down to death; her steps take hold on hell'
   (Proverbs 5:3–5).

From *The Prince's Progress*

This extract (ll. 481–540) was first published in *Macmillan's Magazine*
7 (May 1863), p. 36. The complete poem first appeared in *The Prince's
Progress* (Macmillan, 1866), for which DGR provided two illustrations.
In this poem, a prince who is 'Strong of limb if of purpose weak' (l. 47)
procrastinates on his journey to rescue his princess, and arrives to find
she has died waiting. In this extract, he is addressed by someone in her
funeral cortège.

25. *poppies* signify sleep.
58. *roses* symbolize love and beauty.

The Queen of Hearts

Composed 3 January 1863. *The Prince's Progress* (Macmillan, 1866).
See DGR's 'The Card-Dealer'.
13. *prepense* planned or intended in advance, premeditated.

From *Monna Innominata*

Composed *c.*1879–80. *A Pageant and Other Poems* (Macmillan, 1881).
English translations of the epigraphs from Dante's *Divine Comedy* and
Petrarch's *Canzoniere* are by Charles Cayley (1823–83), scholar and
close personal friend of CGR. Although she turned down his marriage
proposal, CGR became his literary executor after his death.

Title. 'unnamed lady' (Italian).

Prefatory note. Beatrice muse of Dante Alighieri – see title note for
DGR's 'On the "Vita Nuova" of Dante'; *'altissimo poeta . . . cotanto
amante'* the greatest poet and lover combined (Italian), i.e. Dante, see
Inferno 4.80; *Laura* muse of Petrarch (1304–74), Italian scholar and
poet; *Albigenses* members of a Provençal religious movement that
preached a dualistic doctrine of material evil and spiritual good;
Troubadours lyric poets of southern France from the twelfth and
early thirteenth centuries; *Great Poetess* Elizabeth Barrett Browning
(1806–61).

I

Epigraph. 'Since morn have said Adieu to darling friends' (*Purgatorio*

8.3); 'Love, with what force thou dost me now o'erthrow' (*Canzoniere* 85.12).

4

Epigraph. 'Great fire may after little spark succeed' (*Paradiso* 1.34); 'Take flight all thoughts and things that it contains, / And therein Love alone with you remains' (*Canzoniere* 72.44–5).

8.   *weights and measures* 'Diverse weights, and diverse measures, both of them are alike abomination to the Lord' (Proverbs 20:10).

7

Epigraph. 'Here spring was always, and each plant' (*Purgatorio* 28.143); 'Love with me walks and talks, and with him I' (*Canzoniere* 35.14).

5.   *Love builds the house on rock and not on sand* 'And everyone that hearest these sayings of mine, and doeth them not, shall be likened unto a foolish man, which built his house upon sand' (Matthew 7:26). See also Matthew 7:24 and Luke 6:48.
13–14. *Though jealousy be cruel . . . love is strong as death* 'Set me as a seal upon thine heart, as a seal upon thine arm: for love is strong as death; jealousy is cruel as the grave: the coals thereof are coals of fire, which hath a most vehement flame' (Song of Solomon 8:6). See also l. 1 of 'An End': 'Love, strong as Death, is dead.'

8

Epigraph. 'And breathe to God, "Nought recketh me, but thou"' (*Purgatorio*, 8.12); 'I hope to miss not pardon – pity I mean' (*Canzoniere* 1.8).

1.   *'I, if I perish, perish' – Esther spake* ' . . . and so will I go in unto the king, which is not according to the law: and if I perish, I perish' (Esther 4:6).
4.   *slake* here, to quench or extinguish.
8.   *Harmless as doves and subtle as a snake* 'Behold, I send you forth as sheep in the midst of wolves: be ye therefore wise as serpents, and harmless as doves' (Matthew 10:16).
9.   *She trapped him with one mesh of silken hair* see l. 14 of DGR's 'Body's Beauty' (Sonnet LXXVIII of *The House of Life*): 'And round his heart one strangling golden hair'.

11

Epigraph. 'Let people talk, and thou behind me go' (*Purgatorio* 5.13); 'Counting the chances that our life befall' (*Canzoniere* 285.12).

5. *prate* chatter idly.
13. *make it plain* 'And the Lord answered me, and said, Write the vision, and make it plain upon tables, that he may run that readeth it' (Habbakuk 2:2).

14

Epigraph. 'In His good pleasure we have each his peace' (*Paradiso* 3.85); 'Alone with these my thoughts, with altered hair' (*Canzoniere* 30.32).

4. *roses* emblems of beauty.

Babylon the Great

The Face of the Deep (1892). First poetry volume *Verses* (1893). See 'The World'.

Title. 'And upon her forehead was a name written, MYSTERY, BABYLON THE GREAT, THE MOTHER OF HARLOTS AND ABOMINATIONS OF THE EARTH' (Revelation 17:5).

3. *mesh thee in her wanton hair* see l. 14 of DGR's 'Body's Beauty' (Sonnet LXXVIII of *The House of Life*): 'And round his heart one strangling golden hair'.
7. *No wine is in her cup, but filth is there* 'And the woman was arrayed in purple and scarlet colour, and decked with gold and precious stones and pearls, having a golden cup in her hand full of abominations and filthiness of her fornication' (Revelation 17:4).
13. *Her scarlet vest and gold and gem and pearl* see note for l. 7. See also Revelation 18:16.
14. *set on fire* 'Therefore shall her plagues come in one day, death, and mourning, and famine; and she shall be utterly burned with fire: for strong is the Lord God who judgeth her' (Revelation 18:8).

On Keats

Composed 18 January 1849 – noted as the 'Eve of St Agnes' in the original text. *New Poems* (Macmillan, 1896).

Title. See title note for DGR's 'John Keats'.

3. *strong man grown weary of a race* 'Which is as a bridegroom coming out of his chamber, and rejoiceth as a strong man to run a race' (Psalm 19:5).
4–5. *Unto him . . . there thorns are not* this refers to Christ's parable of the sower. See Matthew 13, Mark 4 and Luke 8.
6. *daisies* emblem of innocence. Daisies feature frequently in Keats's poems.

10–11. *Here lies one whose . . . In water* Keats's epitaph. See also ll.
12–13 of DGR's 'John Keats': 'not writ / But rumour'd in water'.
12.   *basil* alludes to Keats's 'Isabella or The Pot of Basil' (1820).

Portraits

Composed 9 May 1853. *New Poems* (Macmillan, 1896). The poem's first stanza portrays WMR, while WMR and DGR are the subject of the second stanza. See Biographical Notes.

In an Artist's Studio

Composed 24 December 1856. *New Poems* (Macmillan, 1896). According to WMR, this poem was inspired by the paintings and drawing of Elizabeth Siddal during CGR's visit to DGR's studio. See DGR's 'The Portrait' (1870) and 'The Portrait' (Sonnet X of *The House of Life*). See also Arthur O'Shaughnessy's 'Paros' and Philip Bourke Marston's 'Love Past Utterance'.

The P.R.B.

Composed 10 November 1853. *FLM* 1. First poetry volume *The Poetical Works of Christina Georgina Rossetti*, ed. WMR (Macmillan, 1904). See DGR's 'To the P.R.B.' and 'St Wagnes' Eve'. See also WBS's 'To the Artists Called P.R.B.' and John Tupper's 'A Quiet Evening'.

Title. The Pre-Raphaelite Brotherhood. Everyone mentioned in the poem is a member. See also Biographical Notes.
2.   *Woolner in Australia* sculptor Thomas Woolner moved briefly to Australia to search for gold.
3.   *Hunt . . . Cheops* painter WHH was preparing for a painting trip to Egypt and Palestine.
4.   *shuns the vulgar optic* DGR, stung by negative reviews of his work, was refusing to exhibit publicly.
5–6. *William M. Rossetti* 'It means that I, as art-critic of *The Spectator*, abused in that paper my fellows in the Praeraphaelite Brotherhood, and that no one heeded my reviews. This joke was not historically true . . .' (WMR's notes to *The Poetical Works of Christina Georgina Rossetti*, p. 491); *Coptic* the liturgical language of the Coptic Church.
7.   *Stephens* Frederic George Stephens, an art critic who began as a painter.
9.   *Millais* John Everett Millais.
11.   *A.R.A.* JEM was made an Associate of the Royal Academy of Art in 1853.

ARTHUR HUGHES

To a Child

Composed 1886. *PP*. Title given by Kineton Parkes.

In a Letter to William Bell Scott at Penkill

Composed 1887. *PP*. Title given by Kineton Parkes.

Title. William Bell Scott see Biographical Notes; *Penkill* a Scottish castle in Ayrshire dating from the sixteenth century. Unhappily married, WBS began an affair with its owner, Alice Boyd, which was tolerated by his wife. In 1864, he moved to Penkill, where he died in 1890. WBS painted murals for the castle, and WM designed some of its tapestries.

1. *Scotus* nickname for WBS.
14. *Michael's Mount* St Michael's Mount, tidal island off the south coast of Cornwall.

WILLIAM MORRIS

All poems first appeared in (and are taken from) WM's first book of poems, *The Defence of Guenevere and Other Poems* (Bell and Daldy, 1858), except where otherwise noted. Poems from this volume were composed between 1856 and 1858.

The Chapel in Lyoness

Oxford and Cambridge Magazine (1856).

Title. Lyoness Arthurian kingdom.
Subtitle. Sir Ozana le Cure Hardy minor knight in King Arthur's court whose career is undistinguished. As is often the case with WM, the poet compresses, modifies or alters episodes of the Malory narrative for dramatic effect. This poem conflates events of Ozana's story with Galahad's search for the Holy Grail. See Malory, Book 10, chapters 11 and 13; Book 18, chapters 10 and 11; and Book 19, Chapter 1. *Sir Galahad* son of Lancelot and Elaine of Corbenic, distinguished for his purity. *Sir Bors de Ganys* grail-seeker, along with Sir Galahad.

11. *parclose* a screen.
15. *samite* silk fabric interwoven with silver and gold threads.
41. *ween* thought, supposed.
51. *drouth* drought.

Riding Together

Oxford and Cambridge Magazine (1856).

12.   *helms* helmets.
18.   *rood* crucifix.
40.   *mazed* confused, dazed.

The Defence of Guenevere

Title. The Arthurian tale of Queen Guenevere's (also spelled 'Guinevere') trial and rescue by Lancelot which inspires this poem can be found in Book 20, chapters 1–8 of Malory. See also WM's 1858 painting *La Belle Iseult* (also called *Queen Guenevere*), now in Tate Britain. For a similar experiment in *terza rima*, see Robert Browning's 'The Statue and the Bust' (1855).

8.   *Gauwaine* (also spelled 'Gawain') a knight of the Round Table.
13.   *wot* knows.
34.   *choosing cloths* pennants, banners; see also ll. 22 and 33.
149. *certes* assuredly, I assure you.
153. *your mother* Morgawse, sister of Arthur, mother of Mordred, wife of King Lot. She is murdered by her son Gaheris (Gauwaine's brother) for becoming Sir Lamorak's lover in Malory, Book 10, Chapter 24.
156. *drouth* drought.
157. *Agravaine* brother of Gauwaine and Gaheris. He accuses Guenevere of adultery with Launcelot and is killed by Launcelot. See Malory, Book 20, chapters 1–4.
168. *Mellyagraunce* a knight whose love for Guenevere is unrequited. After abducting the queen and accusing her of treason, he is killed by Launcelot. See Malory, Book 19, chapters 1–9.
169. *la Fausse Garde* Mellyagraunce's castle.
173. *blood upon my bed* when climbing into Guenevere's chamber through the window, Launcelot cuts his hand and bleeds on her sheets. Mellyagraunce later sees the blood and accuses her of adultery, and therefore treason, with a wounded knight. See Malory, Book 19, Chapter 6.
201. *weet* know.
211. *caitiff* coward.
220. *shent* disgraced, shamed.
222. *blent* blended.

The Gilliflower of Gold

Title. Gilliflower emblem of unfading beauty and bonds of affection.

2. *helm* helmet.
3. *tourney* tournament.
4. *la belle jaune giroflée* the pretty yellow gilliflower (French).
10. *steel-coat* chain mail.
25. *'Honneur aux fils des preux!'* honour to the sons of the brave (French).
53. *mazed* confused, dazed.

The Judgment of God

31. *thwart* across.
46. *recreant* cowardly, disloyal.
67. *sere* withered.

Spell-Bound

See Tennyson's 'Mariana' (1830) and John Keats's 'La Belle Dame Sans Merci' (1820). See also CGR's 'The Prince's Progress'.

24. *samite* silk fabric interwoven with silver and gold threads.
39. *burden* refrain.

The Blue Closet

See William Allingham's 'The Maids of Elfen-Mere'.

Title. DGR painted a watercolour of this subject, with the same title, in 1857; now in Tate Britain.
Stanza title. Damozels see note for l. 1 of 'The Blessed Damozel'.

5. *'Laudate pueri'* praise, oh you servants (Latin).

The Tune of Seven Towers

Title. Inspired by DGR's 1857 watercolour of the same name, now in Tate Britain.

26–7. *coif . . . kirtle* cap and gown.

Golden Wings

Jehane's story echoes that of the Lady in Alfred Tennyson's 'The Lady of Shalott' (1832). See also William Allingham's 'Lady Alice'.

47. *Castel beau* beautiful manor.
51. *fille de fay* daughter of Fay (French).
74. *Undern* mid-afternoon.
87–8. *Arthur . . . Avallon* Avalon, the mythical island to which King Arthur is brought after his final battle, and from which it is hoped

he will return one day. See 'Near Avalon' and WBS's 'I Go to be Cured at Avilion'.

104. *She murmur'd: 'He will be here soon'* see the refrain of Tennyson's 'Mariana' (1830):

> She only said, 'My life is dreary,
> He cometh not,' she said;
> She said, 'I am aweary, aweary,
> I would that I were dead!'

174. *pennon* a long, triangular or swallow-tailed flag, a pennant.
235. *draggled* made dirty and wet.

The Haystack in the Floods

Inspired by events of the Hundred Years' War as described in the *Chronicles* of Jean Froissart (*c*.1337–*c*.1405). While some details have historical merit, the incident and characters are WM's creation.

9.   *kirtle* a woman's gown or outer petticoat.
34.   *That Judas, Godmar* presumably a French enemy, but the link to Judas opens the possibility that he is an English traitor; possibly based on Froissart's Godmar du Fay in *Chronicles*, Book 1 (1322–77).
36.   *pennon* a long, triangular or swallow-tailed flag, a pennant.
39.   *Robert* an English military leader.
42.   *coif* close-fitting cap.
45.   *Poictiers* the battle of Poitiers, 1356, won by the English during the Hundred Years' War.
52.   *Chatelet* the Grand Châtelet, in Paris, destroyed under Napoleon I in the early nineteenth century. Used from the Middle Ages for common-law jurisdiction, it contained a prison and a court, and was famous for confessions being extracted by torture.
69.   *Jehane* French lover of Robert.
95.   *in such wise* in this manner.
153. *fitte* section of a poem.

Two Red Roses Across the Moon

WM's 'lady' echoes Alfred Tennyson's 'Mariana' (1830) and 'The Lady of Shalott' (1832). In an 1872 volume entitled *Fly Leaves*, C. S. Calverly wrote a parody, using the refrain '*Butter and eggs and a pound of cheese*'. It concludes, 'And as to the meaning, it's what you please.'

3–4. *And ever she sung . . . across the moon* see note for l. 103 of
'Golden Wings'.

5–10. *There was a knight . . . past the hall* compare with Lancelot's
arrival in 'The Lady of Shalott', ll. 74–105: 'He rode between the
barley-sheaves . . . '

29.   *trow* think, believe.

30.   *draggled* made dirty and wet.

33.   *may* hawthorn.

Near Avalon

Title. After King Arthur's final battle, he is taken in a barge to the island
of Avalon, accompanied by three queens, Morgan le Fay, the Queen of
the Waste Lands and Nyneve, the chief Lady of the Lake. See also WBS's
'I Go to be Cured at Avilion'.

11.   *heaumes* helmets.

Praise of My Lady

This poem's lady, with her thick hair, long neck, pale skin and mournful,
large eyes typifies the Pre-Raphaelite feminine ideal. George du Maurier
parodies this ideal of beauty in his 'A Legend of Camelot', which
appeared in *Punch* (March 1866). It also targets the medievalism of
DGR's poetry and WM's other Arthurian poems.

4.   *Beata mea Domina* my blessed lady (Latin).

67.   *pennon* a long, triangular or swallow-tailed flag, a pennant.

FROM *THE EARTHLY PARADISE*

The following three extracts were first published in (and are taken
from) *The Earthly Paradise*, vol. 1 (F. S. Ellis, 1868).

An Apology

The first section of *The Earthly Pardise*. Compare with DGR's 'A Sonnet
is a moment's monument'.

The Wanderers

This extract reproduces ll. 1–16 from the second section of *The Earthly
Paradise*, 'Prologue: The Wanderers'.

8.   *Levantine* from the Levant, the eastern part of the Mediterranean.

12.   *napery* household linen.

13.   *Guienne* a region of southern France.

14.   *Geoffrey Chaucer* see note for l. 118 of WBS's 'Morning Sleep'.

15. *lading* cargo.

May

This extract reproduces ll. 1–21 from the section of *The Earthly Paradise* entitled 'May'.

14. *Eld* former times, old times.
16. *ousel* bird.

ALGERNON CHARLES SWINBURNE

Unless otherwise noted, texts here are taken from the six-volume edition of *The Poems of Algernon Charles Swinburne* (Chatto & Windus, 1904), which is generally regarded as more reliable than the twenty-volume Bonchurch edition of Swinburne's complete works (1925–7). Poems from *Poems and Ballads* and *Poems and Ballads II* are taken from vols. 1 and 2 respectively. Poems from *Tristram of Lyonesse* are taken from vol. 4, those from *The Heptalogia* from vol. 5 and from *A Midsummer Holiday* from vol. 6.

A Ballad of Life

Poems and Ballads (Moxon, 1866). Withdrawn in 1866 by its original publisher, Edward Moxon, the volume was republished by John Camden Hotten in the same year.

11. *cithern* a stringed instrument similar to a lute.
29. *upon this wise* in this manner.
76. *Borgia* Lucrezia Borgia (1480–1519), Italian noblewoman who made three political marriages and is popularly regarded as a *femme fatale*.

Laus Veneris

Composed 1862. *Poems and Ballads* (Moxon, 1866). ACS prefaces the original poem with a French epigraph taken, he claims, from Maistre Antoine Gaget's *Livre des grandes merveilles d'amour* ('Book of the Wonders of Love'). The epigraph and its author are both ACS's own inventions. The poem is inspired by the fifteenth-century German Tannhäuser legend, about a minstrel knight who lives in sin with Venus until he is overcome with guilt. He journeys to Rome to ask the Pope's forgiveness, which the Pope denies him. The Pope decrees that, just as it is as impossible for flowers to bloom from his staff, it is impossible for Tannhäuser's sin to be forgiven. After Tannhäuser leaves, flowers do indeed bloom from the Pope's staff, but the knight never hears of this, and dies thinking he is damned.

Title. Laus Veneris in praise of Venus (or love) (Latin). Also the title of an EBJ painting (1873–5), now in the Laing Art Gallery, Newcastle upon Tyne.

1. *Asleep or waking is it* see l. 80 of John Keats's 'Ode to a Nightingale' (1819): 'Fled is that music: – Do I wake or sleep?'
16. *feet and hands . . . were priced* refers to Christ's crucifixion to save mankind.
25. *Horsel* Hörselberg in Thuringia, the location of the underground palace of Venus.
26. *wot* knows.
133. *Adonis* the mortal object of Venus's love. Though she warns him to be careful when hunting, Adonis is killed by a wild boar. Venus transforms his blood into anemones, delicate, short-lived flowers.
172. *Nathless* nevertheless.
197–9. *Egyptian lote-leaf is . . . suckling snake of gold* a reference to Cleopatra (69–30 BC), ancient Egyptian queen known for her seductive charm and political acumen. Legend has it that she committed suicide by holding an asp to her breast.
200. *Semiramis* the mythological daughter of an Assyrian king and a goddess, wife of Nineveh's founder, known for her great beauty and sexual appetite.
252. *teen* suffering, grief.
271. *springe* a snare.
272. *gin* a trap or snare.
278. *vair* fur used for trimming garments.
283. *Magdalen* see note for l. 25 of WBS's 'Rosabell'.
296. *guerdon* reward, recompense.
299. *bay-leaf* worn to signify poetic talent.
350. *Who in the Lord God's likeness bears the keys* the keys to the kingdom of heaven entrusted by Jesus to Simon Peter, and part of the papal insignia ever since.
365. *wist* learned, came to know.
390–91. *As when she came . . . whereon she trod* evoking the birth of Venus, who, according to classical mythology, rose fully formed from the sea.
398. *swart* black.
417. *till the thunder in the trumpet be* see 1 Corinthians 15:52: 'In a moment, in the twinkling of an eye, at the last trump: for the

trumpet shall sound, and the dead shall be raised incorruptible, and we shall be changed.'

424. *The thunder of the trumpets of the night* see the note to l. 417.

A Match

Poems and Ballads (Moxon, 1866).

25.   *thrall* slave.
26.   *page* servant, attendant.

A Cameo

Poems and Ballads (Moxon, 1866). See CGR's 'The World'.

8.   *pashed* smashed, crushed.
14.   *Peradventure* maybe, by chance, perhaps.

The Leper

Composed 1857–8. *Poems and Ballads* (Moxon, 1866). The original poem contains a French postscript supposedly from *Grandes Chroniques de France, 1515*, which, like the epigraph of 'Laus Veneris', is Swinburne's creation. Compare with 'Laus Veneris', DGR's 'Jenny' and WM's 'The Gilliflower of Gold'. See also Robert Browning's 'Porphyria's Lover' (1836).

19.   *wattled* constructed by interweaving stakes with twigs or branches.
30.   *privy* hidden, secret.
140. *The old question. Will not God do right?* see l. 60 of Browning's 'Porphyria's Lover': 'And yet God has not said a word!'

A Ballad of Burdens

Poems and Ballads (Moxon, 1866).

Title. See title note for DGR's 'The Burden of Nineveh'. Like that poem, 'A Ballad of Burdens' makes use of all meanings of 'burden'.

61.   *garner* granary.
L'Envoy. The short, final stanza at the end of a poem, commonly used in French poetic forms such as the *ballade* or *chant royal*; from the Middle French *envoy* (the act of sending or dispatching).

The Garden of Proserpine

Poems and Ballads (Moxon, 1866).

Title. Proserpine Roman name for the Greek goddess Persephone, who is abducted by Pluto and made queen of the underworld. Her mother

Demeter (or Roman 'Ceres', see note for l. 59) refuses to let spring come to the earth until her daughter returns. Persephone is allowed to return, but because she has eaten some pomegranate seeds in the underworld, she is obliged to remain there for part of each year. See also CGR's 'Dream Land'.

23. *wot* know.
27. *poppies* emblems of sleep.
28. *Green grapes of Proserpine* see l. 4 of John Keats's 'Ode on Melancholy' (1820): 'ruby grape of Proserpine'.
59. *the earth her mother* Proserpine's mother is Ceres, goddess of plants and the harvest.
93. *vernal* of or relating to spring.

Before Parting

Poems and Ballads (Moxon, 1866). See DGR's 'The Honeysuckle' and Sonnet XXIX, ll. 13–16, of George Meredith's *Modern Love*.

4–5. *And that strong . . . has burst* see ll. 27–8 of John Keats's 'Ode on Melancholy' (1820): 'Though seen of none save him whose strenuous tongue / Can burst Joy's grape against his palate fine'.
11.   *wise* way.
31–2. *leaves your hair . . . hid spice* see ll. 396–7 of 'Laus Veneris': 'Her hair had smells of all the sunburnt south, / Strange spice and flower . . .' See also ll. 14–15 of John Keats's 'Ode to a Nightingale' (1819): 'Dance, and Provençal song, and sunburnt mirth! / O for a beaker full of the warm South!'

Love and Sleep

Poems and Ballads (Moxon, 1866). See DGR's 'Nuptial Sleep'.

8.   *wist* know.
12. *hair smelling of the south* see note for ll. 31–2 of 'Before Parting'.

The King's Daughter

Composed 1860. *Poems and Ballads* (Moxon, 1866). This poem's subject matter is obscure. Clyde K. Hyder suggests that its events are taken from a popular ballad, 'The King's Dochter Lady Jean', where a woman is raped by a stranger who turns out to be her brother. Brother and sister both die in the end. Hyder speculates that the king's son in ACS's poem has chosen the one maiden out of the ten who is his sister. See Clyde K. Hyder, 'Swinburne and the Popular Ballad', *PMLA* 49.1 (March 1934), pp. 295–309.

11. *may* maiden.

37. *goodliest* the best quality.
55. *streek* prepare a corpse for burial.

A Ballad of Dreamland

Belgravia (September 1876). First poetry volume *Poems and Ballads II* (Chatto & Windus, 1878). See CGR's 'Dream Land'.

8.   *Only the song of a secret bird* see ll. 1–2 of CGR's 'A Birthday': 'My heart is like a singing bird / Whose nest is in a watered shoot'.
14.   *hope deferred* a biblical allusion much favoured by CGR. See l. 2 of 'A Pause of Thought': 'And hope deferred made my heart sick in truth'.
15.   *dispart* to separate, divide.
Envoi. See note for 'L'Envoy' in 'A Ballad of Burdens'.

Sonnet for a Picture

The Heptalogia (Chatto & Windus, 1880), a volume of parodies of contemporary poets. This one parodies DGR's poetic style as well as poking fun at his painting.

5.   *rutilant* glowing with red or golden light.
7.   *shewbread* loaves of bread as offerings to God.

From *Tristram of Lyonesse*

Tristram of Lyonesse and Other Poems (Chatto & Windus, 1882). This extract reproduces ll. 1–75 of 'I. The Sailing of the Swallow'.

Title. From an Arthurian legend in which Tristram travels to Ireland to win Yseult (also spelled 'Iseult') of Ireland's hand in marriage for King Mark of Cornwall. During the return voyage to Cornwall, Tristram and Yseult begin a tragic affair after drinking a love potion intended for Yseult and King Mark. Yseult marries King Mark while Tristram marries Yseult of Brittany, known also as Yseult *aux Blanches Mains* ('of the White Hands'). After Tristram is mortally wounded, Yseult of Ireland voyages to heal him, but arrives too late and dies of grief. This is an outline of the story's basic events; there are many different versions and variations. *Lyonesse* legendary home of Tristram, said to border Cornwall.

8.   *high Carlion* Caerleon-upon-Usk, Wales, the site of one of King Arthur's main residences; sometimes identified with Camelot.
10.   *Tintagel* Mark of Cornwall's castle. Also where King Arthur is conceived.
11.   *stem* bow of a ship.

36. *plenilune* full moon.

57–63. *The whole fair body . . . star and plume* Compare with DGR's description of 'The Blessed Damozel' in the first two stanzas of that poem.

A Death on Easter Day

Composed 1882. *Tristram of Lyonesse and Other Poems* (Chatto & Windus, 1882).

Title. This sonnet is about DGR, who died on Easter Sunday, 1882. See WMR's 'Dedication'.

A Ballad of Appeal

A Midsummer Holiday and Other Poems (Chatto & Windus, 1884).

Subtitle. To *Christina G. Rossetti* see Biographical Notes for CGR. ACS dedicated *A Century of Roundels* (1883) to her.

1–2. *Song wakes . . . only feel* see l. 1 of CGR's 'A Birthday': 'My heart is like a singing bird'.

15. *keen* wail; also 'sharp'.

19. *clave* split.

27. *lave* wash (from the French *laver*).

JOHN PAYNE

All poems were first published in (and are taken from) *New Poems* (Newman and Co., 1880), unless otherwise noted.

This is the House of Dreams. Whoso is fain

The Masque of Shadows (W. H. Allen, 1870).

From *Sir Floris*

The Masque of Shadows (W. H. Allen, 1870). This extract from *Sir Floris* reproduces ll. 1–77 of 'I. The First Coming of the Dove'.

Subtitle. Coming of the Dove later in this poem, a dove appears to Sir Floris, leading him on a quest.

5.   *castellain* governor or constable of a castle.

22. *morion* crested metal helmet.

26. *clarion* trumpet.

49. *disport* amusement.

53. *demesne* domain.

57. *idlesse* idleness.

A Birthday Song

See CGR's 'A Birthday'.

1.   *roses* emblems of love and beauty.

Dream-Life

10.   *cloud-wrack* a group of drifting clouds.

Love's Amulet

Title. *Amulet* charm worn to protect the wearer from harm.

10.   *Roses* emblems of love and beauty.
11.   *Lilies* emblems of innocence.
28.   *thorow* through.

Rondeau

Title. *Rondeau* short lyrical poem based on two rhymes, with the opening words used as an unrhymed refrain.

12.   *roses* emblems of love and beauty.

Sad Summer

9.   *guerdon* reward; *lay* medieval narrative poem.

ARTHUR O'SHAUGHNESSY
Ode

Music and Moonlight (Chatto & Windus, 1874).

19.   *Nineveh* see title note for DGR's 'The Burden of Nineveh'.
20.   *Babel* in Genesis 11, God punishes the hubristic builders of the Tower of Babel by confounding their language, so that they can no longer understand one another.

Song ['I made another garden, yea']

Music and Moonlight (Chatto & Windus, 1874).

Song ['I went to her who loveth me no more']

Music and Moonlight (Chatto & Windus, 1874). See ACS's 'A Match' and 'The Leper'. See also Robert Browning's 'Porphyria's Lover' (1836).

The Great Encounter

Music and Moonlight (Chatto & Windus, 1874).

5–11. *My old aspiring self ... curse and fell* see ll. 10–14 of DGR's
'Lost Days':

> God knows I know the faces I shall see,
> Each one a murdered self, with low last breath.
> 'I am thyself, – what hast thou done to me?'
> 'And I – and I – thyself,' (lo! each one saith,)
> 'And thou thyself to all eternity!'

Living Marble

Songs of a Worker (Chatto & Windus, 1881).

5. *unchid* unscolded, unchided.
7–8. *vain-hearted queen ... wayward Venus* Venus is the Roman
goddess of beauty and sensual love; see also ACS's 'Laus Veneris'.

The Line of Beauty

Songs of a Worker (Chatto & Windus, 1881). See John Keats's 'Ode
on a Grecian Urn' (1820).

11. *consummate* perfect, complete.
14. *God become human and man grown divine* see ll. 386–7 of
Swinburne's 'Laus Veneris: 'And lo my love, mine own soul's heart,
more dear / Than mine own soul, more beautiful than God'.

Pentelicos

Songs of a Worker (Chatto & Windus, 1881).

Title. Greek mountain, known for its fine marble.

Paros

Songs of a Worker (Chatto & Windus, 1881). See DGR's 'The Portrait'
(1870), Elizabeth Siddal's 'The Lust of the Eyes' and CGR's 'In an Artist's
Studio'.

Title. Greek island, known for its white marble.

3. *consummate* perfect, complete.
12–14. *Not simply woman ... eternal being* see ll. 12–14 of DGR's
'The Portrait' (Sonnet X of *The House of Life*): 'Her face is made
her shrine. Let all men note / That in all years (O Love, thy gift is
this!) / They that would look on her must come to me.'

Carrara

Songs of a Worker (Chatto & Windus, 1881). See Percy Bysshe Shelley's 'Ozymandias' (1817). See also John Ruskin's 'The Hills of Carrara' and DGR's 'The Burden of Nineveh'.

Title. See title note for Ruskin's 'The Hills of Carrara'.

4. *scathe* harm, injury.
6. *laths* straps of wood forming a foundation for the laying of a roof, wall or fence.
13. *shriven* absolved.
26. *chidden* scolded, chided, rebuked.

PHILIP BOURKE MARSTON

All poems were first published in (and are taken from) *Song-Tide and Other Poems* (Ellis and Green, 1871), unless otherwise noted.

Love's Shrines

See DGR's 'Without Her'.

Love Past Utterance

See DGR's 'The Portrait' (Sonnet X of *The House of Life*), Arthur O'Shaughnessy's 'Paros' and CGR's 'In an Artist's Studio'.

Love's Warfare

See Sonnet VI of George Meredith's *Modern Love*.

Stronger Than Sleep

See DGR's 'Nuptial Sleep'.

5. *roses* emblems of love and beauty.

The New Religion

All in All: Poems and Sonnets (Chatto & Windus, 1875). See DGR's 'A Sonnet is a moment's monument'.

1. *lays* medieval narrative poems, meant to be sung.
11. *He that hath ears to hearken, let him hear* a common biblical injunction which refers to mankind's ability to perceive God. For example, Deuteronomy 29:4: 'Yet the Lord hath not given you an heart to perceive, and eyes to see, and ears to hear, unto this day.'

OLIVER MADOX BROWN

Both poems first published in *The Dwale Bluth, Hebditch's Legacy, and Other Literary Remains*, vol. 2 (Tinsley Brothers, 1876).

Sonnet: Written at the Age of Thirteen for a Picture by Mrs Stillman

Title note. Mrs Stillman Mrs William James Stillman, née Marie Spartali. A painter in the Pre-Raphaelite style and model for Pre-Raphaelite painters, she modelled for Oliver Madox Brown's father, FMB, with whom she also studied painting.

Index of Titles

Page numbers in italics refer to the Notes. Where there are two italicized numbers, the first refers to the introductory note to a group of poems. Where an individual poem is not annotated, the italicized number refers to the introductory note. For an explanation of how the source details for the poems are shown in the Notes, please see p. 322.

Index of First Lines

Page numbers in italics refer to the Notes. Where there are two italicized numbers, the first refers to the introductory note to a group of poems. Where an individual poem is not annotated, the italicized number refers to the introductory note. For an explanation of how the source details for the poems are shown in the Notes, please see p. 322.

PENGUIN CLASSICS

LIVES OF THE ARTISTS VOLUME I
GIORGIO VASARI

'In this painting of Leonardo's there was a smile so pleasing
that it seemed divine rather than human'

Giorgio Vasari (1511–74) was an accomplished painter and architect, but it is for his illuminating biographies that he is best remembered. Beginning with Cimabue and Giotto in the thirteenth century, he traces the development of Italian art across three centuries to the golden epoch of Leonardo and Michelangelo. Great men, and their immortal works, are brought vividly to life, as Vasari depicts the young Giotto scratching his first drawings on stone; Donatello gazing at Brunelleschi's crucifix; and Michelangelo's painstaking work on the Sistine Chapel, harassed by the impatient Pope Julius II. The *Lives* also conveys much about Vasari himself and his outstanding abilities as a critic inspired by his passion for art.

George Bull's introduction discusses Vasari's life and influences, and the political and historical background of sixteenth-century Florence. This volume also includes notes on the artists by Peter Murray and a list for further reading.

'The most influential book about the history of art ever written'
New York Review of Books

A selection translated by George Bull, with notes on the artists by Peter Murray

PENGUIN CLASSICS

LIVES OF THE ARTISTS VOLUME II
GIORGIO VASARI

'Enterprises endowed with virtue and talent …
never pause or rest till they have reached the height of glory'

In his *Lives of Artists of the Italian Renaissance*, Giorgio Vasari (1511–74) demonstrated a literary talent that even outshone his outstanding abilities as a painter and architect, revealing both a deep understanding of human nature and perceptive responses to great works of art. Through character sketches and anecdotes he depicts Piero di Cosimo shut away in his derelict house, living only to paint; Giulio Romano's startling painting of Jove striking down the giants; and his friend Francesco Salviati, whose biography also tells us much about Vasari's own early career. Vasari's original and soaring vision, and his acute aesthetic judgements have made him one of the most influential art historians of all time.

In his introduction, George Bull discusses Vasari's life and works, and his development as an artist. This edition includes notes on the artists by Peter Murray and suggestions for further reading.

'It is his unfailing enthusiasm for art, his delight in artists and their artistic temperament, and his sensitivity, which make his books so valuable' *The Times*

A selection translated by George Bull, with notes on the artists by Peter Murray

PENGUIN CLASSICS

THE NEW PENGUIN BOOK OF ROMANTIC POETRY

'And what if all of animated Nature
Be but organic harps, diversely framed'

The Romanticism that emerged after the American and French revolutions of 1776 and 1789 represented a new flowering of the imagination and the spirit, and a celebration of the soul of humanity with its capacity for love. This extraordinary collection sets the acknowledged genius of poems such as Blake's 'Tyger', Coleridge's 'Khubla Khan' and Shelley's 'Ozymandias' alongside verse from less familiar figures and women poets such as Charlotte Smith and Mary Robinson. We also see familiar poets in an unaccustomed light, as Blake, Wordsworth and Shelley demonstrate their comic skills, while Coleridge, Keats and Clare explore the Gothic and surreal.

This volume is arranged by theme and genre, revealing unexpected connections between the poets. In their introduction Jonathan and Jessica Wordsworth explore Romanticism as a way of responding to the world, and they begin each section with a helpful preface, notes and bibliography.

'An absolutely fascinating selection – notable for its women poets, its intriguing thematic categories and its helpful mini biographies' Richard Holmes

Edited with an introduction by Jonathan and Jessica Wordsworth

PENGUIN CLASSICS

THE LETTERS OF VINCENT VAN GOGH

> 'Be clearly aware of the stars and infinity on high.
> Then life seems almost enchanted after all'

Few artists' letters are as self-revelatory as Vincent Van Gogh's, and the selection included here, spanning the whole of his artistic career, sheds light on every facet of the life and work of this complex and tortured man. Engaging candidly and movingly with his religious struggles, his ill-fated search for love, his intense relationship with his brother Theo and his attacks of mental illness, the letters contradict the popular image of Van Gogh as an anti-social madman and a martyr to art, showing instead that he was capable of great emotional and spiritual depths. Above all, they stand as an intense personal narrative of artistic development and a unique account of the process of creation.

The letters are linked by explanatory biographical passages, revealing Van Gogh's inner journey as well as the outer facts of his life. This edition includes the drawings that originally illustrated the letters.

'If ever there was any doubt that Van Gogh's letters belong beside those great classics of artistic self-revelation, Cellini's autobiography and Delacroix's journal, this excellent edition dispels it' *The Times*

Selected and edited by Ronald de Leeuw
Translated by Arnold Pomerans

THE STORY OF PENGUIN CLASSICS

Before 1946 ...'Classics' are mainly the domain of academics and students, without readable editions for everyone else. This all changes when a little-known classicist, E. V. Rieu, presents Penguin founder Allen Lane with the translation of Homer's *Odyssey* that he has been working on and reading to his wife Nelly in his spare time.

1946 *The Odyssey* becomes the first Penguin Classic published, and promptly sells three million copies. Suddenly, classic books are no longer for the privileged few.

1950s Rieu, now series editor, turns to professional writers for the best modern, readable translations, including Dorothy L. Sayers's *Inferno* and Robert Graves's *The Twelve Caesars*, which revives the salacious original.

1960s The Classics are given the distinctive black jackets that have remained a constant throughout the series's various looks. Rieu retires in 1964, hailing the Penguin Classics list as 'the greatest educative force of the 20th century'.

1970s A new generation of translators arrives to swell the Penguin Classics ranks, and the list grows to encompass more philosophy, religion, science, history and politics.

1980s The Penguin American Library joins the Classics stable, with titles such as *The Last of the Mohicans* safeguarded. Penguin Classics now offers the most comprehensive library of world literature available.

1990s The launch of Penguin Audiobooks brings the classics to a listening audience for the first time, and in 1999 the launch of the Penguin Classics website takes them online to a larger global readership than ever before.

The 21st Century Penguin Classics are rejacketed for the first time in nearly twenty years. This world famous series now consists of more than 1300 titles, making the widest range of the best books ever written available to millions – and constantly redefining the meaning of what makes a 'classic'.

The Odyssey continues ...

The best books ever written

PENGUIN 🐧 CLASSICS

SINCE 1946

Find out more at www.penguinclassics.com